Homesteads
Ungovernable

NUMBER THREE

Jack and Doris Smothers Series
in Texas History, Life, and Culture

MARK M. CARROLL

HOMESTEADS UNGOVERNABLE

Families, Sex, Race

AND

the Law in
Frontier Texas
1823-1860

UNIVERSITY OF TEXAS PRESS, AUSTIN

Publication of this work was made possible in part by support from the J. E. Smothers, Sr., Memorial Foundation and the National Endowment for the Humanities.

Requests for permission to reproduce material from this work should be sent to:

Permissions
University of Texas Press
P.O. Box 7819
Austin, TX 78713-7819.
www.utexas.edu/utpress/about/bpermission.html

∞ The paper used in this book meets the minimum requirements of ANSI/NISO z39.48-1992 (R1997) (Permanence of Paper).

LIBRARY OF CONGRESS CATALOGING-IN-PUBLICATION DATA
Carroll, Mark M. (Mark McNeese)
Homesteads ungovernable : families, sex, race, and the law in frontier Texas, 1823–1860 / by Mark M. Carroll.—1st. ed.
    p.   cm.
Includes bibliographical references and index.
ISBN 0-292-71227-8 (cloth : alk. paper)—ISBN 0-292-71228-6 (pbk. : alk. paper)
    1. Family—Texas—History—19th century.   2. Sex role—Texas—History—19th century.   3. Domestic relations—Texas—History—19th century.   4. Frontier and pioneer life—Texas—History—19th century.   5. Texas—Race relations.   6. Texas—Social life and customs.   I. Title.
HQ536.15.T4 C37   2001
306.85'09764'09034—dc21   00-044351

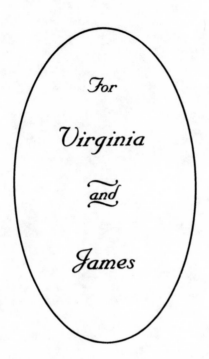

For

Virginia

and

James

Contents

Acknowledgments

I heartily thank those who aided me in the writing of this book. Foremost among those to whom I am grateful is Robert C. Palmer, who supervised the doctoral dissertation at the University of Houston from which this book is derived. His teaching spurred my interest in the history of society and law, and his careful reading of the dissertation and criticisms were invaluable. The astute appraisals that Steven Mintz, Stanley Siegel, Laura Oren, James W. Paulsen, and A. Mark Smith provided were particularly helpful in expanding the parameters of the study, reconceptualizing the organization of my argument, and otherwise preparing the manuscript for book publication. My editors at the University of Texas Press deserve special recognition for their cogent assessments of my work, unstinting professionalism, and cheerful guidance. The comments and suggestions of Theresa May, Sheryl Englund, Rachel Chance, and Leslie Tingle on matters of style and organization were critical in helping me to extract from a rather voluminous dissertation a much more accessible and focused piece. Letitia Blalock copyedited the manuscript with great care, and her sensitivity to the subject matter and cooperative spirit were a pleasant bonus. While the contributions of these individuals have helped to produce a more subtle and sophisticated book, responsibility for its shortcomings, of course, rests entirely with its author.

My family was a constant source of encouragement. Without them the project would have been less meaningful. Deep personal thanks, in particular, go to my parents. Their support, patience, and generosity have been unswerving and the value of their reassurances incalculable.

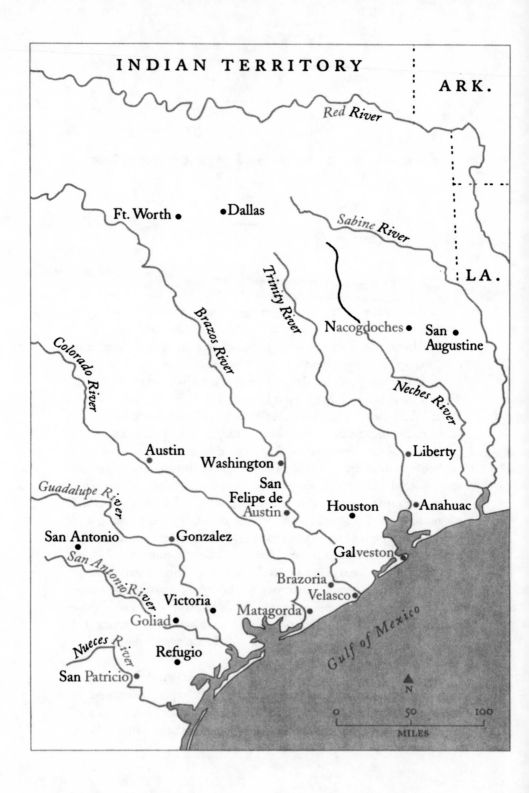

INDIAN TERRITORY

ARK.

LA.

Red River

Sabine River

Ft. Worth ● ●Dallas

Trinity River

Brazos River

Nacogdoches ● ●San Augustine

Colorado River

Neches River

Austin ●

Washington ●

●Liberty

San Felipe de Austin ●

Houston ●

●Anahuac

Guadalupe River

San Antonio ●

Gonzalez ●

Galveston ●

San Antonio River

Brazoria ●

Velasco ●

Victoria ●

Matagorda ●

Goliad ●

Nueces River

Refugio ●

San Patricio ●

Gulf of Mexico

N

0   50   100

MILES

Introduction

The world of Harriet Ames was not the world of republican companionate marriage or of plantation patriarchy. She and Solomon Page arrived in Mexican Texas from New Orleans just before the Anglo-Texan War of Independence. In keeping with the customary way of dealing with the shortage of Catholic priests, required by law to perform weddings if they were to be valid, the couple married contractually, or by bond, in the District of Brazoria. Like so many southern women and men seeking a fresh start in Texas, no sooner had the two established this makeshift marital relation than Solomon obtained for them the more than 4,600 acres of land available to settling spouses. Rather than help cultivate the new tract, which the pair owned coequally under the Hispanic regime, Solomon gambled away all their meager belongings. Shortly thereafter, he abandoned Harriet and her two small children to join General Houston's army. As Solomon decamped, Harriet made her feelings clear with the comment: "I hope . . . the first bullet . . . fired will pierce your heart, and just leave you time enough to think of the wife and children . . . you left to die of starvation in this wilderness."[1]

Santa Anna's army soon approached, and Harriet joined the wild scramble to the east, commonly referred to as the "Runaway Scrape." During this chaotic episode she met the notorious Colonel Robert Potter. A former member of Congress from North Carolina, the colonel was known throughout the South for "Potterizing," or castrating, a Methodist preacher and seventeen-year-old boy whom he had suspected of having sexual relations with his wife. A singularly beautiful woman, Harriet quickly stimulated Robert's interest. As the newly appointed Secretary of the Texas Navy, he persuaded Harriet to lodge with him on board ship in Galveston Bay. After rebuffing the entreaties of Solomon to return and learning that her unsolemnized bond marriage with him did not legally bind her in any case, she agreed to settle down with the colonel. She then sealed with him her second bond marriage. Following independence from Mexico, Robert applied for and obtained for them the full headright of land available to married men in the new Republic of Texas.[2]

For six years, the Potters worked their homestead in the Old Red River County. Along with Harriet's children, they established themselves in the area as a bona fide family. Solomon Page filed for divorce in 1840, but this caused the couple little concern. When Harriet received notice of the suit, Potter advised her to "give herself no trouble about the matter, but leave it with him and he would attend to it." Harriet easily discarded her failed "marriage" to Solomon, but dire events beset her and Robert in the spring of 1842. At that time, the colonel prevailed upon the Texas Congress to issue a requisition calling for the citizens of the republic to bring William Pinkney Rose to justice, dead or alive, for the murder of the Panola County sheriff. "Old Rose," leader of the Harrison County regulators, and John W. Scott, his son-in-law, decided to exact vengeance. They and nine other men descended upon the Potter homestead at dawn one morning. Harriet reminded the colonel that they had a cannon and plenty of firearms and urged him to stand with her and fight to the death. Instead, Robert fled on foot toward Caddo Lake, about a hundred yards behind the house. Diving into the water just steps ahead of his pursuers, he never had a chance. Scott shot the colonel dead when he came to the surface for air. Having loaded the small artillery piece with buckshot, Harriet accosted Rose and snarled, "If only I had a match to touch off this cannon, I would shoot your tongue down your throat." The regulators left her unmolested and departed, after Scott had impressed upon Rose that she was "too brave a woman to kill." Harriet held on to the land for many years, but was finally dispossessed. She died in New Orleans at the age of eighty-four, a gritty survivor of a violent and unruly frontier.[3]

Harriet's life with Robert was hardly amenable to republican matrimonial ideals or southern patriarchal gentility. It seems unlikely, however, that she ever gave much thought to how frontier pressures had intertwined with the peculiar practice of marriage by bond, the Hispanic matrimonial regime, land-grant policies, and Anglo-Texan hegemony to shape her "domestic" life in distinctive ways. On the other hand, any jurist familiar with antebellum Texas would have rejected out of hand the proposition that the post-independence law relevant to families, sexual behavior, and kinship simply replicated that found in the urbanizing republican North or the more settled plantation South.

Historians writing about the family and its institutional context have provided important, yet circumscribed, approaches for an integrated study of the law relevant to frontier households and sexual intimacy in antebellum Texas. Beginning in the early 1960s, scholars committed to the "new social history" began relying on demographic information to assess the material existence and everyday lives of common people. This approach, however, viewed the law and the mechanisms of governance as essentially superstructural and thus deemphasized the legal system.[4] In the late 1970s, historians turned their focus from the inner aspects of family life outward to the laws, state apparatuses, and policies that established normative relations within the family and sanctioned deviance among its members. While revealing the inextricable connection of state power, private life, and culture in nineteenth-century America, the new scholarship usually concentrated on treatise writers, appellate justices, and legislators. By the same token, these scholars often ignored how flesh-and-blood individuals actually interacted with the law and its institutions in particular social situations.[5] In essence, legal historians interested in the family focused too much on the "top" in their effort to improve an approach that had concentrated too much on the "bottom."

Michael Grossberg's *Governing the Hearth* marked an important departure in this line of inquiry. He perceived a substantial shift in the nineteenth century from patriarchal family norms to more egalitarian household relations—a result of republican idealism. In his view, the nineteenth century was the time when jurists, legislators, and commentators fundamentally redirected governance of the home. Legal changes attendant on industrialization and urbanization created a new distribution of power among spouses and their children, and between the household and the state. Under this "republican family" orientation, the rights and status of its members were made more equal.

Society viewed marriage in more consensual terms, and consequently men and women based their marriages on companionate ideals. As husbands shouldered responsibilities in the marketplace, wives became custodians of a restricted "domestic sphere." Spouses placed a new emphasis on romantic love, reciprocal obligations and duties, mutual respect, and the importance of child-rearing. The United States bench, a "judicial patriarchy," correspondingly assumed the primary burden of state intervention to inculcate and support this new version of the family.[6]

While perpetuating the nearly hermetic study of lawmakers, rule structures, and cultural ideals, Peter Bardaglio argued that Grossberg's conceptualization has questionable relevance to the Old South. Building on the theory of southern exceptionalism, his *Reconstructing the Household* constituted the first effort to analyze comprehensively domestic relations and the law governing them in the nineteenth-century southern states.[7] This work particularly emphasized the inapplicability of Grossberg's explanation to a society that often defined the household to encompass not only white family members but also slaves and their children, including those who had slave-owning patriarchs as fathers. Given the inherent inequities of this arrangement, a middle-class, egalitarian system of family government hardly explained the development of southern domestic relations and pertinent law.[8]

Bardaglio argued that the antebellum South saw itself as the defender of the traditional patriarchal household. In this conception, the broader Victorian culture encouraged more equality and affection among southern spouses and their children. The family, however, remained the chief vehicle for the exercise of authority. As in the colonial period, the rule of fathers and husbands, a powerful ethos of male honor, and strong kinship bonds continued to provide the key sources of order and stability, reducing the role of the state in household regulation. Reflecting the conclusions of Catherine Clinton and Bertram Wyatt-Brown, Bardaglio maintained that southern family relations consequently rested more on hierarchy and dependence than on egalitarianism and consent. The sexual access of slave-holding men to their wives and bondwomen forged patriarchy as a system shaping both race relations and gender. With the support of their planter allies, southern lawmakers worked to maintain this arrangement. While imposing legal changes on society that marginally liberalized the law of slavery, married women's property, divorce, and child custody, they worked systematically to secure the dominance of both common and elite white men.[9]

A growing body of research reveals the inadequacy of a monolithic patriarchal model to describe antebellum southern family mores and the relevant law.[10] Several works in the past fifteen years show that analyses built exclusively on planter hegemony and the cult of male honor are too blunt to account for the considerable variety in family relations within particular regions and among various groups. Victoria Bynum's *Unruly Women*, for example, showed how both white and black women in the North Carolina Piedmont Region resisted male dominion and the efforts of courts to enforce ideals of domesticity.[11] Bynum's work revealed that differences in wealth, class, kinship affiliation, local economies, and neighborly relations figured heavily in the pattern of female resistance and independence. Suzanne Lebsock's *The Free Women of Petersburg* examined well-to-do white women in Petersburg, Virginia, from 1784 to 1860.[12] A significant number of these women found work for wages and acquired separate estates in marriage, or otherwise refrained from matrimony and thus experienced increasing independence. This assertive female response to agricultural depressions arose in the face of an antifeminist and patriarchal culture.

Scholarship utilizing an expanded conception of gender has laid the groundwork for a history of family and law in the antebellum South that transcends the reductionist patriarchal paradigm. In the last decade, feminist historians have made gender central to theoretical thinking about social history. As early as 1975, however, Natalie Davis suggested that investigation of the ways that societies and institutions have constructed gender should consider women and men equally. Especially since the publication of Joan Wallach Scott's *Gender and the Politics of History*,[13] numerous historians have utilized the postmodern and poststructuralist theories of Jacques Derrida and Michel Foucault to deconstruct gender regimes defining femininity and to question the notion of an unchanging definition of maleness. These historians have "problematized" masculinity and male sexuality, opening them up to closer scrutiny and examining much more carefully their transformations across time and space.[14]

In *A Family Venture*, Joan Cashin built on advances in the study of gender to explore planter women and men who migrated to the Old

Southwest.[15] This work showed that the loss of extended family networks in the seaboard South and a socially unchecked "manly independence" on the frontier induced radical alterations in sex roles and in the traditional paternalistic relationships of planter couples and their slaves. Cashin's book undoubtedly relied on an interpretive framework more sophisticated than that which earlier historians of southern women and the family had used. It did not, however, explore thoroughly the relationship between frontier conditions, the relationships of settling women and men, and the law. Nor did it examine the mores of the preponderant yeoman class or the fundamental social and legal transformations occurring in Texas as white insurgents from the United States displaced Mexican authority there in the mid-1830s.

Investigations of modern imperialism and the work of postcolonial theorists suggest that a thorough study of families and the law in the Old South should transcend the traditional focus on white society and African-American slaves. Three decades ago, Philip Mason's *Patterns of Dominance* described the sexual and reproductive implications of racial ordering for an array of colonized groups in the Americas, Africa, and Asia during the age of European imperial expansion.[16] George M. Fredrickson's *White Supremacy* identified these processes among enslaved blacks and whites in the Old South.[17] While more recent postcolonial scholars often emphasize the impossibility of objective historical analysis and the invalidity of "univocal" narrative, their work has reinforced the determination of researchers to question hegemonic discourses and reinstate the marginalized within historical writing.[18] Postmodern scholars and those working in the empirical humanist tradition have thus provided the conceptual means for a description of the sexual relationships, family mores, and pertinent legal regimes that developed on the multiracial southwestern frontier during the antebellum period. Such an approach, furthermore, usefully emphasizes that "family" included not only legal spouses and their children but also couples and blood kin whose connections were not necessarily contained neatly within the discrete racial and legal categories shaping conceptions of appropriate social organization.

New historical methodology concentrating on gender suggests that investigations of the Old South have unnecessarily delimited scholarship dealing with the family, sexual mores, and their relationships to the law. Feminist historians have emphasized the need to explore the construction of gender through the examination of topics not traditionally associated directly with women, such as high politics and the myriad uses of public power.[19] Several recent works examining sex roles in the multicultural colonial South have expanded the matrix of analysis by combining the study of legal discourses, race, and class.[20] Most research on legal development and the family in the Old South, however, has dealt primarily with the private laws and institutions explicitly affecting the relationships of white family members and, to a lesser extent, their slaves. A more comprehensive study would also examine the ways state power, in behalf of nominally public purposes, interacted with the law of domestic relations to shape family norms, sexual mores, and gender among the full array of racial groups that inhabited the expanding antebellum South.

Developing approaches in legal history indicate the insufficiency of a model of law and society in the Old South that concentrates on the ways patriarchal lawmakers systematically protected their economic interests and imposed their dominance and ideals on the lower orders. Historians have come to recognize, first of all, that antebellum southern law retained autonomous Anglo-American common-law principles in the face of economic forces associated with slavery and the initiatives of elites.[21] Legal historians have increasingly emphasized, furthermore, that nineteenth-century United States law and society changed synergistically, rather than simply "from the top down."[22] Building on the work of S. F. C. Milsom, English legal historian Robert C. Palmer revealed the often unanticipated patterns of social and legal change, rooted in a dynamic interaction among society, government, courts, legal practitioners, and litigants.[23] No study of the Old South, however, has examined the development of law, society, and the family from this perspective. Much less has there been heretofore an attempt to describe legal change relevant to families, sex roles, and race that includes the ecology and demography of the antebellum southern frontier within an interactive framework.

A substantial body of scholarship indicates a rough description of antebellum Anglo-Texan families and the law relevant to them. Traditional studies show that white southerners arriving in Texas after 1821 built a loosely organized and precarious social order based on land greed and rampant individualism. A number of historians have revealed the exceptional unruliness of frontiersmen in antebellum Texas and, more recently, the unusual autonomy of women settling there.[24] Joseph W. McKnight and others have identified how the Hispanic community property regime and homestead exemption laws met the needs of early settlers.[25] Few scholars, however, have attempted to reconcile these findings or describe the entire array of law relevant to the sexual and marital relationships of Anglo-Texan men and women.

Traditional studies and contemporary research suggest the outlines of a transracial pattern of intimacy and social-legal ordering that developed in Texas during the four decades preceding the Civil War. The pioneering work of Harold Schoen in the late 1930s and, more recently, Ann Patton Malone's *Women on the Texas Frontier* explored the sexual involvements of black women and white men in Texas amid hardening institutional and social restraints stemming from Anglo-American racism and slavery.[26] Jane Dysart similarly analyzed the legal and extralegal relationships of Hispanic women and men within the increasingly dominant group between 1830 and 1860. Arnoldo De León's *They Called Them Greasers* examined racist Anglo-American attitudes undergirding this development.[27] Historians have given very little attention, however, to the larger patterned interrelationship of Texas public and private law, families, sexual behavior, and gender. Nor have they examined how frontier conditions, slavery, and white supremacy affected sexual relationships and family mores within the distinctive multiracial and multicultural setting of the state.

In an ethnically complex and rapidly transforming frontier polity, circumstances like those Harriet Ames encountered produced problematic family norms that would test singularly the skills and creativity of Texas lawmakers. Her pioneering career and adventures with Robert Potter were certainly spectacular. Her relationships with both Solomon Page and Potter, however, highlight some of the more distinctive features of Anglo-Texan matrimony. Like the colonel, many homesteaders from the more settled South easily escaped failed marriages. In a poorly organized society with little public surveillance, pragmatic immigrants—often fleeing debt—established and terminated their own marital relations with limited consideration of legal niceties. In primitive conditions, the practical benefits of marriage and, for much of the period, the lure of inexpensive land being sold in larger portions to those with spouses prompted hastily arranged and unstable unions. Stressful circumstances, the inaccessibility of courts and officials, and the scant regard for marital procedures also encouraged informal coupling and uncoupling, illicit co-habitation, bigamy, and adultery. Like Page, immigrant southern men were frequently self-absorbed and devoid of a sense of family obliga-tion. More than a few, like Potter, were violent and jealous of their wives. On the other hand, many homesteading women, like Ames, were more mesquite than shrinking violet and certainly tough enough to meet the challenges of the frontier. In an erstwhile Mexican prov-ince inhabited by wary Tejanos, often hostile Indians, and immigrant Ameses, Pages, and Potters, Anglo-Texan law relevant to sex and the family would have to be different from that of the more civilized states of the nation. In order for invading Anglos, eager to reinforce slavery and secure their dominance, to establish a functional law of domestic relations and sexual intimacy, it had to be pragmatic, neither imported nor idealistic.

The present study will show how frontier society and public insti-tutions both shaped and responded to family and sexual norms in antebellum Texas in ways radically different from those of the urban-izing North and the more settled states of the slave South. Republican idealism, patriarchy, and racism certainly affected the development of society and family life in Texas from 1823 to 1860. The frontier, how-ever, channeled these influences in extraordinary ways, which often resulted in unintended social and legal patterns. Stressful living condi-tions, institutional disarray, land-grant rules designed to promote rapid settlement, and a dysfunctional law of matrimony made settling Anglo-Texan families highly unstable, as did the often self-indulgent and sex-ually promiscuous behavior of Anglo-Texan men. Post-independence law adjusted to a double standard that permitted these men sexual lib-erty with Indian, Tejano, and black women but made relatively scarce Anglo women accessible to them usually only through marriage. Even so, pioneer conditions, land policy, and the Hispanic matrimonial prop-erty regime prompted homesteading spouses to work cooperatively and often ruthlessly as conjugal joint venturers, grounding their marriages in survival and economic imperatives rather than in republican fam-ily ideals.

With only tenuous connections between common folk and the legal system, Texas law relevant to sex and the family developed reciprocally with frontier social transformation. To a large degree, the law devel-oping after Anglo-Texan independence was progressive and pragmatic, bolstering Anglo families and their property rights. Building on and deviating from Hispanic legal principles, the law empowered Anglo-Texan women to function in their autonomous marital roles, ensured them the material rewards of their arduous settlement efforts, and provided them relief from abusive and neglectful husbands. In pioneer circumstances, patriarchal authority gave ground to female autonomy. Legal rules accommodated both the frontier conditions inducing extramarital sexual relations among women and men and the practical considerations discouraging marital dissolution. Innovative domestic relations law and rules relevant to sexual behavior, however, also worked within a larger institutional construct of Anglo-Texan supremacy to position Anglo families atop a racial-caste hierarchy that subjugated slaves and subordinated free blacks, Indians, and Tejanos.

ONE

Ardent Adventurers

AND

Borderland Beauties

*Tender Ties beyond
the Pale*

A multiracial frontier provided novel mating choices for men who rebuilt their personal lives in the northernmost province of the new Republic of Mexico. In 1826, after four years of marriage, William Smith of Missouri abandoned his wife, Harriet Stone, and their three children and headed for Texas to start over. Converting nominally to Catholicism in order to become a Mexican citizen, the enterprising civil engineer first settled in Gonzales. After four years of rediscovered "bachelorhood" in this rough-and-tumble town, during which time he changed his name to John W. Smith, he moved to San Antonio. There he began a relationship with María Jesusa Delgado, a woman from a prominent San Antonio family. Claiming to have immigrated from North Carolina and concealing from María his existing marriage to Harriet and his Missouri children, John married María in a festive ceremony before the town's only

Catholic priest on 22 February 1830. Thereafter, the Mexican government granted to John an hacienda amounting to more than 5,750 acres, including the extra one-fourth available to immigrant men who married Mexican women.[1]

After playing a critical role in the siege of San Antonio in 1835 and fortuitously eluding death at the Alamo, the veteran of the Texas War of Independence returned to María and their children and built an important political career. Thanks to Delgado family influence, John repeatedly won elections to the mayorship of San Antonio between 1837 and 1842. His courageous efforts in resisting and helping to expel Mexican troops who invaded the town in March 1842 further solidified his reputation and leadership stature. In 1844 and 1845 John served as senator from Bexar County in the Texas Congress.[2]

As the years passed, María may well have learned of John's prior marriage. Harriet divorced him in 1833 and moved to Texas six years later with their children and a new husband. Even if María did learn of Harriet, however, she appears to have enjoyed a satisfying life with John until his death on 12 January 1845. According to his obituary in the *Texas National Register,* John W. Smith "was of most benevolent disposition, a devoted patriot, and an affectionate husband and father. . . . A wife and five children survive to grieve for this afflicting dispensation of Providence."[3]

It does not seem Harriet and her children agreed entirely with this glowing encomium. Soon after John's death, his children by Harriet filed suit in Bexar County Court to claim their father's expansive estate and exclude María and her children. The basic allegation was that María could not have legally married John in 1830 because of his undissolved marriage to Harriet. The unsavory implication of the suit was that María had been an illicit consort and the children she had with John were all bastards. Protracted litigation worked its way up to the Texas Supreme Court twice in the ten years following John's death. In the 1846 decision of *Smith v. Smith* and the 1856 ruling in *Lee v. Smith,* the high court expansively interpreted Spanish doctrine to uphold María's bigamous marriage to John, her right to a one-half community share in the estate, as well as the inheritance claims of her and John's Anglo-Hispanic children.[4]

The rulings of the Texas Supreme Court certainly provided María and her children a just result. Less obvious is how a multiracial pattern of sexual intimacy rooted in frontier demography and cross-cultural interaction prompted the relationship of John W. Smith and María Delgado. Most contemporary jurists perusing the decisions of *Smith v. Smith* and *Lee v. Smith,* at least, would be hard pressed to glean simply from the language of the opinions the ethnocentric, pragmatic, and political considerations undergirding the union of John and María.

As much as any other development, a distinctive pattern of population growth facilitated the intimate relations of Anglo-Texan men with indigenous women and Tejanas[5] in antebellum Texas. John W. Smith's resettlement there in 1826 was part of a massive Anglo-American migration beginning after Mexican independence. Immigrants from the United States, along with smaller numbers from Europe, flooded the province. This ever-growing movement was in response to generous land allocation policies of the Mexican government and those of the Republic of Texas and the State of Texas. Beginning with the initial settlement of the Old Three Hundred in Stephen F. Austin's colony, the number of land-hungry Anglo-Americans immigrating to Texas between 1823 and 1836 rose from approximately 1,200 to 30,000. Like Smith, most of these settlers came from the states of the upper South. The population doubled approximately every seven years from 1840 to 1860. Immigration during the 1850s was particularly voluminous. A significant number of settlers arrived from European nations such as France, Germany, Ireland, Scotland, Poland, Czechoslovakia, and Switzerland. By the early 1850s, from 10,000 to 12,000 had immigrated to the upper fringes of the polity from the Ohio Valley and the northeastern United States. But the great majority of those settling in East Texas were from the states of the seaboard and lower South. By 1860, the population of Texas had grown to 604,215, including 412,649 Anglos.[6]

Land-grant policies under both Mexican and Anglo-Texan rule encouraged the immigration of unaccompanied Anglo men. The Mexican colonization laws and their included rules for the distribution of land certainly prompted families to settle in Texas. Usually through generously compensated *empresarios,* the majority of immigrant men received enlarged grants because they were heads of a family: 4,428 acres (one *sitio*) if they were ranchers, or 177 acres (one *labor*) if they were farmers. Family heads claiming both to ranch and to farm, which was common, thus received about 4,605 acres. Less generous than the

Mexican government, the immigration policy of the Republic of Texas included a headright system until January 1842 that amply rewarded husbands and fathers; a first-class headright, for example, provided a family man as much as 4,605 acres, comprising a *sitio* and a *labor;* a fourth-class headright, as well as various colonization contracts, provided 640 acres to men with families. On the other hand, the 1825 state colonization law offered a single man about 1,151 acres if he ranched and farmed. A first-class headright for a single man under post-independence rules included about 1,476 acres, while a fourth-class headright and the standard colonization grant offered single men was 320 acres. Between 1845 and 1853, preemption and homestead legislation of the Republic of Texas and State of Texas made 320 acres available to both men and women settlers, while the 1854 Pre-emption Act provided settlers of both sexes 160 acres for as little as fifty cents per acre.[7]

In response to offers of inexpensive land and extraordinary opportunity, a surplus of Anglo-American men arrived in Texas without the company of a wife or children. It is not surprising that John W. Smith did not remarry while living in the town of Gonzales from 1826 to 1830; land-grant rules drew many more solitary men than unaccompanied women. Even after Texas law made land available to single women, settlement in the wilderness continued to be difficult and dangerous; it also continued to require intensive heavy labor. Relatively few unmarried women thus were eager to join the migration alone. From the earliest years, consequently, Texas exhibited an acute imbalance of men over women. According to Newton and Gambrell, a visitor in Texas in 1835 estimated there were 10 men to every woman. These authors considered this guess probably to be incorrect, but concluded, "It is evident that there were relatively few [white] women in the colonies." In newer settlements and western fringe areas, the sex ratio ran as high as 150 to 200 unaccompanied Anglo-Texan men for every 100 solitary Anglo-Texan women. The United States Census listed a male-female sex ratio for the State of Texas of 115 to 100 in 1850 and of 112 to 100 in 1860. In 1850, men outnumbered women by 15,704, and in 1860 by 36,000. The imbalance of men over women thus continued to the end of the antebellum period, with more pronounced imbalances occurring in newly settled areas.[8]

Mexican culture and law posed no barrier to the marriage of Anglo-Texan men with either Mexican or Native American women. John W.

Smith almost certainly faced no racist objections among the Mexican inhabitants of San Antonio to his marriage with María Delgado. Hispanic society was accustomed to *mestizaje,* or racial mixture. Mexicans accepted marriage among Indians, blacks, and criollos, that is, persons of mixed but predominantly European ancestry. They inherited this attitude from early Spanish colonizers who had developed it during many centuries of experience in the Iberian Peninsula and during the early Spanish colonial period, initially in the Valley of Mexico. Hispanic Catholicism as well did not impede the marriage of Indians with pure-blood Spaniards and blacks. By 1821, in fact, the new mestizo race born of this intermixture constituted the Mexican population almost entirely.[9]

Mexican colonization law purposely promoted the marriage of Anglo-Texan men and Tejanas. Mexican law substantially rewarded men like John W. Smith who married native-born residents. The Imperial Colonization Law of 1823 expedited naturalization for immigrants who married Mexican women and provided such men "particular merit" in the eyes of the government. Article 15 of the 1825 colonization law allowed the Mexican government to grant an unmarried immigrant man a plot of land equal in size to about one-fourth of that available to a head of family. After he had actually settled, he could enlarge this to a family-sized grant simply by marrying, and he could increase it by another fourth if he married a Mexican.[10]

Settling Anglo-Texan men had strong prejudices against marriage with Tejanas and Indian women. Anglo-Americans arriving in early Texas believed that Indians were heathens, witches, and devilish agents. In particular, they perceived Native American women as unchaste and therefore unsuitable marriage partners. Despite his marriage choice, it is unlikely John W. Smith was entirely free of these aversions or of the equally common Anglo-Texan prejudice against Tejanos in general, particularly those of apparently mixed race. Anglo-Texans frequently likened Tejanos to Indians and looked down on them. Because of the racial prejudice and xenophobia of Catholics and Spaniards, Anglos perceived Tejanos as "mongrels," uncivilized, morally deficient, and un-Christian. From the beginning, Anglo-Texans publicly condemned marriage with Native American women and mestizas.[11]

On the other hand, the characteristics of many Anglo-American men settling in Texas strongly encouraged them to form relationships with indigenous women and Tejanas. Most of the men settling in

Texas were quite young. Approximately 77 percent of them were under forty at the time the United States government took its first census in 1850. A large percentage of the young men in this cohort certainly came to Texas to escape debt and make a new life for themselves. Many, like John W. Smith, however, also came with the purpose of abandoning bad marriages. Those in Smith's situation were thus strongly predisposed to commence new relationships with the opposite sex. As was the case on other western frontiers, Anglo settlers in Texas were committed to farming and ranching and lived in relative isolation. The consequent absence of social restraints and surveillance thus permitted a large segment of the Anglo-Texan male population to have considerable autonomy regarding their sexual activities and matters matrimonial. Harsh living conditions, physical danger, and resource scarcity, furthermore, placed a premium on intensive pair-bonding, which improved the chances for survival and lessened its rigors.[12]

Weak commitment to the larger immigrant community in early Texas made marriage and sexual interaction with Indians and Tejanas more acceptable to many Anglo-Texan men than if these connections had been strong. Stanley Siegel pointed out not all who came to Texas were fugitives from justice, but that "enough undesirables did come . . . to give credence to the characterization of the new area as the 'Botany Bay' of the United States." Many of these men were arch individualists and social misfits escaping personal and legal troubles. To this extent, they were not strongly devoted to any coherent Anglo-American communal vision or to any particular collective goal to carve out a new social order. The tendency of southerners to make Indians and other peoples with dark skin out-groups in order to enhance a definable collective Anglo-American identity was greatly subdued among these men. In this way at least, cooperation with Mexicans and Indians and integration into their societies, even if only temporarily, were not particularly objectionable to them. As a consequence, marriage and sexual interaction with the women from these groups were also unobjectionable.[13]

The large number of southern men who settled in Texas after 1836 brought with them a sex role predisposing them to interact sexually with the women already residing there. Most of the immigrants to Texas after 1836 were from the seaboard and lower South. A new masculine ideal that emerged among the men from these regions beginning in the late 1820s stressed self-absorbed behavior and risk-taking.

This ideal of "manly independence" quite prominently glorified sexual prowess and unrestrained sexual interaction with young women, especially those with darker skins. Many of the men who immigrated to Texas after 1836 certainly had the same motivations and personal characteristics as those in the first wave of immigration. But the men arriving after 1836 exhibited, in the words of Jane Dysart, an "exaggeratedly masculine style of behavior" approximating the emergent southern ideal. Given the continuing shortage of Anglo-Texan women and frontier pressures, unaccompanied men settling in Texas after independence from Mexico were strongly inclined to indulge expansively their new sex role by forming relationships with indigenous women and Tejanas.[14]

Commercial interaction was fundamental to the relationships Anglo-Texan men cultivated with Indian women. In the late eighteenth century, Anglo-American frontiersmen, having displaced the French, first began to develop a trade in guns with the Comanche, other Plains tribes, and the Wichita. These Indians sold horses and bartered with Anglo-Americans throughout the colonial settlements. By 1820, enterprising Anglo-Americans were trading regularly with many of the tribes in fur pelts, whiskey, guns, and ammunition in the wilds of southeastern Texas, especially around Nacogdoches. By 1830, Anglo and Hispanic traders alike involved themselves in an emerging regional market system in which the members of numerous immigrant and indigenous tribes participated, including the Cherokee, Creek, Chickasaw, Choctaw, Shawnee, Delaware, Kickapoo, Quapaw, Biloxi, Ioni, Alabama, Coushatta, and Caddo of the Neches. Armed conflict between Anglo-Texans and Plains tribes, such as the Kiowa and Comanche, and sometimes between Anglo-Texans and the more cooperative immigrant tribes, occurred frequently and destabilized everyday life. This conflict, however, did not deter trade with them.[15]

Beginning in the early Mexican period, some Anglo-Texan tradesmen and adventurers made homes with Indian women in their villages. Since first contact with the southern tribes, European men had perceived Indian women as sexually assertive and uninhibited.[16] Anglo-American men traveling or settling in Texas commonly found resident Indian women physically attractive and admirable. Francis S. Latham, for example, wrote of a striking raven-haired and olive-skinned Lipan Apache woman he observed near San Antonio in 1842:

> Her forehead and nose were admirably Grecian; her form and limbs delicate and handsome; a graceful and flowing carriage, which, disdaining the Grecian hump or bow attitude, assumed the erect and stately figure of the forest pine. . . . She moved a native queen of the prairie, an imposing model of savage beauty.[17]

From the earliest times, Anglo-American traders succumbed to natural urges, overcame ethnocentric predispositions, and married Native American women according to tribal custom and their own frontier tradition. This pairing-off usually occurred in pioneer areas near fledgling Anglo-American settlements, such as Nacogdoches, where the shortage of Anglo women was most acute and where Anglo-Texan society was least organized. In these circumstances, enterprising Anglo-Texan men made homes and had children with Indian women. Marriage and cohabitation of Anglo men with Indian women, however, usually occurred beyond the observation of Anglo-Texan society.[18]

The experiences of Native Americans in Texas with Spanish, French, British, and United States tradesmen on earlier frontiers had generated a cautious but favorable attitude among Native Americans toward marriage of their women to immigrating white men. Marriage of Indian women with pure-blood Spaniards and criollos had its roots in early Spanish colonization. Hispanic settlers and Franciscan friars established control of the labor and lives of numerous Texas tribes within the northward extension of the mission and presidio system in the early eighteenth century. Mestizo soldiers and frontiersmen took Indian women as concubines and sometimes married them as part of this larger process of subjugation. The aggressiveness of the mestizo settlers revealed to the independent Texas tribes the hopelessness and dangers of marriage and assimilation with European groups. The trade interaction of indigenous and southern immigrant Texas Indians with French, English, and United States frontiersmen, however, seemed to present the opportunity for cooperation and mutual coexistence. As an integral feature of trade relations, these Native Americans were often eager for women in their tribes to marry white tradesmen who lived among them in accordance with tribal customs. Initially at least, marriage of Indian women with Anglo-Texan men was economically and politically beneficial and presented no perceivable threat to tribal solidarity and well-being.[19]

The most extensive sexual interaction between Anglo-Texan men and Native American women occurred before statehood. Anglo-Texan and Indian populations in East Texas were then much more comparable in size and lived in closer proximity than later. Before the Indian Removal between the summer of 1839 and late 1842, it was the almost universal practice of Anglo-Texan men living even temporarily in the Cherokee Nation to marry a woman from this tribe. Along the Louisiana border, there flourished a virtual subculture of cross-racial interaction, including marriage of Anglo-Texan men and Indian women from various indigenous and immigrant tribes. The men who took Native American wives included some of the most prominent Anglo-Texan leaders, from George Washington Paschal to Sam Houston.[20] The forced removal of the tribes and the continuing impact of epidemic disease, however, greatly reduced the number of Native Americans living in East Texas. The explosive population increase of Anglo-Texans after independence dwarfed the population of the remaining bands of Cherokee, Chickasaw, Delaware, and Shawnee. Texas law and Anglo society thereafter compelled these groups, as well as bands of Waco and Tawakoni, to live far apart from areas of Anglo settlement. This policy greatly reduced the amount of trade, the degree of social interaction, and the number of marriages between Native Americans and Anglo-Texans.[21]

Anglo-Texan men often viewed their Native American wives as servants and as a form of property. In the estimation of most frontiersmen, Indian husbands treated their wives as mere commodities. Reflecting conceptions originating on earlier southern frontiers and a delimited understanding of customary female roles among the tribes, Anglo men in early Texas commonly believed the required bestowal of marriage gifts upon the bride's parents or kinsmen meant Indian families simply sold their daughters. Anthony Glass, for example, who lived among the Wichita in 1808 and 1809 in a village on the Red River, surmised that when a man wanted an Indian wife he "purchased" her from the uncle or brother of the woman, with the general "price" being two horses. According to Colonel Richard Dodge of the United States Army, who traveled among the Texas Plains tribes in the 1850s and later, the new husband of an Indian woman became her absolute owner. As such, he concluded, the husband could sell her, with no one having the right to interfere. In his words, the newly acquired Indian wife was "more ab-solutely a slave than any Negro before the war of rebellion," since she could be sold or given away by her husband at his pleasure and without her consent. Compounding these perceptions was the frequent obser-vation that wife-lending and bartering were common practices among most of the Texas tribes.[22]

Notwithstanding these views, Native American women were valu-able helpmates and a key to survival for the Anglo-Texan men who took them as wives. After marriage, the life of an Indian woman be-came more arduous than in her maidenhood. Among indigenous Tex-ans, the "good Indian wife" became not only a producer of children but a provider of vital services to her husband and family. According to a former president of the Republic of Texas, David G. Burnet, Coman-che brides quickly became "primarily hewers of wood and drawers of water." The pride of an accomplished Plains Indian wife was to permit her husband to do nothing for himself. A competent wife cared for her babies, cooked her husband and children's food, made and mended the lodge and her husband's clothing, prepared the skins, butchered the game, dressed the meat, and always went after and saddled her hus-band's horse. Upon relocation of the village, a dutiful wife moved the lodge, superintended the march, unpacked the animals, pitched the new lodge, and made the beds. As Sylvia Vankirk has pointed out, regarding the mixed marriages of fur traders on the eighteenth- and nineteenth-century Canadian frontier, an Indian wife was a valuable asset for white frontiersmen. Such women were, in fact, remarkable economic partners, possessing a wide range of skills and wilderness know-how quite foreign to most women of European descent.[23]

The sex-based division of labor among Native Americans allowed Anglo-Texan frontiersmen to maintain Indian marriages in accord-ance with their ambulatory and cross-cultural lifestyle. Recent schol-arship suggests that trade interaction with Europeans, beginning in the sixteenth century, generated a division of labor among the southern Woodlands Indians and Plains tribes that had substantially circum-scribed the traditional role of indigenous females and reduced their status by the time European men ventured into Texas. Even so, warfare and hunting were then usually the exclusive activities of warriors, that is, accomplished adult males. Perhaps more than in previous centuries, the primary center of activity for an Indian woman was the lodge. Tra-ditional or not, this division of labor necessarily meant that husbands routinely spent extended periods of time away from home. In essence, Indian marital norms and the division of labor among the sexes permitted Anglo-Texan men the freedom to maintain marriages with Native Americans without residing continuously in villages and to interact freely with both Indian and white society.[24]

Preexisting Hispanic sexual mores provided the basis for the informal relationships that Anglo men developed with Tejanas. For the majority of women in New Spain and then Mexico, marriage certainly provided the most acceptable and secure social status and economic position. Given the traditional Spanish preoccupation with "limpieza de sangre" (pure blood; racial purity), marriage to a darker-skinned woman was a step down in the social scale for Hispanic men with *peninsular* (Spanish) or even criollo lineage; informal cohabitation rather than marriage for these men was the most workable alternative. Concubinage, or *barraganería*, was an institution deeply rooted in Hispanic culture. Higher-status Spanish men typically maintained lower-status women of Indian or mixed racial stock as concubines. Women who adopted this role, in the conception of Hispanic society, were useful and tolerated but not suited for marriage with even a criollo gentleman.[25]

Since few *españoles*, from Spain, ever lived in Texas, the social structure of Texas did not mirror the more clearly stratified order of the interior of Mexico. That society placed *peninsulares* at the top, ranked criollos next, and relegated mestizos, *indios*, and *africanos* to the bottom. Most of the Tejanos in La Bahía del Espíritu Santo were descendants of Tlascalan Indians and mestizo soldiers from Coahuila. Those who lived in Nacogdoches were the descendants of children whom mestizo soldiers had with Native American and black women from Louisiana. The early soldier-settlers of San Antonio were also of mixed-race heritage; almost all of the early recruits for settlement in San Antonio de Béxar were mulattos, *lobos* (of black and Indian descent), *coyotes* (of mestizo and Indian descent), and mestizos. Many of the prominent families in San Antonio, however, descended from the mixed-race Mexican soldier-settlers and Canary Islanders, or *isleños*, who settled in Béxar during the initial distribution of farm and ranch lands, from 1730 to 1760. *Isleños* and Mexicans of mixed race, as early as the 1740s, however, intermarried, reducing social and racial distinctions between the two groups. With racial lineages intertwined in this manner, the social hierarchy of San Antonio was based more on socioeconomic and cultural differences than on race. The town thus included usually a "well-bred" governor, a captain, troops and their families, civilian settlers, and Indians who resided nearby in the mission-controlled *villas*, at least until 1793–1794 when the Spanish crown secularized them.[26]

Regardless of the blurring of racial lines among Tejanos, *barraganería* was widespread in military outposts from the earliest days of colonization. In eighteenth-century Texas, the degree of sex imbalance of men over women induced mestizo presidial soldiers and male settlers to mix freely with subjugated Indian women from local missions. Native American women around San Antonio, Nacogdoches, and La Bahía also lived in concubinage with these men in the nearby Indian *villas*, while their children were almost always Hispanicized. The institution of *barraganería* was by far the most common form of domestic interaction, and Mexican officials rarely enforced criminal penalties for out-of-wedlock *coito*. After 1800 Tejanos often married among themselves, but both Indian and mixed-race women continued to adopt the role of *concubina* and to adhere to the expectations that Mexican society created for them. Certainly John W. Smith's mating options were not limited to formal marriage with a Tejana in 1830. The custom of *barraganería* was firmly established in San Antonio when he and other Anglo-American traders, hunters, and adventurers first began to enter the city.[27]

As in Hispanic society, Anglo men arriving in early Texas conceptualized women in moralistic terms and mutually exclusive categories. Like their Tejano male counterparts, Anglo-Texan men were familiar with social idealizations that placed women in two diametrically opposed categories: the chaste, respectable, and marriageable lady; and the unchaste, unmarriageable mistress or concubine. In keeping with the "true woman" ideal emergent in the urbanizing North and perhaps its exaggerated form among some urban middle-class and elite southerners, Anglo-Texan men idealized a respectable woman as not only chaste but also as submissive, dependent, and pious. In normal social circumstances, female behavior failing to comport with this ideal was inherently suspect and rendered a woman disreputable and unfit for marriage. This did not mean, however, that unmarriageable women were not fit for sexual relations as mistresses or prostitutes.[28]

Ethnocentric prejudices permitted most Anglo-Texan men to place dark-skinned Tejanas in the unchaste and unmarriageable category of women that Hispanic society and their own culture had constructed. The Tejano practice of nude public bathing and the sensuous movements of Tejanas who danced nightly at the balls in San Antonio often shocked and dismayed Anglo-American men traveling or residing there. They also regarded the low-cut dresses of the Tejano village women and their uncorseted figures as both immodest and indecent. Anglo-Texan men living in San Antonio almost always concluded they were morally lax. Most Anglo men, however, held the opinion that moral laxity among Tejanas was largely confined to the darker-skinned women, that is, mestizos and mulattos from the lower *castas*. To many southern men, not surprisingly, the institution of *barraganería* strongly resembled the cohabitative unions of white men and black women with which they were familiar. This perception also reveals, however, the association they made between Tejanas who were mestizas, black women, and lasciviousness.[29]

Regardless of these negative views, Anglo-Texan men found Tejanas extremely appealing. By 1830, John W. Smith had very likely become quite familiar with the perception, common among Anglo-Texan men, that Tejanas were especially pleasing when it came to intimate matters. Although these men adjudged mestizas to be morally lax and of unmarriageable quality, they regularly concluded that Tejanas of all classes and racial categories had kind dispositions and "tender sympathies." Beginning in the early Mexican period, Anglo-Texan men traveling in Hispanic regions frequently commented about the allure of Tejanas. At the same time, they indulged the firm belief that Tejanas were also unusually passionate sexual partners.[30] Latham, for example, wrote in 1840 of new female acquaintances who instructed him in the Spanish language: "[T]hey really *look* as if they could love *harder* and more *devotedly* than any other women."[31] Frederick Benjamin Page wrote similarly of the Mexican women he observed while traveling in the Republic of Texas:

> Voluptuous and fascinating as the Mexican women are, they are never more so than when excited by soft music and the rapturous *fandango* of which they are so fond. Love then sparkles in their eyes, and their sensitive hearts yield irresistibly to the pleasures which it awakes.[32]

Anglo-Texan men frequently took Tejanas as mistresses, especially after independence from Mexico. Except in Nacogdoches, most Anglo-American settlers had little contact with Tejanos before the Texas War of Independence, since they were concentrated in settlements far to the south and west of newer Anglo settlements. There was thus only a limited amount of sexual interaction between Anglo-Texan men and Mexican women before 1836. After independence, however, Anglo-Texans began to migrate southward and westward. San Antonio became the prime military outpost and trading center in Texas, and thus received an unusually large number of unaccompanied Anglo-Texan men. Even more ventured into southern Texas during and after the Mexican War. Anglo-Texan men who traveled to San Antonio or La Bahía, or who resided in these towns from time to time, had frequent involvements with Tejanas. Living and working in close proximity, many of them slept together, once the men had succumbed to the charms of the alluring señoritas and had dealt with their ethnocentric predispositions and emotional conflicts. By the late 1850s, in places as far west as El Paso, most Anglo-Texan men residing in Hispanic communities kept Tejano mistresses.[33]

The Hispanic custom of *barraganería* was well suited to the mobile lifestyle of typical Anglo-Texan frontiersmen. Tejano men usually lived with their mistresses. Anglo men, however, generally lived apart from them, moving freely in and out of the homes of their consorts. The transformation of Tejano mistresses into occasional sexual companions lends credence to Dysart's conclusion that *barraganería* provided a partial substitute for a typical frontier institution, the bawdy house. Post-independence criminal law facilitated the practice, furthermore, since it conspicuously omitted to penalize fornication.[34]

In actuality, the same interplay of sexism and prejudice that encouraged Anglo-Texan men to take Tejano mistresses also prompted them to seek out Hispanic prostitutes with special vigor. Recent Texas history scholarship has described well the Anglo women who flocked initially, in the early 1830s, to nascent towns such as Galveston and Houston to establish thriving brothels. The small hotel and entrepôt for paid sex in La Grange that the notorious "Mrs. Swine" established in 1844 with young women she brought from New Orleans flourished infamously, unabatedly, and with the cooperation of local lawmen for almost 130 years. Even so, organized prostitution developed in Texas long before the Anglo invasion. Hispanic courtesans plied their services in San Antonio when Texas was still a Spanish province, and Hispanic ladies of the night continued to be active there from the earliest days of Anglo-Texan rule. Tejano prostitutes in Corpus Christi catered to the men in General Zachary Taylor's army during its eight-month stay before invading Mexico in 1846, and Tejanas found regular work in the brothels of El Paso accommodating the flood of forty-niners traveling to the goldfields. In 1850, an observer noted that the town of Brownsville, deep in Hispanic southern Texas, was "infected with lewd and abandoned women" who kept "dens of corruption." Lower-class Tejanas, and thus usually those of mixed racial stock and with darker skins, provided the bulk of the workforce in these houses of ill fame. In the view of ethnocentric Anglo-Texan men who nurtured female idealizations that equated chastity and respectability with lighter hues, the mestizo denizens of frontier bawdy houses seemed particularly well suited for their profession. While Tejanas clearly did not monopolize the bawdy house trade in antebellum Texas, the particularly strong appeal of these women to their Anglo-Texan clientele ensured them a steady business.[35]

Some Mexican women viewed marriage to an Anglo-American man as desirable simply because they found these men physically attractive. The adventurer and veteran of the Texas War of Independence John C. Duval, for example, concluded that the señoritas preferred "the blue-eyed fair complexioned young Saxon to their copper-colored beaux."[36] In a similar vein, Kendall observed that Mexican women were particularly fond of "blue-eyed light-haired Americans." According to him,

> In Mexico all light-haired men are termed *guerros*—yellow locks, blue eyes, and a fair complexion, are so uncommon in that country, that the possession of them is a passport directly to the affections of the opposite sex.[37]

The northern critic of slavery Frederick Law Olmstead, while traveling in Texas in 1856, came to a similar conclusion:

> There was testimony of [frequent sexual relations between Mexican women and Anglo-Texan men] in the various shades and

features of their children; in fact, we thought the number of babies of European hair and feature exceeded the native olive in number.[38]

William P. Zuber observed that Tejanas at the fandangos held in Nacogdoches in the late 1820s sometimes preferred to dance with visiting Anglo "redlanders" rather than with the Tejanos in attendance, exciting their jealousy and hatred. He also noted that Tejanas who preferred not to dance with the Anglos were sometimes forcibly pulled to the floor and compelled to do so.[39] There may well be merit in Arnoldo De León's suggestion that racist and psychically conflicted Anglo-Texan men only imagined the Tejanas they found so attractive returned the sentiment.[40] Even so, the notable frequency and openness of sexual relations involving Anglo-Texan men and Tejanas alone makes the contemporaneous conclusions of Olmstead and others quite plausible.

Many upper-class Tejanas viewed marriage with an Anglo-Texan man as a means of maintaining or elevating their own status and that of the children resulting from such unions. In 1830 María Delgado very likely saw her marriage to a fair-skinned Anglo in decidedly positive terms. Mexican mores and racial attitudes developed long before Anglo-Texan immigration placed a premium on a light skin tone. Well-to-do Tejano families prided themselves on their European lineage and looked down on those with Native American or black ancestry. An enduring social stigma attached to mixed race, and the additional taint of slavery attached to mulattos in most of Mexican society. Use of the term "mulatto" in a derogatory manner, continued employment of separate and severe punishments for lawbreakers of mixed race, and the frequency of "passing" all demonstrate that palpable distinctions existed, making the lighter racial categories preferable to most Tejanos. In traditional Hispanic society, furthermore, marriage to a man of European ancestry was a prime vehicle for women of mixed race to elevate themselves and their children and for those with European ancestry to maintain their social rank. That upper-class Tejanas considered Anglo-Texan men preferable as spouses, in racial terms at least, represents but a mere corollary to this preexisting Mexican norm.[41]

The comportment and status of Anglo-Texan men made them attractive marriage partners to socially prominent Tejanas. María Delgado may well have found John W. Smith an attractive marriage prospect for reasons other than his fair complexion. The behavior of immigrant Anglo-Texan men was highly consistent with Mexican prescriptions for a desirable husband. The emergent Anglo-Texan male gender role, to a large degree, paralleled some of the more salient aspects of customary Hispanic maleness. The independence, autonomy, and exaggerated masculine style of Anglo-Texan men, in fact, were largely in accord with traditional Hispanic machismo. At the same time, however, increasingly influential Anglo-American idealizations of marriage posited marital relations in more egalitarian terms. In theory at least, this placed limits on Anglo machismo, a change that educated and rich Tejanas with more liberal views may well have welcomed. Lucrative land grants available to enterprising Anglo-Texan men also made them upwardly mobile. This, along with their increasing political hegemony after 1836, also placed them in good stead as husbands and providers, in keeping with traditional Tejano matrimonial standards.[42]

The racial admixture of upper-class Tejanas made marriage to them appealing to many Anglo men. Given the prominence of her family, it seems quite likely María Delgado possessed physical characteristics that John W. Smith deemed appropriate for a respectable wife. The racial composition of well-to-do Tejanas often diminished or removed entirely the barriers that Anglo men perceived to marriage with those of more obvious mixed race. Anglo-Texan men found Tejanas who had lighter complexions and more European features particularly attractive. According to Latham, these women were "very fair, handsome and even beautiful. Their universally black, silken hair, and full, dark eye, modestly beaming with the most intense and expressive emotion."[43] The Anglo who married a well-born Tejana showing a "trace of rich Castilian lineage," in fact, received none of the reproach from his own people that would have followed his taking an Indian, black, or mestizo wife.[44]

Compatible female and male sex roles also induced marriage of upper-class Tejanas and Anglo-Texan men. Immigrant Anglo-Texan men commonly believed that Tejanas made unusually loving and devoted wives. The subservience, deference, and well-mannered behavior of Tejanas, fostered by Hispanic customs, also approximated a long-standing feminine ideal among the Anglos. Both immigrant Anglo-Texan men and Tejanas accepted the cultural prescription that women should occupy a subordinate role; whereas men appropriated and dominated business and politics, a woman's place was in the home. For some Anglo-Texan men, concern about continued dominance of male over female, in the face of the burgeoning women's movement in the United States, might well have made the more traditional Tejana quite appealing. Firmly rooted in a culture that severely restricted their public roles and opportunities, Tejanas presented a striking contrast, especially for southern men who preferred for their women to display humility, grateful affection, self-renouncing loyalty, and subordination.[45]

A significant minority of upper-class Tejanas married immigrant Anglo-Texan men, beginning most notably in the early 1830s. John W. Smith was not alone in his selection of a rich Tejano bride. In April 1831, later hero of the Alamo James Bowie married Ursula María de Veramendi, daughter of wealthy San Antonio–born Juan Martín de Veramendi, first alcalde of the town in 1824 and governor of Coahuila and Texas in 1832 and 1833. James Hewetson, merchant and *empresario*, fortified his position in Coahuila by marrying wealthy widow Josefa Guarjardo in April 1833. Anglo-Hispanic marriages of this kind, however, occurred more frequently after 1836, when Anglos and Tejanos came into closer proximity in and around San Antonio. Like Smith and Bowie, Anglo-Texan men settling there usually married women from the small Tejano upper class, particularly those who traced their ancestry back to the founding of the town. Civil marriage records dating from 1837 to 1860 in Bexar County reveal that out of 994 Tejanas who married during the period, 88, or approximately 9 percent, married Anglos. Of the marriages of Tejanas to Anglo-Texan men in Bexar County from 1830 to 1860, almost half were from well-to-do San Antonio families.[46]

In the view of many prominent Tejano families, marriage of their daughters to Anglo-Texan men was desirable because it helped maintain family economic and political position within a polity in which Tejanos were rapidly becoming a threatened minority. As early as 1830, when rumblings of Anglo-Texan independence increased notably, María Delgado's family could easily have anticipated the considerable benefits deriving from her marriage to a well-situated Anglo. Before the outbreak of hostilities in 1835, some upper-class Tejanos identified their own political liberalism with Anglo-American ideals and were eager to seal marriages between their young women and Anglo-Texans. After independence, when the Anglos often viewed Tejanos as enemies and suspected disloyalty among many of those who remained, it was politically and economically advantageous for well-to-do Tejano clans to establish family connections with members of the newly dominant group. Such marriages joined Anglo-Texan political influence and Tejano landed wealth, with the aim, quite frequently, of taking an Anglo son-in-law as protection against the loss of extensive holdings. Numerous Tejano families with wealth and power married one or more daughters to Anglos to reinforce their economic and political position. The two decisions the Texas Supreme Court handed down after independence upholding María Delgado's marriage, her community property rights, and the inheritance of her children represent, in fact, one of the most notable successes of this strategy during the antebellum period.[47]

Particularly after 1836, there were substantial political rewards for Anglo-Texan men who married upper-class Tejanas. John W. Smith's marriage to María Delgado situated him well to pursue a successful political career in San Antonio as Anglo-Texans asserted their dominance over the Hispanic population. Although the number of Spanish-surnamed officeholders in San Antonio declined after 1840, the Tejano vote remained an important factor in elections. Anglo men with family ties in the Tejano community consistently won elections to city office during the 1840s and 1850s. Horace "Horatio" Alsbury, who played an important role in the Texas revolt, lived in San Antonio after the war and held numerous offices with the support of his Tejano wife and family. Influential and politically active veteran of the war Erastus "Deaf" Smith similarly received the backing of his wife, Juana Navarro, and the benefit of the intimate connections she had with the Veramendi clan. Like John W. Smith, Edward Dwyer was elected mayor of San Antonio during the republic after first marrying into a leading San Antonio family. John Williamson Moses of Banquete married Victoriana Cuellar in November 1857, and ascended to such offices as justice of the peace and postmaster.[48]

The substantial economic benefits for Anglo-Texan men who married prominent Tejanas continued after independence. The government of the Republic of Texas granted land in larger portions to family men. Marriage to a Tejana thus continued to provide at least this bonus. Given the Hispanic inheritance rules that Texas adopted after independence, however, such a marriage provided much more lucrative opportunities to men who married well-to-do Tejanas. Under the Spanish regime, daughters inherited property on an equal basis with sons. The law thus provided a powerful incentive for enterprising

Anglo-Texan men like Bowie and Hewetson to marry a Tejana from one of the older and wealthier families.[49]

The public and private lives of John W. Smith indicate several important aspects of a cross-cultural dynamic at work in early Texas which encouraged Anglo-Texan men to form intimate relationships with Tejanas and indigenous women. From the earliest years of Anglo-Texan settlement, Anglo men venturing into Hispanic areas found Tejanas particularly attractive. They also commonly believed all Tejanas were unusually passionate lovers and devoted mates. Often isolated from well-organized Anglo communities, immigrant men with broken families and failed marriages overcame ethnocentric predispositions and took advantage of the anonymity and personal liberty the frontier provided to establish interracial sexual relationships.

Smith's marriage to María Delgado, however, also indicates the combined racist and pragmatic impulses of both the arriving Anglo-Texan men in need of female companionship and of the Tejanas who sometimes married them. Anglo men who married "Spanish" women with light complexions and European cultural roots received relatively little criticism from Anglo-Texan society. Significant economic and political advantages accruing to such men further eroded ethnocentric barriers. The Smith-Delgado marriage, however, also reflects the ethnocentric and pragmatic impulses of the native "Castilian" residents. Marriage of a daughter to a fair-skinned Anglo met their own racial preferences. Such marriages also cemented ties to the ascendant Anglo-Texan majority and ensured a beneficial influence for prominent Tejano families within the highest levels of the new Anglo government.

In actuality, a number of ecological and demographic conditions combined with cross-cultural reinforcements to prompt Anglo-Texan men to form sexual and conjugal ties with Native American women and Tejanas. Predisposing Anglo-Texan immigrant men to take these steps was a shortage of marriageable women, the pressures of frontier survival, tolerant Hispanic culture and law, and a southern masculine ideal placing a premium on sexual prowess. Particularly before Indian Removal, tradesmen of European descent frequently married Indian women according to native custom and lived with them among the tribes. While Anglo-Texan men viewed their Native American wives as chattel-servants, the women usually functioned as valuable trade liaisons and helpmates. Reinforcing Hispanic and Anglo-American gender norms and racial-caste conceptions promoted the marriage of Anglo-Texan men and upper-class Tejanas. These same conceptions more frequently, however, encouraged Anglo-Texan men to sexually exploit mestizas and take them as mistresses. Tejana concubinage and Native American marital norms comported with the Anglo-Texan frontiersmen's mobile lifestyle. Marriage of Anglo-Texan men with prominent Tejanas, furthermore, enriched and improved the prospects of Anglo-Texan husbands, reinforced the economic position and status of their wives, and bolstered the political influence and property rights of the families of well-to-do Tejano brides.

TWO

Eros

AND

Dominion

Indians, Tejanos, and Anglos

ad Sam Houston known that one day he would lead the Texas War of Independence, he might well have thought more carefully before reexploring his Indian roots as intimately as he did. After learning within days of his marriage to Eliza Allen that she loved another, the humiliated governor of Tennessee resigned his office and headed for the southwestern frontier. Following a packet trip down the Red River in the late spring of 1829, the thirty-six-year-old Houston traveled overland and reunited with the Cherokee at Tahlontuskee in Indian Territory. He wasted little time in ministering to his wounded pride. At the annual Green Corn Dance in July, Houston rekindled a relationship with Tiana Rogers, a sweetheart from his early life among the Indians in East Tennessee and North Carolina. Thirty years old and a widow, Tiana was the tall and beautiful mixed-race daughter of Captain John "Hell-Fire Jack" Rogers, one of the most prominent white men in the Cherokee Nation. Viewing his marriage to Eliza as no hindrance, Houston began living with Tiana and thus married her according to Cherokee custom. The two established their wigwam on the Neosho River, just a few miles north of Canton-ment Gibson. The setting, however, hardly would have been conducive to domestic tranquility with a respectable white wife. As the western-most military outpost on the United States frontier, Fort Gibson was a wild place, known as the hellhole of the Southwest, where gamblers, ad-venturers, soldiers, Indians, and tradesmen intermingled freely.[1]

During his time with Tiana, Houston lived a dissipated and reck-less existence, while pursuing various opportunities to advance him-self. Now a full-fledged member of the Cherokee tribe, Col-lon-neh (the Raven) established himself at Fort Gibson in the merchant trade, speculated in land, and served as a liaison between the Indians and the Jackson administration. Houston was constantly in motion, making numerous trips back east and to Texas. He traveled to Tennessee four times and, at least on two occasions, visited Eliza, who had experienced a change of heart and wanted to reunite with her runaway husband. During his lengthy absences from Tiana, Houston maintained rela-tions with at least two other Indian wives in and around the territory. All the while, Tiana devotedly maintained their home, the Wigwam Neosho, ministered to the personal needs of her husband, and kept his store. When not traveling, Houston played cards and drank with the soldiers and gamblers at the fort. So frequently was Col-lon-neh in-toxicated in the streets of Gibson, the Indians renamed him Oo-tse-tee Ar-dee-tah-skee (Big Drunk).[2]

After several years, the Raven became restless and desired to rejoin white society. With growing interest in the Anglo-American indepen-dence movement brewing south of the Red River, he decided to leave the wigwam and his Cherokee wife. In November or December of 1832, he said good-bye to Tiana and headed for Nacogdoches. As he set up his Texas law practice, the forty-year-old Houston began court-ing seventeen-year-old Anna Raguet, a slender, blue-eyed blonde and a member of one of the most prominent Nacogdoches families. He pursued Anna devotedly through the Battle of San Jacinto, but after the new president of the republic scandalized the young woman with a controversial divorce from Eliza that smacked of secrecy, fraud, and political influence, her feelings toward him cooled. Sometime in 1838 Houston once again turned to female Indian companionship, marrying the daughter of Duwali, or Chief Bowles, leader of the East Texas Cherokee. The marriage didn't last long, and Houston certainly did not bother to obtain a legal divorce. During an 1839 trip to Alabama in search of financial capital for his Texas enterprises, he met Margaret Moffat Lea of Mobile, the charming widow of a Baptist minister. Sam proposed within a month and legally married the poised, violet-eyed brunette on 9 May 1840. In the view of close friends and acquaintances, the Raven's regeneration was complete.[3]

While he ultimately returned to his own people and married a white woman, the Texas public and Houston's own family hardly approved of his relationships with Native American women. His open and notorious relationship with Tiana had provided his political enemies ample grist with which to ridicule him. The picture conveyed in openly partisan attacks against him in the press "was that of the former governor of Tennessee living at the lowest depths of humanity with a filthy Indian squaw."[4] Members of Houston's family came to accept grudgingly that Sam had lived with Tiana, but for years they refused to believe the two had been husband and wife in the legal and moral sense. Amid rumors that the Father of Texas had begotten numerous Indian children, the Houston family displayed considerable animus toward any public discussion of his renegade sexual past or suggestions that members of the family were related by blood to Indians.[5]

Regardless of the difficulties Sam Houston's family had in accepting his involvement with indigenous women, most settlers were quite familiar with the way some white men associated with female Indians. It seems much less likely, however, that many Anglo settlers thought much about the way their own ethnocentrism and notions about femininity encouraged and shaped the relationships of white frontiersmen with both indigenous women and Tejanas. That these cross-racial and cross-cultural connections comported with an institutional design structuring the sexual relationships of Indians, Tejanos, and Anglos in accordance with white hegemony after independence from Mexico, however, almost certainly would not have surprised any thoughtful contemporary observer.

Ethnocentrism shaping the involvement of Anglo-Texan men and Indian women stemmed from substantial differences in the way their respective cultures organized domestic relationships. Frontiersmen who formed sexual connections with Indian women dealt invariably with people who viewed marriage as an informal arrangement. There were no binding betrothals or marriage vows in any of these societies. Only the Caddo surrounded a wedding with any kind of festivities or attached any religious significance to marital union. In the fashion of the 1829 Cherokee wedding of Sam Houston and Tiana Rogers, simple cohabitation worked to solemnize a marriage among most of the tribes. This usually occurred, however, only after the groom had provided gifts to the parents of the bride or her male kin.[6]

Among all the Indians in Texas, marriage essentially benefited families. Native Americans viewed marriage from an integrated social and economic context in which clans and extended families were the basic social constructs for production and survival. Marriage between women and men from different bands brought to families and clans the valuable economic skills of newly acquired spouses. Male deaths resulting from warfare with whites may well have circumscribed the traditional role the tribes prescribed for women by the time southern whites began filtering into Mexican Texas. Even so, families prized new daughters-in-law as childbearers and domestic managers, and as food growers and preparers. They valued new sons-in-law as providers and protectors, and expected them to devote themselves to hunting and warfare. Though obligations to individual spouses and children were important, Texas Indians regarded the services of both spouses to the extended family and clan as primary obligations.[7]

Polygamy among the tribes reinforced interfamily bonds. The Cherokee hardly could have viewed Sam Houston's legally undissolved marriage to Eliza Allen as an obstacle to his marriage to Tiana Rogers. The Cherokee accepted polygyny, or the custom among high-status men of taking multiple wives. Stemming in part from the ancient imperative of maximizing births, this practice was quite common among all the tribes residing in Texas. Polygyny, however, usually involved the sororate, that is, the marriage of a man to the sister or sisters of his wife. The much less common practice of polyandry similarly entailed the levirate, or the marriage of a woman to the brother or brothers of her husband. Both the sororate and levirate reinforced family connections and clan alliances, especially upon the death of a spouse. If a wife died, for example, the immediate family of the woman provided her husband a new spouse, unless he had already married one or more of his deceased wife's sisters. In this way, death did not jeopardize the linkage between the two families. Among the Comanche, the levirate functioned with particular effectiveness, since husbands were frequently killed in warfare. So vital were these practices among the Kiowa and Kiowa Apache that custom required a man to pay substantial compensation to the widow of his brother if he refused to marry her.[8]

The Indian custom of wife lending, so shocking to whites, derived from the determination to maintain interfamily relationships. Among most of the tribes in Texas, men sometimes authorized their wives to have sexual relations with friends or highly esteemed guests. Particularly among the Tawakoni, husbands were often deeply offended if a guest refused this hospitality and sometimes inflicted horrific punishment on men guilty of such an egregious faux pas. Both wife lending and husband lending, however, usually occurred when a man or woman encouraged a spouse to have sexual relations with his or her sibling. Anthropologists, however, have characterized the more common practice of wife lending as "anticipatory levirate," that is, authorized sex between wife and brother-in-law in anticipation of their future marriage. In societies where the life expectancy of warriors was short, such as that of the Comanche, sexual relations between brother-in-law and wife merely laid the foundation for a marriage that would maintain family alliances in the not unlikely event of a husband's death. In this context, Texas Indians did not view relations between a woman and the likely replacement of her spouse as harmful. Certainly the tribes did not consider this kind of extramarital sexual activity adulterous but rather a proper exercise of family duty.[9]

Indian divorce customs made it fairly simple for spouses to sever relations with one another. The tribes from which Sam Houston selected his Indian wives almost certainly could not have faulted him for the manner in which he terminated his marriages with them or for his abandonment of Eliza Allen. The vital role marriage played in cementing bonds between families did not preempt spouses from dissolving unsatisfactory unions. Marriage was a provisional arrangement either husband or wife could terminate at will. Texas Indians usually divorced, however, when a woman was unfaithful, when a man failed to provide, or when a man mistreated his wife. Indian divorce seemed ridiculously easy to white observers. A Caddoan man, for example, divorced his wife by leaving home. Women from the Cherokee and Choctaw tribes divorced their husbands by putting them and their possessions out of the lodge.[10]

Texas Indians often effected divorce and remarriage simultaneously. Among the Plains tribes, either a man or woman could instantaneously divorce and remarry by the single act of abandonment of an existing spouse and the taking of a new one. Among the Kiowa, either spouse could divorce and remarry by simply "eloping" with a new partner. The sole condition was that the new husband render some form of material compensation to the old one, usually horses or firearms.[11]

The delimited understanding Anglo-Americans had of indigenous cultures and their attitude of superiority prompted them to place little stock in Indian marriages and family integrity. Most whites had little respect for Indian marriage customs because of the perceived mercenary practice of parents selling daughters to the highest bidder. Equally disconcerting was the informal nature of the marital agreement and the ease with which Indian spouses dissolved their unions. Anglo-Americans, furthermore, believed Indian marriages created no discernible binding obligations. That they did not appear to impose duties of mutual fidelity, exclusive intercourse, and cohabitation particularly disturbed whites. All of these views encouraged Anglo-Americans to believe that Indian women and men did not take their marriages seriously. Reflecting a sexist double standard at work within white society, informal coupling and uncoupling among Indians reinforced the view that indigenous women, in particular, were promiscuous, unchaste, and adulterous. The custom among the Comanche of punishing an unfaithful woman by cutting off her nose appears to have reinforced this impression. The practice of polygyny, furthermore, suggested Native American marriages were not only immoral and heathenish but also exploitative of Indian women. Whites commonly perceived Indian husbands as treating their multiple wives like so many chattel-servants, since women assumed the bulk of domestic labor within the tribes.[12]

Whites approached Indian marital customs with beliefs suited to the socioeconomic organization of their own society. In a turbulent and rapidly expanding nation, extended family structures provided both fewer restraints and fewer safeguards for most Anglo-Americans than they had in the British colonial period. For nineteenth-century whites, marriage was basically a private contract between property-owning and property-conscious individuals. Legal marriage led to mutually accumulated material wealth, inheritance rights to such property, and the future security it provided. Monogamous marriage and the nuclear family provided the vital mainstays of physical security, emotional support, companionship, and mutual aid for family members. Divorce was objectionable because it entailed the abrogation of a solemn vow. White society also condemned divorce because the well-being of its members, as well as good social and moral order, vitally depended upon binding, lifelong marriage. For these reasons, rigorous social and institutional support of matrimony seemed imperative.[13]

Anglo-Americans generally failed to apprehend that Native American divorce virtually never created the reprehensible consequences it did in white society. While commenting on the flexible mating customs of the Plains tribes, Dodge observed, "[I]t is very remarkable that so many [of the women] are chaste, and that . . . exchanges of husbands are the exception and not the rule."[14] When divorce and remarriage did occur, however, it was orderly and rarely produced discord among family and clan members. Dissolution of marriage did not ordinarily involve disputes over personal property. Because the concept of real estate was alien to most Indians, squabbles over that form of wealth among divorcing spouses was virtually unknown. Since a decedent's personal belongings were usually buried with him or her, children did not have to concern themselves with later asserting rights to inheritance against the children of their remarried parents. Extended family and clan structures, in fact, provided a functional economic and emotional support network for women who divorced, especially within the much more common matrilineal and matrilocal tribes. In these societies, divorced women and their children continued to have the benefit of support and kinship associations they had enjoyed throughout their lives.[15]

Anglo-Texan men routinely exploited Native American divorce customs to desert their Indian families. Sam Houston's abandonment of his Indian wives and his ultimate return to white society were hardly atypical. White men almost never wed their indigenous consorts in accordance with Anglo law. Since they placed little stock in Indian marriages, they usually simply left their Indian wives when they wished to rejoin white society. To some extent, abandonment of Native American families was consistent with the personal histories of many Anglo-Texan frontiersmen. Given their low estimation of Indian women, however, desertion of an Indian wife for most of these men posed much less of a moral dilemma than abandonment of one who was white. While Anglo-Texans condemned casual marriage and divorce among the tribes, white men who married Indian women almost always took advantage of the ease with which they could exit these customary relationships. They seldom made efforts, furthermore, to provide for the families they left behind.[16]

The sexual relations of Anglo-Texan men with Native American women reveal a classic pattern of white supremacy. From the earliest years in Mexican Texas, marriage with an Indian woman was a temporary and extremely casual relationship for most white frontiersmen. They rarely brought their Indian wives and Anglo-Indian children into their own families or white society before large-scale Indian Removal or thereafter. While white men certainly appreciated the practical benefits their Indian consorts provided, they did not ordinarily consider them bona fide spouses. Like the members of Sam Houston's family, white Texans viewed the Indian wives of frontiersmen as concubines or temporary and expedient sexual partners. By the same token, they viewed the children born of these exploitative relations as inferior. This pattern correlates strongly with that evident in other colonial societies in which dominant Europeans subordinated and excluded darker-skinned consorts and mixed-race children from their own societies.[17]

The risk was slight to abandoning white men that their Indian wives or Anglo-Indian children would actually make claims to their estates. The apparently complacent behavior of the numerous Indian women whom Sam Houston left behind had deep roots in Indian culture and folkways. When white men deserted their Native American families, the consorts they left behind usually perceived that the separation itself effected a valid divorce and did not consider pursuing one in a court of law. Since divorcing spouses in Native American societies did not involve themselves in extensive property settlements, the abandoned Indian wives of Anglo-Texan men were not predisposed to enter white courts of law to make marital property claims. And since Texas Indians bequeathed little or no property, Indian wives and Anglo-Indian children ordinarily did not give much thought to asserting claims to inheritance. They would have seldom known when and where absconding husbands and fathers had died in any case. Only the very rare Indian woman or Anglo-Indian child who had taken significant steps toward assimilation was predisposed to make estate claims in the alien and highly formalized tribunals of the white man.

Even if abandoned Indian wives and Anglo-Indian children did assert claims, the law worked with frontier mores to deny them. Many antebellum jurists spurned Indian marriages because couples could terminate them at will. In the case of mixed marriages, justices routinely noted the problem of distinguishing female Indian concubinage from "real" matrimony. But a number of state supreme courts claimed principles of comity, and the United States Constitution required them to recognize such relationships. In actuality, these courts usually relied on common law marriage rules, which recognized a union when a couple agreed to marry or when they cohabited and were reputed to be spouses. Moreover, they almost always used "habit and repute" evidentiary rules in probate proceedings when mixed-race children asserted claims to the estates of fathers who had deserted them and returned to white society many years earlier. Consequently, validation was usually forthcoming only if a man had lived with his Indian family in a white community, or if he had returned to white society, acknowledged his Indian child, and supported the child. The rules thus proved useless to most potential Anglo-Indian claimants. Tribal customs and the expectations, conduct, and assertions of the Indian women whom frontiersmen left behind usually did not help abandoned family members to obtain relief, since they almost never appeared in court to establish claims. Judges thus concerned themselves almost exclusively with the very few Anglo-Indian children for whom some white men had voluntarily assumed some long-term responsibility.[18]

Only toward the end of the antebellum period were Texas trial courts predisposed to consider Anglo-American jurisprudence regarding marriages of Native Americans and Anglo-Texans. Mexican law certainly did not recognize informal Indian marriages or those based on "habit and repute," nor did the Texas Supreme Court through the years of the republic. Shortly after statehood, in compliance with constitutional precepts, the high court in Texas recognized the right of the tribes to govern their own domestic relations. And in 1847, it adopted common law marriage.[19] But the high court never dealt with the validity of Anglo-Indian marriages before 1860. Texas trial judges, however, typically looked to other United States jurisdictions for precedents on unsettled points of law. It thus seems quite likely that lower Texas courts between 1847 and 1861 would have utilized mainstream United States doctrine to adjudicate Anglo-Indian marriages on those rather infrequent occasions when the children resulting from them asserted their validity in probate proceedings.[20]

Further indicating this conclusion is the only nineteenth-century appellate ruling in Texas dealing with a cross-racial Indian marriage. About 1845, William T. Patterson began living in Indian Territory with Mrs. Alcy, a Creek woman. She gave birth to a female child in 1848 and cohabited with Patterson for several more years before he abandoned her and their child and resettled in Texas. Patterson died in June 1891, and his forty-three-year-old Anglo-Indian daughter sued Patterson's white heirs in Travis County District Court for the $2,000 constituting his estate. The ostensible issue identified at trial, and on appeal, was whether informal Creek marriage customs could sustain the legitimacy and inheritance claims of Alcy's daughter.[21] In its 1896 decision *First National Bank of Austin v. Sharpe,* the Texas Court of Civil Appeals conceded the Creek had no written laws concerning matrimony or ceremonial marriage rites, but stated that constitutional principles compelled recognition of their informal usages. Writing for the court, Associate Justice William Mercer Key noted there was some evidence presented at trial that showed Patterson never believed he had actually married Alcy and had never intended to do so. On the other hand, Justice Key concluded there was enough evidence to support the jury finding.

> [T]hey agreed to be husband and wife . . . and the evidence is quite clear . . . they cohabited with each other for a considerable time before and after appellee was born, and publicly recognized and treated each other as husband and wife . . . and for years afterwards he acknowledged appellee as his child, and contributed to her support.[22]

As in most cases of this kind in other United States jurisdictions, the recognition of the court actually turned on common law marriage principles rather than on Creek matrimonial customs, the testimony of tribal members familiar with the marital relationship, or the assertions of a former Indian wife. Of equal importance, the decision rested essentially on Patterson's acknowledgment to Travis County whites of his daughter and lifelong support of her.

While white prejudice and tribal customs encouraged frontiersmen to abandon their Indian wives and children, antebellum Texas law ratified exclusion of the abandoned family members from Anglo-Texan society. Only if lower Texas courts had deviated substantially from the mainstream policy in the United States regarding validation of mixed tribal marriages would the courts have legitimated the casual sexual relationships that white men formed briefly within the tribes. As did Sam Houston on numerous occasions, Anglo-Texan men could discard their Indian consorts and children at will, with impunity, and without the necessity of utilizing divorce courts. Few Native American women would have resorted to an affiliation proceeding to establish the paternity of their illegitimate child even had the procedure been available.[23] Even so, the statutory omission legally insulated white men from financial responsibility for their Indian children. The law of informal marriage and bastardy thus empowered Anglo-Texan men to keep Native American women as concubines without risking diversion of personal wealth or white family property to them or to the children resulting from such unions.

The regime of private law that encouraged the exclusion of Indian wives and Anglo-Indian children from white society was only part of a more fundamental scheme of racial ordering that Anglo-Texans instituted after independence from Mexico. Rejecting Mexican law that acknowledged political rights for Indians, leaders in the new republic denied Native Americans participation in republican government and thus an equal status with whites. Taking the first steps toward establishing a racial-caste system, Anglo-Texans expelled most of the East Texas Indians beginning in 1839 and segregated the remaining few from white society. While treaties settled the Alabama and Coushatta briefly on a reservation, homesteaders and white authorities stripped almost all indigenous peoples in East Texas of their lands. After statehood, Texas leaders granted the remaining Native Americans citizenship and the derivative right to receive new lands from the government, but only on the condition that they pay taxes.[24] Payments of this kind hardly appealed to the independent Native Americans, since they inevitably perceived them as tribute and an implicit abdication of their sovereignty. Payment of taxes was also ill-suited to their barter economy, which generated little cash. Homesteading on lands the government might have granted also required Indians to separate from their tribes and become isolated agriculturalists, a change so radical and undesirable as to guarantee their rejection of this offer. Ethnocentric mores and legal precepts effectively denying the Indian consorts and their children by Anglo-Texan men a place in white society thus worked within a larger exclusionist framework of public law.

After independence from Mexico, Texas leaders contemplating statutory rules about Indian-Anglo marriage and sex did so just as they were rapidly developing a negative assessment of Native Americans. Into the 1820s, many leaders in the United States continued to believe matrimony of this kind might provide a solution to the problem of frontier conflict and a humane dispensation for the tribes. A number of philanthropists, reformers, and politicians maintained that assimilation through marriage would "civilize" and "Christianize" the Indians and thus save them from extermination.[25] In an 1808 speech to a group of Native Americans, for example, Thomas Jefferson announced, "You will mix with us by marriage, your blood will run in our veins, and will spread with us over this great island."[26] To a large degree, this belief derived from the positive theories of a group of scientists denominated "monogenists." Since the American Revolution, these ethnological theorizers had argued that Native Americans belonged to the same species as Caucasians. By the early 1830s, however, new ethnological theorists asserted that the various races of humankind were, in fact, different species. In their view, Indian inferiority was thus innate rather than the result of insufficient education. For whites, assimilation of Indians through formal intermarriage became unthinkable.[27]

The rhetoric attending the drastic policy of Indian Removal that President Mirabeau B. Lamar instituted reveals the distinctive racist conceptualization working against the incorporation of Indians into white society. By 1839, Texas leaders had embarked upon establishing a new republic with an emergent collective identity rooted in the concept of "Anglo-Saxonism." This idea clearly drew on the same pseudoscientific theories characterizing Native Americans, for the first time, as a separate and inferior species.[28] Lamar's justification for the forced removal of the tribes posited rather clearly the inherent superiority of Anglo-Texans over Indians and the notion that the tribes present in the polity were irredeemably primitive and unassimilable:

> The proper policy to be pursued towards the barbarian race, is absolute expulsion from the country. . . . The white man and the red man cannot dwell in harmony together. Nature forbids it. They are separated by the strongest possible antipathies, by colour, by habits, by modes of thinking, and indeed by all the causes

which engender hatred, and render strife the inevitable consequence of juxtaposition.[29]

Lamar was not alone in popularizing natural Indian inferiority. An
editor on the western Texas frontier in 1840 wrote, "An Indian has not
one redeeming quality in his composition: the whole race are thieves
and murderers. . . . Lying, stealing, and murdering are their nature, and
it cannot be reclaimed from his [sic] brutality. . . . These . . . [are the]
lowest of all created beings."[30] In a more scholarly manner, Dr. Samuel G. Morton, a well-known Philadelphia ethnologist, asserted the
inherent deficiency of Native Americans in a widely published essay the
Houston Morning Star carried in installments through 1843. Morton
concluded that all the "aboriginal nations" of North and South America were "decidedly inferior to the Mongolian stock. . . . averse to the
restraints of education . . . [and] incapable of a continued process of
reasoning on abstract subjects."[31]

As these editorials and the address of President Lamar indicate,
more negative views of Native Americans emerged among Anglo-
Texans in tandem with increasingly hostile relations between the two
groups. Adverse "scientific" conceptions of Indians intensified in the
United States as white settlers swept westward after the War of 1812
and as frontier warfare with Native Americans increased in the 1820s
and 1830s.[32] After 1836, Anglo-Texans engaged in chronic and particularly bloody strife with various independent Texas tribes, including the
Tonkawa, Lipan Apache, and Comanche.

The memoirs and diaries of homesteaders attest to the venom resulting from the growing conflict. A. J. Sowell, for example, recounted
a "depredation" that occurred in Nacogdoches County one night in
1838. Nine armed men who were on patrol, looking for some offending
tribesmen, came to the Hutchinson homestead for a respite. The obstreperous Indians, "hideously painted," appeared unexpectedly during
supper. While the men ran to an adjacent building for their muskets,
Mrs. Hutchinson "seized a heavy iron shovel . . . commenced a most
furious attack . . . and succeeded in beating one of them to the floor
before she was tomahawked." Her daughter Anna similarly flew at the
intruders "with a weapon of some kind . . . but she was also struck on
the head and fell to the floor lifeless." The attackers cut out Anna's left
breast and set the house ablaze before Mr. Hutchinson and the other
men could get organized and summon up the courage to wade into

the brawl.[33] While these tribesmen escaped without a single casualty, Anglo-Texan settlers routinely committed depredations of their own. Sowell commented on a militia expedition of forty men that tracked down a band of Native Americans encamped on the Trinity River in the early fall of 1842:

> Here the Indians had a village with growing corn, pumpkins, and water melons. The settlers furiously charged in among them, and a short, but bloody fight ensued. The Indians soon gave way and fled through the bottoms, leaving fourteen of their number dead on the ground. . . . The village was set on fire . . . and the pioneers returned to their homes, having broken up one of the strongholds of the hostiles.[34]

Regardless of growing hatred of Native Americans and hardening conceptions of them, Texas legislators enacted no law prohibiting whites from having sexual relations with Indians or marrying them. The vigorous public condemnation of Sam Houston's sexual escapades among the tribes certainly demonstrates the contempt many Anglo-Texans had for white men who married Indian women. Even so, the first Texas antimiscegenation act, passed in 1837, resembled those of most other southern states, banning and penalizing only the marriage of persons of African ancestry to persons of European descent. A revision of the act in 1858 also prohibited and punished intermarriage of only persons from these two racial groups.[35] While post-independence law aimed at the general population penalized "living in fornication," the long-standing custom of female Indian concubinage on earlier southern frontiers and in Mexican Texas militated against prosecutions.[36] White settlers and leaders concerned themselves little with white men who lived with Indian women unobtrusively beyond the pale. Enforcement of white law among the independent tribes was virtually impossible in any case. After 1845, furthermore, the Texas Supreme Court explicitly recognized the United States Constitution prohibited the state government from interfering in the self-rule and domestic relations of the Indian Nations.[37]

To some extent, Anglo-Texans may have refrained from banning the marriage or sexual intimacy of whites with Native Americans simply because of contraindicating United States legal tradition. Mexican law had accepted marriage between Indians and whites and imposed no special penalties on Indians and Tejanos who engaged in out-of-wedlock *coito*. Laws banning interracial sex and marriage during the British colonial period in North America certainly reveal that attitudes toward tawny-skinned Indians and black-skinned Africans differed substantially. Colonial legislators, however, aimed such laws almost exclusively at relationships of blacks and whites. Public disapproval of unions between Indians and whites notwithstanding, only North Carolina and Virginia forbade the marriage of Indians and whites. No colonies applied special penalties for the fornication of Indians and whites, as they often did for relationships involving blacks and whites. Only a few states, furthermore, passed statutes banning or penalizing sex and marriage between Indians and whites.[38]

Another consideration militating against the adoption of a ban against sex and marriage between Indians and whites was the rapidly changing demography. Even at the time Sam Houston married the daughter of Chief Bowles in 1838, whites greatly outnumbered Native Americans in East Texas. The percentage of men in the Anglo-Texan population who might have involved themselves with Indian women was much smaller than ever before and likely to become even smaller. By the same token, the threat that Native Americans might absorb whites through intermarriage was rapidly disappearing. Indian Removal from the summer of 1839 through 1842 greatly reduced the probability that sexual involvements between Indians and whites would occur very often, especially since Anglo-Texans had driven most of the immigrant tribes north of the Red River and thus into the Indian Territory. By the late 1840s, the Anglo-Texan population dwarfed that of the few segregated bands remaining. Unusually aggressive warfare with the Comanche and Kiowa along the line of settlement and further west through the 1850s alienated whites from Native Americans more than ever. Under these circumstances, a criminal penalty for marriage or sexual relations between them was almost pointless.[39]

Some Native Americans in Texas after Indian Removal certainly made efforts to make a place for themselves in the new racial order. A few indigenous women continued to join their Anglo-Texan husbands in white society. Lawyer George Washington Paschal, for example, lived in Galveston and then in Austin after 1847 with his Cherokee wife, Sarah Ridge, while working to establish the claims of her tribe against the United States government. Thanks to the efforts of Sam Houston in his second administration, various Shawnee and Delaware bands maintained cooperative relations with Anglo-Texans along the margins of settlement. Many members of these tribes, however, were the offspring of mixed marriages resulting from generations of white contact. Mixed-race warriors who straddled both worlds, like John Connor, served as scouts, interpreters, and guides for Texas militiamen and Rangers. Other Anglo-Indians, like Jim Sagundai and Jack and Joe Harry, also worked their dual status as messengers and mediators between Anglo-Texan leaders and the staunchly resistant Comanche through to the Civil War. Also notable in this regard was Jesse Chisolm, the Anglo-Cherokee trader and close relative of Tiana Rogers.[40]

At least one Anglo-Indian woman turned the emerging white supremacy to her own advantage. Rebecca McIntosh Hagerty was the daughter of William McIntosh, the half-Scottish chief of the Lower Creek, and his second wife, Susanna Coe, a Creek. Having been expelled from Georgia in 1825, Rebecca and her family resettled with their slaves near Fort Gibson. In 1831, she married Benjamin Hawkins, an educated Anglo-Creek and sometime business partner of Sam Houston. Late in 1833, the couple moved to Texas, settled near Nacogdoches, and had two daughters. After Hawkins was murdered—apparently for conspiring with Houston to introduce a large Creek settlement into Texas—Rebecca began to purchase land and slaves. In 1838, she married Spire M. Hagerty, a planter with large holdings of land in Harrison County. While her marriage to Hagerty was troubled from the beginning, Rebecca continued to acquire land. By 1860 she was one of the richest planters in antebellum Texas and the only woman there who owned more than a hundred slaves. It thus appears that having some European ancestry and success at obtaining the penultimate emblems of white hegemony qualified even women with Native American blood and acculturation to secure a place in the dominant racial caste and to marry men within its highest echelon.[41]

In many respects, however, Anglo-Texans did not deny Indians admission into white families and society. For the most part, Texas leaders could rely on the enmity and customs of the tribes to deter extensive intimacy between Native Americans and Anglo-Texans; the independent tribes hardly wished a place for themselves among people they regarded as their enemy. Their hostility to white encroachment and continual warfare with advancing settlers clearly testify to this. By 1860, very few Texas tribes had agreed to residence on reservations. Few Indians, furthermore, had departed from their clans and attempted to join white communities. On the other hand, the resistance of the independent Texas tribes comported quite well with the pattern of sexual ordering that dominant Anglo-Texans preferred.

White racial hegemony also affected the relationships Anglo-Texan men had with Tejanas. Tejano men often made enduring commitments to their *concubinas* and the children they had with these women. Spanish law legitimating the children of parents who married and permitting a man to acknowledge legally his bastard child both facilitated and ameliorated the custom of *barraganería*. For the most part, white men sexually exploited their Tejano mistresses and made few efforts to provide for them or their Anglo-Hispanic children. These men, in fact, usually viewed their Tejano consorts as occasional sexual partners rather than as bona fide mistresses or wives. Certainly most of these relationships did not reach the level of stable, long-term, cohabitative unions. Post-independence legislation perpetuated Mexican law that permitted colonial couples to legitimate their children by marriage, and a statute implemented after statehood revived a Hispanic notarial device permitting men to adopt their out-of-wedlock offspring. Anglo men, however, seldom took advantage of these rules to take responsibility for the illegitimate children they fathered with their mistresses.[42]

Some Anglo-Texan men simply abandoned their Tejano mistresses and Anglo-Hispanic children rather than assume responsibility for them. As Frederick Olmstead traveled along the Rio Grande in 1856, he and his party came upon a "strikingly attractive Mexican woman" with a mixed-race child "dressed entirely in American garb." The anxious mother had stationed herself at the crossroads to inquire of all who passed if they had seen her white husband further west. A knowledgeable Mexican man traveling with Olmstead, however, told him the two had simply been lovers, and the man had abandoned her after she became pregnant. The woman reported, however, that her former companion had promised to return in a year after completing a trip to California. According to Olmstead, three years had passed since she had heard from him.[43]

As Olmstead's encounter indicates, Tejano mistresses and their mixed-race children rarely became part of white society. Tejanas usually raised their out-of-wedlock children without the assistance or regular presence of the Anglo-Texan men who fathered them. According to Jane Dysart, "[C]oncubinage without the sustained contact of sharing the same household was unlikely to promote Americanization of the Mexican woman or her mixed-blood children, at least not to the extent *barraganería* had Hispanicized many of the Indians." The children that white frontiersmen had with Tejanas out of wedlock, in fact, usually assumed the surname of their mothers and maintained an exclusive affiliation with their matrilineal kin. They were, consequently, usually acculturated in Hispanic society.[44]

The Texas law of marriage and bastardy worked to deny important property rights to the Tejano mistresses of white men and the children they had together. In Mexican Texas, Hispanic law and related Catholic Church rules certainly did not view a man and a woman who cohabited as husband and wife. By the same token, Tejanas did not presume a marriage in this situation or that their Anglo-Hispanic children were legitimate. Texas courts were not predisposed to validate the sexual relationships of Anglo-Texan frontiersmen and Tejanas after the judicial adoption of common law marriage in 1847. Like Anglo-Texan society in general, ethnocentric judges were not inclined to characterize these sporadic interracial connections as lawful marriages. With no affiliation procedure available, furthermore, Tejanas could not impose financial responsibility for their children on the Anglo-Texan men who fathered them even when they wanted to do so.[45] Tejano mistresses thus usually had no matrimonial property rights and their Anglo-Hispanic children ordinarily had no cognizable claims to patrimonial inheritance. The support that extended Tejano families and communities provided to such women and children, however, worked to induce the acquiescence of mistresses to the situation and to ameliorate it.

The pattern of marriage between Tejanas and Anglo men also comported with Anglo-Texan dominance. The xenophobia and racism of Anglos impeded the marriage of Tejanas and Anglo men through the antebellum period. While the number of matrimonial ties involving Anglo men and Tejanas increased notably after independence, these unions constituted a decreasing proportion of all Texas marriages. By 1860, only 6 of 1,055 married couples were Anglo-Tejano.[46] Those marriages sealed after 1836 in San Antonio, furthermore, occurred as that town became a commercial and military center which Anglo-Texans dominated economically, politically, and socially. Of equal importance, Anglo-Texan men there usually married high-status Tejanas. The marriage of John Smith to María Delgado reflected this trend, exemplifying the tendency of dominant males within a conquering group to marry only select high-status women from subordinated groups. That prominent Tejano families married their daughters to Anglo-Texan men as a hedge against loss of property and political influence reflects a complementary aspect of this sexual-political pattern.[47]

In rural areas, Tejanas and the children they had with Anglo-Texan husbands had little opportunity to assimilate into Anglo society and made few efforts to do so. On *ranchos* and in small villages in Hispanic areas south of San Antonio, Tejanas who married Anglo men associated almost exclusively with their own families and provincial Tejano society. These women, consequently, reared their mixed-race children in this setting. In the Lower Rio Grande Valley in the 1850s, Anglo-Hispanic children even attended schools in Mexico. Both wives and children had little or no contact with the families of Anglo-Texan husbands and fathers. In these circumstances, Tejano wives and Anglo-Hispanic children were neither situated nor predisposed to assimilate into Anglo-Texan society. Consequently, they were thoroughly Hispanicized.[48]

Even in town settings, the Tejanas whom Anglo-Texan men married and their children received no strong reinforcements for Americanization. Tejano wives maintained close ties with kinship groups homogeneously Hispanic. Consequently, they took charge of the socialization process of the children they had with their Anglo husbands. Whether the father was Catholic or not, these women customarily saw to it that their children were baptized in the Roman Catholic faith. Most of them received typically Spanish names. In several instances, Anglo-Hispanic families shared the same household with Tejano grandparents. The godparents, or *padrinos*, of Anglo-Hispanic children were almost always Tejanos.[49]

Many legitimate mixed-race children in San Antonio, however, made determined efforts to gain acceptance among Anglo-Texans. Since Anglo and Hispanic families were not segregated residentially there, mixed-race children had frequent contacts with their Anglo-Texan neighbors. Children born of mixed marriages attended schools with white children. The great majority of upper-class Anglo-Hispanic children made consistent efforts, in adulthood at least, to establish identity with the racial group of their father rather than that of their mother. By the time they became adults, the majority had Anglicized their given names. Some became Protestant or attended English-speaking Roman Catholic churches. With rare exceptions, neither the sons nor daughters married Tejanos. In short, this generation moved significantly toward assimilation with Anglo-Texan society.[50]

Most of the Tejanas who married Anglo-Texan men and their mixed-race children found the dominant group had erected almost insurmountable obstacles to complete assimilation with them. While legitimate Anglo-Hispanic children often made determined efforts to Americanize and move into Anglo society, they still occupied a lower status within it. Only well-to-do Tejano wives with light skin and mixed-race children with Anglo-American surnames and fair complexions had a reasonable chance to escape the full impact of the stigma attached to their Mexican ancestry. The pressures urging Anglo-American conformity were intense. The obstacles to full acceptance in Anglo-Texan society, however, were virtually insuperable. The nativist movement of the 1850s exacerbated hostilities against non-Anglo-Saxon and Catholic groups. Anglo-Texans laid upon the Tejanos an onus of guilt for the Alamo and Goliad. The basis of discrimination and violence that prevented full assimilation and equal status for Tejano wives and their children, however, was the sense of racial and cultural superiority that Anglo-Texans cultivated. Anglos continued to view Tejanos as inferior and as a threat to economic and political progress. Tejanas and their legitimate Anglo-Hispanic children thus consistently experienced racism and exclusion rather than social equality with the Anglo majority.[51]

Anglo-Texan law facilitating the relationships of Anglo men and Hispanic women emerged amid conflicting conceptions of Tejano fitness. While most Anglo-Texans viewed themselves superior to Tejanos, the basis of this belief was not clear in the colonial period. To a large degree, negative perceptions of Tejanos then had their origins in cultural differences between the two groups. Many in the growing majority, however, also believed the "backwardness" of Tejanos was simply the result of their mixed racial composition.[52]

Anglo-Texans were decidedly opposed to accepting Tejanos in the new polity during the struggle for independence. Through the conflict, Anglo settlers hounded suspect Tejanos out of Texas and seized their lands illegally. Without their farms and ranches, many Tejano families found themselves dispossessed, ostracized, and homeless. Amid the heated passions of war, most of the Anglos were determined to create a homogeneously Anglo citizenry.[53]

Anglo-Texans established their own political order amid the increasingly common view that Tejanos were inferior, not simply as a matter of culture, but strictly as a matter of race. The determination of Anglo-Texans during their struggle for independence to justify slavery and then Indian Removal occurred in step with an increased emphasis on the inherent superiority of Anglos. Indeed, as race-conscious Anglos grew more aware of the "affinity" of mestizos and Indians, they associated Indian treachery and cruelty to this blood connection. Anglo-Texans also began to note an even more disturbing affinity between their slaves and the Tejanos. For this reason, Anglo-Texans often falsely accused Tejanos of slave theft and of encouraging runaways. In any case, new ideas positing the racial inferiority of Tejanos began to vitiate the hope of regenerating them with the imposition of a superior—that is, Anglo-Saxon—cultural and political environment.[54]

Acceptance of Tejanos within the new political order also seemed to imply Anglo-Texan racial attenuation and thus degradation. Southern whites perceived a fundamental linkage between citizenship, suffrage, and marital freedom.[55] Political equality of Anglo-Texans and Tejanos was clearly inconsistent with the imperatives of Anglo-Saxonism, since it also suggested social equality and thus the possibility of unimpeded Anglo-Hispanic marriage. As Texas Anglos conceived of themselves and other cultural groups in terms of inherent racial qualities, interbreeding with dark-skinned Tejanos seemed, more than ever, a threat to Anglo society. Anglo-Texans saw "degeneration," in the case of the Tejanos, almost exclusively as the result of *mestizaje*. Spanish marriage with Indians and blacks, whom Anglo-Texans now characterized as naturally inferior, had produced a "mongrel race" incapable of advancement or self-government. The Tejano represented, more than ever, the degenerate Spaniard, a "white man gone bad." The Tejano thus became a negative example of special relevance to Anglo-Texans who nurtured growing fears that interracial marriage and "amalgamation" might sabotage their own special destiny.[56]

The positive role that many Tejanos had played in the successful war of independence, however, mitigated adverse Anglo-Texan attitudes toward those who remained and provided a marginal political presence for such Tejanos. Texas Anglos were not prepared to discriminate too much against the Mexican people who had risked their lives and fortunes to establish and defend the republic. The 1836 constitution consequently provided citizenship for Tejanos, albeit under strict and precarious terms. It made eligible only those who had actively supported the revolt against Mexico. The new constitution empowered Anglo-Texans to seize the lands of Tejanos who had fled to avoid participation in the war. It also denied these people rights of citizenship, which would have qualified them for new land grants. Since the constitution denied citizenship to "the descendants of Africans, and Indians," the position of Tejanos in the new republic was even more tenuous. Anglo leaders, however, never strictly construed the constitutional language. A respect for due process thus had deterred the disfranchisement of Tejanos and mitigated their despoilment. By the end of the 1830s, some Anglo-Texans even welcomed loyal and hard-working Tejanos as citizens and landholders.[57]

As the mutual enmity cooled in the late 1830s, some Anglo-Texans decided the "problem" with the remaining Tejanos lay in a cultural legacy of Spanish misrule that might be rectified. Anglo leaders and many Tejano liberals came to believe the insidious power of the Catholic Church over the Mexican people had induced the disturbing apathy the Tejanos seemed to display. These leaders also conjectured the anti-liberalism of the authoritarian Mexican political and military hierarchy had reinforced habits of docility among the Hispanic inhabitants. This view of Tejano deficiency in some quarters, however, at least held out the hope of regenerating those who had survived the purge.[58]

On the heels of renewed tensions with Mexico in the early 1840s, the Anglo-Texan estimate of Tejanos deteriorated. The year 1841 appears to have been the high-water mark for Tejanos. In the next several years tensions with Mexico increased rapidly, as the possibility loomed of "annexing" New Mexico. Texas political leaders frequently distinguished "good Mexicans" from "bad Mexicans," noble Castilian federalists from semisavage mixed-race centralists. A number of other developments combined also to produce a marked reaction among Anglo-Texans against the Tejano population. These included the involvement of Texas in the Mexican federalist wars, the tensions which the renewed conflict with Mexico along the southwestern frontier aroused, the malaise gripping the republic in the difficult depression years of the 1840s, and some very tangible evidence in 1842 of disloyalty on the part of several prominent Tejano patriots of the war of independence.[59]

A formal proposal attendant on statehood regarding the franchise drew resurgent Anglo intolerance of Tejanos to a head. The incorporation of Tejanos as citizens in the new state of Texas was clearly distasteful to most Anglos. During the constitutional convention of 1845, a proposal to extend the franchise only to Indians who paid taxes and "free white males" precipitated a debate over the necessity of the explicitly racial designation. Those who favored the extension of the franchise to Tejanos urged that the word "white" be deleted. On 23 July, Francis Moore, Jr., delegate from Harris County, expressed his fears in no uncertain terms. He argued that by deleting the word "white," the state would be vulnerable later to "hordes of Mexican Indians" who might come from the west and "vanquish the Anglos at the ballot box." The next day, Moore renewed his attack, based on the standard litany that uneducated, inferior Mexicans were not fit to vote but only to have their votes manipulated or bought and sold.[60]

Moore's strident objection to Tejano enfranchisement generated trenchant countervailing debate. Henry L. Kinney of San Patricio launched a rebuttal to Moore's charges. Kinney's arguments focused on how few Tejanos had been allowed to stay, their demonstrated loyalty, their willingness to fight in the war of independence, and their taxpaying status.[61] Thomas Jefferson Rusk of Nacogdoches, the president of the convention, also spoke in favor of political rights for Tejanos. He argued that "to exclude [those] . . . we found in possession of the country when we came here. . . . [w]ould be injurious to the people, to ourselves, and the magnanimous character which the Americans have ever possessed."[62] Apparently swayed by these arguments, the majority of the delegates overcame their prejudices and voted to exclude the word "white" from the franchise provision.[63]

The delegates also took this step because of the difficulty of fashioning language that would distinguish Tejanos from Indians and blacks. Ultimately a large majority of the framers of the new constitution agreed the "white" restriction was not only unnecessary but also potentially troublesome because of the varied composition of the Tejano population. The inclusion of the word "white," along with explicit references to blacks and Indians, might be construed to place Tejanos with the two disfranchised racial groups. At the same time, the legal construction of a racial category that would include language distinguishing Texans of Mexican ancestry on the one hand and Indians and "persons of African ancestry" on the other would have been extremely difficult to fashion, if not totally arbitrary and unworkable. The designation "Mexican" covered a racial spectrum that included Hispanicized Indians with no trace of European blood, old Spanish families in San Antonio of mostly European extraction, and mestizos with various degrees of black and Indian ancestry. As James Ernest Crisp has pointed out, the Hispanic concept of *la raza* was simply not analogous to the color-oriented Anglo-Texan concept of race.[64]

The decision of Texas lawmakers to permit Anglo-Hispanic sex and marriage implicated some of the same considerations dealt with in deciding political rights for Tejanos. The antimiscegenation law of 1837 and its 1858 revision banned only marriage of persons of European extraction and persons of African ancestry. Having granted Tejanos citizenship, denying them marriage and sexual relations with Anglos would have relegated them to a status inconsistent with those rights—indeed, lowering them to the status of free blacks and slaves. Not only would this have represented a glaring inconsistency in law and principle, it would have ignored the underlying considerations compelling post-independence lawmakers to extend citizenship status to some Tejanos in the first place, that is, their native birth, sacrifices, and loyalty to the republic. The diverse racial composition of Tejanos, furthermore, represented a conceptual barrier to the formulation of statutory antimiscegenation language precise enough to be functional. In the final analysis, sexual and marital liberty for Tejanos constituted a blend of fundamental justice, political expediency, white supremacy calculations, and pragmatism.

The weight of legal tradition also militated against a proscription of Anglo-Hispanic matrimony and sex. Even if Anglo-Texan lawmakers had given full vent to their prejudices and managed to formulate a functional statute to proscribe Anglo-Hispanic mixing, such a law would have represented a significant break with Spanish, Mexican, and United States legal development. A law proscribing marriage or sexual relations between Tejanos and Anglo-Americans, in fact, would have been wholly unprecedented. None of the British North American colonies or jurisdictions of the United States had ever established such a rule, either judicially or legislatively. Certainly the law of New Spain or of Mexico had never erected barriers to interracial sexual relations or marriage.[65]

The connection of prominent leaders to Tejano families also thwarted a proscription of Anglo-Hispanic matrimony. Texas lawmakers certainly had to consider the substantial number of white immigrants who had married Tejanas. More than a few Anglo-Texan politicians, such as John W. Smith of San Antonio, had a special interest in maintaining the legitimacy of such unions, given their political influence derived from powerful Tejano families. Anglo politicians from predominantly Hispanic districts who were joined by marriage with leading Tejano families could hardly have wanted to institute laws relegating their own wives, affinal kin, and children to a lower status. Intended or not, the interracial marriage strategy of some prominent Tejano families provided substantial benefits to Texas Mexicans of all *castas*.

Texas leaders also realized that not banning Anglo-Hispanic sex and marriage did not threaten Anglo-Texan preeminence. Political leaders after independence from Mexico knew that the extension of the franchise to a limited population of loyal Tejanos presented no real challenge to them. By the same token, they could predict that marital and sexual freedom for the relatively small number of Tejanos residing in Texas would not significantly undermine Anglo-Texan racial cohesion, unity, and dominance. Continuing immigration of Anglos from the South, statehood, and the victory of the United States over Mexico in 1848 reduced the threat even further. In a letter to her mother from Fort Brown in July 1849, Helen Chapman expressed the continuing aversion that Anglo-Texans felt toward Mexicans and the confidence of the Anglos in their own ascendance:

> [T]here is something in seeing barbarism and civilization side by side, that affects you strongly. You feel the irresistible necessity that one race must subdue the other and, where the moral precepts are not keen and delicate, they, of the superior race, can easily learn to look upon themselves as men of Destiny, impelled to conquer and subdue by the great design of providence.[66]

Inevitable or not, the post-independence regime worked fundamentally to allow the relationships of Anglo men and Tejanas. Anglo-Hispanic sex and marriage typically involved Anglo men and Tejanas in arrangements reinforcing, rather than challenging, Anglo dominance. The omission of a ban on Anglo-Hispanic sex and marriage thus permitted these connections, as did not criminalizing simple fornication. The criminal penalty for "living in fornication" also tolerated the modified form of *barraganería* that white frontiersmen indulged in, since the sanction had questionable applicability to the often intermittent trysts of Anglo men and their Tejano mistresses. After the adoption of common law marriage, Anglo-Texan men and Tejanas involved in a more sustained cohabitative relationship could avoid prosecution simply by claiming to be married. That Anglo men who did so might not live up to the obligations of a legal husband and father would have concerned authorities and common Anglo-Texans very little; the custom of *barraganería* was well entrenched, while racism and moralistic female gender ideals generated little sympathy for the mestizo consorts whom Anglo-Texans often labeled mere harlots.

Female gender constructs went a long way to bolster the transracial sexual double standard permeating the Texas frontier. To a great extent, the prescribed social role for Anglo-Texan women was sufficient to alienate them from potential Tejano and Native American suitors. Most Anglo women in frontier Texas did not have the same opportunities as their male counterparts to make contacts with Indian and Tejano men, given the segregation of these peoples from Anglo-Texans and that trade among the tribes and in Tejano communities was an Anglo male occupation almost exclusively. Anglo women thus resided rather continuously on homesteads and mostly within Anglo-Texan settlements. Consequently, most of those interested in cultivating relationships with the opposite sex had little choice but to select partners from the overabundant population of Anglo men.

The hatred stemming from warfare with the tribes worked powerfully to deter Anglo women from having relationships with indigenous men. Most Anglo-Texans certainly would have condemned any of their women who voluntarily involved themselves intimately with an Indian warrior. Few Anglo men, however, had to deal with this situation. Anglo-Texan women embraced attitudes of superiority and usually indulged strong contempt for Native Americans.[67] Constant hostilities between Native Americans and Anglo-Texans, particularly in the last few decades of the antebellum period, greatly intensified these negative feelings. Comanche and Kiowa war parties frequently slaughtered settling women and men, abducted their children, held them for ransom, and sometimes transformed them into "white Indians." Anglo-Texan women whom hostile bands captured frequently faced torture, enslavement, and forced concubinage. Sometimes the tribes ransomed these women; sometimes they simply killed them, often after an ordeal that had dragged on for years.[68] It is thus not surprising few Anglo-Texan women desired to associate intimately with the tribesmen.

The abuse of captive children particularly stoked the hatred that Anglo-Texan women felt for Indians. Events preceding the famed Council House Fight between Comanche chiefs and San Antonio leaders provide a typical example. On 19 March 1840, Comanche warriors entered the town to discuss a peace treaty. To facilitate the meeting, which ultimately exploded in mayhem, they reluctantly returned fifteen-year-old Matilda Lockhart, who had been captured with her infant sister in December 1838. Mary V. Maverick wrote about Matilda's condition in her memoirs:

> Her head, arms and face were full of bruises, and sores, and her nose actually burnt off to the bone. . . . She told a piteous tale of how dreadfully the Indians had beaten her, and how they would wake her from sleep by sticking a chunk of fire to her flesh . . . and how they would shout and laugh like fiends when she cried. . . . Ah, it was sickening to behold, and made one's blood boil for vengeance. . . . [T]hough glad to be free of her detested tyrants, she was very sad and broken hearted. She said she felt utterly degraded. . . . Yet her case was by no means solitary. She told of fifteen other American captives, all children.[69]

Racism and sexual prescriptions for Anglo women, however, worked most consistently to thwart their interaction with both Indian and Tejano men. Anglo-Texan attitudes discouraging marriage or sex between their women and Native American men prevailed even when the relatively friendly East Texas Indians lived in close proximity to new Anglo-Texan settlements during the Mexican period. Anglo hatred for Indians stemming from warfare and segregation of the races thus cannot explain entirely the exclusionist norm. In actuality, Anglo-Texan conceptions of preeminence intensified an already more restrictive sexual standard for women than for men.[70] This racially energized social construct rose to the level of taboo, strongly discouraging Anglo-Texan women from passing over Anglo men to marry or establish sexual relationships with their supposedly inferior Indian and Tejano counterparts.[71] While Texas lawmakers after independence criminalized "living in fornication," officials did not need to rely on this measure to deny Anglo women mutually consensual relationships with Tejano and Native American men. For those who might cultivate such involvements, however, the sanction certainly constituted a useful tool with which to break them up.

Texas Indians and Tejanos accepted the transracial sexual double standard as part of a strategic capitulation to Anglo dominance. On most interracial frontiers in the age of European imperial expansion, subordinated indigenous peoples allowed their women to marry or have sexual relations with colonizing men, even when the aggressors refused to reciprocate. Done consciously or not, and often at the expense of young daughters, this strategy helped indigenous groups cope with encroachers possessing superior resources, technology, and military power. Subordinate societies thus permitted European men concubinage and marriage with their high-status women to effect good will and seal stable political and economic relations. These women created eradicable blood ties between their own peoples and colonizing whites to discourage aggression and the most intolerable forms of exploitation and oppression. Texas Indians and Tejanos could have forbidden their women to marry Anglo men and refused to accept them or their mixed-race children into their societies. As the interracial marriages of John W. Smith and Sam Houston indicate, however, this was not their policy. Tejanos and most of the Texas tribes, rather, accommodated the sexual double standard to improve their own chances for survival, collective security, and the position of their own propertied and political elites.[72]

The sexual relationships of Sam Houston among the tribes indicate the typical interaction between Anglo men and indigenous women enmeshed in the cross-cultural social matrix that developed on the Texas frontier. Houston traveled constantly from 1829 until he settled down. He thus exemplified the mobile lifestyle common among Anglo-Texan men. In Houston's case, at least, this constituted a modus vivendi that provided him with sufficient time and liberty to cultivate, even if precariously, relationships with both Native American and Anglo women. Like Houston, most frontiersmen frequently formed relationships with Indian women who could serve as attractive sexual companions and frontier helpmates and provide them valuable trade connections with the tribes.

The experiences of Col-lon-neh also indicate how pioneer conditions, prejudice, and the law combined to shape the sexual relationships of Anglo-Texan men and female Indians. Regardless of Houston's well-deserved historical reputation as a committed ally of the friendly East Texas tribes, his various Indian marriages demonstrate the disdainful treatment nineteenth-century frontiersmen often meted out to Native American women. Such men rarely made permanent commitments to their Indian consorts and mixed-race children. Taking advantage of indigenous marriage and divorce customs, Anglo-Texan men usually abandoned their Indian wives and returned to their own people. Post-independence law reflected and promoted the chauvinistic attitudes and racism underlying this practice, neither prohibiting sexual relations and marriage between Indian women and Anglo men nor recognizing the validity of informal unions formed within the tribes.

Ethnocentrism and gender prescriptions, however, worked with law to shape the conjugal relationships of both Anglo-Texan men and women with Native Americans and Tejanos—a pattern that comported entirely with Anglo hegemony. Through the antebellum period, Texas society and law permitted Anglo-Texan frontiersmen sexual and marital freedom with Indian women and Tejanas. Anglo racism and attitudes of superiority, along with the law, maintained an inferior status for Indian and Tejano concubines, their relationships with Anglo men, and the children resulting from such unions. Anglo-Texan society also assigned a subordinate status to well-to-do Tejanas and the children they had with legal Anglo husbands. This same social-legal dynamic and a transracial sexual double standard, however, deterred Anglo women from involving themselves with darker-skinned suitors from subjugated groups.

THREE

Intimacy

AND

Subjugation

Property Rights and Black Texans

Circumstances in early Texas prompted men to form complicated relationships with their slave women that white society in the more settled South would have considered at least highly unorthodox. Columbus R. "Kit" Patton of Kentucky and his brothers pulled up stakes and immigrated to Mexican Texas in the late 1820s. After obtaining an inexpensive tract of land along the Brazos River, young Kit and the few slaves he brought with him began carving a farm out of the wilderness. Amid the difficulties of establishing a new sugarcane and cotton-growing operation in a swampy coastal terrain, Kit began a sexual involvement with Rachel, his mulatto slave. Over the next several decades the relationship deepened. An intelligent and rather haughty woman, Rachel became Kit's supreme confidante and acknowledged mistress of the plantation.[1]

Over the years, Rachel's relationship with Kit became unacceptable to his mother, younger brother Charles, and nephew Matt. Especially galling to them were the open and relatively reciprocal aspects of the connection. That Kit maintained a slave woman, a "Negro," virtually as his wife and permitted her to assume all the prerogatives of that role, within the precincts of the plantation at least, became more than the Pattons could bear.[2]

The Patton family resorted to the courts to fix the problem. By 1853, Kit's impractical plans for the plantation and strange religious ideas disturbed the Pattons, leading them to conclude he had become "eccentric." It was Kit's open involvement with Rachel, however, that most consistently upset the family. While Charles himself was a bachelor who kept a slave mistress on his farm at nearby West Columbia, Rachel's unusually assertive behavior and high position so outraged him that he conspired successfully with Matt Patton in 1854 to have Kit declared non compos mentis. Shortly thereafter, Charles had Kit committed to an insane asylum in South Carolina, where the thirty-nine-year-old died rather mysteriously on 29 September 1856. Having taken charge of his brother's land and slaves, Charles quickly sent Rachel back to the fields.[3]

Not long after Kit's inexplicable death, the appearance of a secret will marred Patton family designs on the property of its errant kinsman. The legal rights of the clan to Kit's estate seemed quite secure initially. In 1857, however, new estate administrator John Adriance produced a will in Brazoria County Court bluntly disinheriting both Charles and Matt and leaving almost the entire estate to a young niece. More outrageous to the Pattons were other provisions in the will providing Rachel a substantial lifetime yearly allowance out of Kit's property and permitting her to live wherever she chose. According to Adriance, furthermore, Kit had drafted the will in 1853 before his declared incompetency and institutionalization.[4]

All hell broke loose during probate administration of the belated will as the Patton family mobilized to suppress it. The thrust of their challenge was that Kit had been deranged when he drafted the document. Of equal importance, they argued, Rachel, his "slave concubine," had improperly influenced him. In their official statement, the Pattons claimed the will had been extorted from Kit by the "threats, fraudulent conduct, and artful devices of a certain negro woman slave named

Rachel" with whom he had "lived in disgraceful intimacy, and who had undue influence and control over [him]."[5]

The Brazoria County Court ultimately capitulated to the pressure. The Pattons worked out a compromise settlement securing most of Kit's estate for Charles. The court, however, honored those portions of the will concerning the supposed Jezebel whom the Pattons claimed had unduly influenced its preparation. Adriance rescued Rachel from the fields, and the court compelled Charles in 1857 to provide her with a separate house. Regardless of her reduced status, Rachel continued to live like the lady of a great plantation. Her undiminished influence among the slaves, however, prompted Adriance in 1860 to relocate her to Cincinnati, Ohio, as Texas braced for war against the North. Taking the name Rachel Bartlett, she lived there independently and with the benefit of her allowance until at least 1868.[6]

Although white immigrants in Mexican Texas certainly looked down on blacks, few witnessed any embroglio similar to that which disturbed the Patton clan in the mid-1850s. Relationships like Kit and Rachel's were certainly not that unusual in the socially fluid, multiracial province. On the other hand, new white supremacy policies and the adoption of laws reinforcing slavery after independence hardly surprised the older settlers, given that immigrants from the Deep South poured into Texas in ever-larger numbers. By the same token, the implementation of statutes banning marriage between persons of African descent and those of European descent was part and parcel of the new dispensation. But only the minority of those who came to Texas as slaveholders, or the relatively few yeomen who moved into the slave-owning class, ever had reason to consider carefully how post-independence antimiscegenation law reinforced slavery and white hegemony but permitted the continuation of sexual intimacy between blacks and whites. The Patton clan came to appreciate with particular incisiveness the limitations of that law in protecting family wealth. They were, however, not alone. While frontier demography and living conditions worked in tandem with immigrant mores to perpetuate black female concubinage, both jurists and legislators were mindful of the threat that sex between blacks and whites and the procreation of mixed-race children posed to Anglo-Texan families in a society built on extraordinarily generous land-grant rules and subject to the Hispanic matrimonial property system.

The unusually open interracial relationships of men like Kit Patton developed initially amid a relatively small black population. Only a few people of African descent lived in Texas before 1821. According to the census of New Spain conducted in the mid-1790s, their number hardly exceeded fifty. Enslavement of Africans, in fact, had begun to disappear in Texas by the time of New Spain's war of independence. The size of the black population in Texas then was extremely small, amounting only to several hundred. The majority of this group, furthermore, were free. These blacks resided around Nacogdoches, the region closest to Louisiana, from which more than a few had escaped slavery. By the time Mexico achieved independence, many of these fugitives had integrated into Texas society, adopted Hispanic surnames, and learned the Spanish language.[7]

The slaves whom immigrant southerners brought with them gradually augmented the free black population. Rachel Bartlett's settlement in Brazoria with Kit Patton in the late 1820s placed her within the first cohort of pioneering African-American women. Slaves from the more settled South were among the earliest colonizers in East Texas. Immigrant Anglo-Americans, mostly from the upper South, began to bring slaves into the Austin Colony in 1823. White settlers slowly increased the African-American population thereafter on the homesteads and plantations they established in the rich valleys along the Brazos, Colorado, and Trinity Rivers.[8]

The opposition of the Mexican government to slavery restricted its growth in Texas before independence. The central government of the Republic of Mexico made vacillating efforts either to abolish or limit the growth of slavery beginning in 1824. Reflecting the initial surge of slave importation into the colony of Stephen F. Austin, slaves represented approximately 25 percent of the population in the State of Coahuila and Texas in 1825. For the rest of the Mexican period, however, slave importation slowed as immigrants from the Deep South grew insecure about their slave titles. Consequently, the number of slaves in Texas did not assume the proportion of the populace they constituted in the states of the more settled South. The ratio of slaves to the total population, in fact, declined in the late 1820s and early 1830s. As of 1836, there were approximately 5,000 slaves in Texas, constituting only 12 percent of the population.[9]

The great majority of white settlers in Mexican Texas did not own slaves, yet their racism made the idea of marriage between blacks and whites objectionable. Most Anglo-American immigrants were non-slave-owning agriculturalists and backwoodsmen from the upper South whose families had previously inhabited the Middle Atlantic regions. Many of them were accustomed to living among free blacks. These southerners, nonetheless, embraced the ideals of the emergent Jacksonian democracy, including the strong alliance of the Democratic Party with the slave power. These settlers resented slave owners and the institution of slavery itself, but supported it because of their fundamental commitment to white supremacy. A key adjunct to this devotion was the exclusion of blacks from white society and a refusal to see African-Americans integrated into Anglo-Texan families by marriage.[10]

Slave owners in Mexican Texas similarly opposed the idea of the marriage of whites with slaves or free blacks. Regardless of his willingness to involve himself sexually with Rachel Bartlett, Kit Patton could hardly have done so without having to deal with conflicting feelings stemming from his early socialization in Kentucky. The minority of southerners who settled in early Texas with slaves idealized their relations with them in paternalistic terms. This ideal, still prevalent in the middle and southern seaboard states, posited slaves as a childlike race in a process of development. This construct helped owners rationalize their exploitation of slaves. It also predicated that they ought to treat their slave dependents with some amount of decency, and it prevented some owners from acting on their worst instincts. Slaveholders in colonial Texas were, nonetheless, firmly committed to maintaining African-Americans in bondage. This determination ruled out the possibility of matrimony among Texas slaves or between Texas slaves and free blacks. It also rejected the gradual emancipation and integration of Texas slaves through marriage with whites.[11]

The frontier situation encouraged men like Kit Patton to involve themselves with their slave women. Fear of Indian attack, resistant Mexicans, and other kinds of physical danger promoted cooperation and solidarity among settling whites and blacks living and working together in isolation. These pressures alone diluted the enmity and mutual distrust that slavery and the racism of immigrant whites otherwise fostered. These circumstances, along with harsh living conditions, also prompted single white men residing with black women, either free or slave, to form sexual relationships with them. The absence of social constraints and public surveillance, furthermore, permitted white men and black women substantial autonomy regarding their relations.[12]

The racism of immigrant white men also encouraged their sexual involvement with black women. In the beginning at least, Kit Patton could have viewed his sexual connection with Rachel Bartlett in customary terms. Southern whites traditionally tolerated the forcible sexual exploitation of black women. They also accepted that many young white men established extensive relationships with slave women to gain sexual experience. The supposed licentiousness of black women and the frequent white characterization of them as temptresses reinforced these attitudes. Southern men settling in Mexican Texas certainly subscribed to well-established views that cast attractive black women as suitable mistresses. Like the seaboard and upper-southern society from which most men emigrated, whites arriving in Mexican Texas were predisposed to tolerate such practices and did not view them as a significant problem.[13]

The culture and laws of Mexico further prompted white frontiersmen to cohabit with black women and sometimes marry them. Spanish-speaking peoples living in East Texas in the late 1820s certainly would not have objected to Kit Patton's relationship with Rachel Bartlett. Immigrant Anglo-American men faced virtually no indigenous social and institutional barriers to marriage with women of African descent or sexual liaisons with them. While slavery had once been a vital element in the economic development of New Spain, Mexican culture maintained a viable social role for free blacks and slaves. In keeping with *mestizaje*, the society in New Spain and then Mexico accepted intermarriage of blacks, Indians, persons of European ancestry, and those of mixed ancestry. Hispanic Catholicism as well did not impede interracial marriage. Under Mexican matrimonial and slave law, *peninsulares* (Spaniards), criollos, and mestizos could legally marry *africanos* and mulattos, free or bonded.[14]

White men in Mexican Texas frequently married or simply lived with female slaves and free black women. While the reaction of the Patton family to the relationship of Rachel and Kit became powerful and hostile, his involvement was not unusual. Many Anglo-Texan men overcame racist aversion and kept slave concubines or married black women from 1821 to 1836. Black female concubinage was often an arrangement based on affection, convenience, and a mutuality uncommon in the more settled South. Black and mulatto women married and lived openly with white men and with significantly less stigma attached to such relationships than in the southern states from which these men immigrated. Particularly around Nacogdoches in the late 1820s, white society accepted black women with white husbands and had significant amicable contacts with them. Mixed marriages were certainly more common and accepted in sparsely settled areas.[15] Nonetheless, according to Woolfolk, this frontier phenomenon, in the context of the Spanish-Mexican culture and law, made "the Texas borderland . . . a true melting pot."[16]

Racism and dominance, however, reveal themselves in the relationships of colonial whites and blacks. The Anglo-Texan drive to act out the concept of white supremacy was certainly muted within a relatively tolerant multiracial setting. As was the case with Kit Patton, however, white men who took black women as concubines or married them did so most often to meet emotional, biological, and practical needs amid a shortage of marriageable white women rather than to cultivate relationships based on mutual esteem. Men who sexually involved themselves with black women, bonded or free, did so on the fringes of a loosely organized pioneer society. In this context, they were only tenuously connected to other settlers and did not have to deal continuously with the stigma that immigrant whites ordinarily continued to attach to marriage between blacks and whites. That many white men maintained their mistresses in slavery or kept free black women as concubines, rather than marrying them, when they could have done so, reflects the lowered estimation such men had of these women. Anglo-Texan men who married black women did not ordinarily bring them or the children they had with them into their white families. The mulatto children whom white men had with black concubines, furthermore, were not legitimate, and many remained in bondage along with their mothers. Most indicative of Anglo-Texan racial dominance, however, is that very few white women married black men or lived with them out of wedlock.[17]

The mixed marriage of John F. Webber reveals how the pressures of white racism limited the efforts of Anglo-Texan men to establish egalitarian relationships with black consorts. Immigrating from Vermont in 1826, Webber settled in Austin's colony. He ceremonially married Silvia Hector, the slave of John Cryer, and obtained a family-sized land grant in June 1832. Shortly thereafter, Webber purchased Silvia, or "Puss" as she was known, and the out-of-wedlock child they had together. The two of them made their home on the very edge of white settlement in Travis County on the Colorado River. Over the years, they had eight more children. Noah Smithwick, who homesteaded on Webber's Prairie, commented on the racial undercurrents affecting John, Puss, and their children:

> The Webber family of course could not mingle with the white people. . . . Still there wasn't a white woman in the vicinity but knew and liked Puss, as Webber's dusky helpmeet was called. . . . [She] was every [sic] ready to render assistance, without money and without price. . . . Beneath that sable bosom, beat as true a heart as ever warmed a human body. . . . Webber and his wife merited and enjoyed the good will . . . and, to a certain extent the respect of the early settlers. . . . The ladies visited Puss sometimes, not as an equal, but because they appreciated her kindness.[18]

The sexual relationships continuing to develop between white men and their bondwomen after independence did so amid a hardening regime of slavery. Anglo-Texans were predisposed to duplicate the brutal system of slavery already established in the more settled southern states. After Texas independence, class tensions certainly increased between immigrant slave owners and nonslaveholders. The practically universal belief among whites that slavery was the only method of coexisting with a growing number of bonded blacks, however, obscured these differences. Anglo-Texans thus came to view slavery both as a system of labor and as a tool for maintaining social order and race control. Rejecting the paternalistic ideal of earlier settlers, Texas slave owners implemented a new scheme of African-American bondage that relied, with less restraint than ever before, on inhumanity, avarice, and brutality.[19]

Through the years of the republic, immigrants from the settled South substantially increased the slave population. After independence from Mexico, slave-owning settlers poured into Texas in much greater numbers than before. Slaves thus came to represent a larger proportion of the East Texas population than they had during the colonial period. In 1840, the number of slaves had grown to 38,753. As such, they constituted fully 20 percent of the Texas populace.[20]

In the fifteen years following statehood, massive southern immigration nearly quintupled the Texas slave population. Kit Patton's relationship with Rachel Bartlett matured in a county with one of the most rapidly expanding slave populations in Texas. From 1845 to 1860, East Texas was among the fastest growing plantation regions in the southern United States. By 1850 there were 56,161 slaves living there. By 1860, the number of slaves had risen to 182,566, constituting roughly 33 percent of the population. The bonded populace was most concentrated around the original Austin colony and inland from the coast along the Brazos and Colorado Rivers. A second zone of concentration centered on San Augustine County and the Nacogdoches area; a third developed in the Red River counties. In the Houston-Galveston area, Austin, and around Nacogdoches after 1850, the ratio of slaves to whites was comparable to that in the black belt of the slave-exporting states to the east. In these intensive cotton producing regions, 50 percent or more of the inhabitants were slaves. In surrounding areas, almost to the full extent of East Texas, the number of slaves ran from 25 to 50 percent of the population.[21]

Regardless of the rapid growth of the slave population, the frontier situation continued to generate a distinctive residential pattern for whites and blacks. In most of the Deep South, about 70 percent of slaves lived on plantations holding more than twenty of them. As in the Mexican period, the majority of bonded African-Americans in Texas from 1836 to 1860 were in the hands of small-scale farmers. In 1850, 69 percent, and in 1860, 60 percent, of all slaves lived on small to medium-sized farms in numbers less than twenty, rather than on extensive plantations. In 1850, owners with fewer than ten slaves constituted about 76 percent of all slaveholders, and roughly 74 percent in 1860. The typical owner, furthermore, held one or only a few slaves. Thanks to land-grant policies providing settlers with unusually large tracts, the majority of Texas slaves lived with whites on widely dispersed and thus isolated homesteads.[22]

Close interaction between Anglo-Texans and their slaves on frontier farms often increased the oppressiveness of bondage. In the words of former bondman Martin Jackson, the regime of slavery on the Texas frontier caused "plenty of cruel suffering."[23] Especially in the 1840s, Texas slave owners had a widespread reputation for "hard driving." Adeline Cunningham recalled they were "rough people and dey treat everybody rough."[24] Adeline Marshall, another former bondwoman in the state, declared that her master treated animals better than he treated his slaves, forcing small children into field labor and beating adults to make them work harder.[25]

The close and constant interplay between owners and bonded servants tempted some men to exploit their slave women with uncommon ruthlessness. From the earliest days of settlement in Texas, white men certainly viewed female slaves as proper objects of sexual exploitation. As the slave regime hardened, however, paternalistic ideals worked less often to restrain them from acting out this conception. Forced sexual intercourse with female slaves was usually a casual undertaking for Anglo-Texan men. Much more than in their relations with other dark-skinned women, these men gave full rein to their "manly independence" when sexually exploiting slave women. Male owners sometimes took young slave women through psychological coercion or by offering them special privileges or perks to make their lives easier or improve the situation of their children. Sometimes they simply threatened female slaves with violence or battered them to have their way. When white men raped slave women, they usually did so in a clandestine fashion.[26]

Law and white ethnocentrism combined to make Texas bondwomen vulnerable to sexual exploitation. Slaves married one another with ceremonies of their own design, recognized the moral validity of their unions, and were deeply committed to their families. Texas slave law, however, denied them legal marriage. Bonded men and women thus could, and sometimes did, sever their unions at will. Because of the informality of slave marriages, owners regarded them somewhat casually. Informal coupling and uncoupling among slaves and African-American mores that permitted a limited amount of premarital sex, furthermore, encouraged slave-owning men to view their female slaves as unchaste, licentious, and suitable for sexual exploitation. Because owners usually tried to place bonded children with their mothers when a trade separated parents, slave husbands and fathers saw their parental roles and marital relationships discounted. This denial of conjugal and filial prerogatives further encouraged slave-owning men to misuse sexually bonded wives and daughters. As in the more settled southern states, Texas law did not protect a slave woman from rape by her owner, whether she was married or not. Slave men thus lacked any feasible means to protect their wives and daughters from sexual aggression, short of rebellion and thus risk of life or limb.[27]

Frontier living arrangements and demography increased the susceptibility of slave women to sexual abuse. On isolated homesteads, where there was little public surveillance, slave-owning men wielded virtually unlimited personal power. In the absence of cohesive slave communities that might have pressured these men to restrain their excesses, bonded females were even more vulnerable to sexual exploitation than they were in the more settled South. Because a shortage of white women often denied Anglo-Texan men conjugal intimacy, female slaves became even more tempting targets of sexual aggression than they otherwise would have been.[28]

The spatial arrangement of owners and slaves also generated unusually close interpersonal relations among some of them. Texas slaveholders were almost never absentee owners; they usually lived in close quarters with their slaves. Especially in the most remote and exposed areas, a strong emotional bond frequently developed between owners and slaves as they dealt with the challenges and insecurities of their new existence. Many accounts attest to this bonding, which rested primarily on mutual dependency and practical necessity. While certainly not equal relationships, they were at least more reciprocal than those common on plantations in the more settled southern states.[29]

The situation on frontier homesteads sometimes encouraged a genuine, albeit limited, affection among slaves and their masters. As was the case throughout the antebellum South, relations between owners and slaves on farms in Texas were more personal than on extensive plantations.[30] In an unusually large number of cases, Texas owners viewed their slaves as household members. While racism and the dictates of slavery certainly constrained this attitude, it often extended to both domestic servants and field workers. Many slaves also perceived themselves, to some extent, as family members. Anderson Edwards, for example, had been a slave on a Texas farm holding three black families. He reported his master had treated him and the other slaves with kindness.[31] Slave testimony, diaries, and wills support the conclusion many Anglo-Texans displayed uncommon familiarity and even trust toward their slaves, particularly those who were older and more loyal.[32]

The enhanced familiarity among white and bonded settlers on frontier homesteads also encouraged Anglo-Texan men to cohabit with their slave women with uncommon frequency. As in Mexican Texas, resource scarcity, harsh living conditions, and a shortage of white women often prompted unaccompanied white men to seek out available slave women as close companions. Female slave concubinage sometimes began under compulsion. As in the case of Kit Patton, however, it frequently developed into a caring relationship. These relationships usually developed when the owner was a bachelor, widower, or otherwise had few contacts with marriageable white women. Slaveholding men kept young slave women as mistresses within relatively cooperative arrangements that were often quite fecund; the mulatto birth rate in post-independence Texas was nearly twice as high as that in the more settled South. While racism and slavery certainly thwarted the development of relationships grounded fully in mutual esteem, many partners displayed a surprising degree of affection and respect for one another. Shielded from constant public scrutiny on isolated homesteads, furthermore, Anglo-Texan men and their slave women had considerable liberty to comport themselves and maintain sexual relationships without much interference from white society. The open practice of female slave concubinage from 1836 to 1860 certainly reflected the brazen sexual conduct southern "manly independence" encouraged in the frontier situation. In more than a few cases, however, cohabiting men and slave women simply continued involvements they had initiated in the relatively tolerant multiracial society of Mexican Texas.[33]

That many Anglo-Texan men cohabited with their slave women through to 1860 is well established. Official documents and private writings attest to numerous relationships similar to that which existed between Kit Patton and Rachel Bartlett.[34] William Oldham, for example, immigrated from Kentucky to Texas shortly before the war of independence. He lived with a beautiful mulatto slave named Phillis in the Brazos bottom from 1839 until his death in 1868. During that time, she helped run the plantation and supervised the dozen or so slaves who worked it, especially in Oldham's absence.[35] John C. Clark moved to Texas from South Carolina in 1822, fought Indians with considerable success along the Colorado River, and established an unusually large plantation in Wharton County. In 1833 or 1834, he purchased a mulatto named Sobrina and cohabited with her until his death in 1862. They ultimately had three children together. Numerous witnesses at the probate proceedings attendant on Clark's death testified that "the two habitually occupied the same bed, and ate at the same table . . . [and] that Sobrina carried the keys and exercised the authority of mistress of the house." Some of the witnesses avowed they sometimes heard Clark speak of Sobrina as his wife. In any case, the arrangement disturbed Wharton County whites very little.[36] According to Edward Collier,

"The general report in the neighborhood in those slavery times was that Clark kept a Negro woman . . . as men frequently did in those days."[37]

Men who kept slave mistresses often gave them and the children they had together affection and substantial material support. The children whom Anglo-Texan men had with black women were sometimes treated preferentially and sometimes not, usually depending on the mutuality and duration of the relationship leading to their birth. Nonetheless, many owners held their concubines and mulatto children in high regard and took extraordinary steps to secure their well-being in the face of rising white supremacy. Petitions and memorials to Texas legislators regularly requested permission to manumit slaves who were the mistresses or children of white owners. Not untypical were the efforts of a man named Fitzgerald from Matagorda County who gave Caroline Hilliard, his reputed "natural" daughter, to another until she was old enough to be set free. Philip "Sunnyside" Cuney, a wealthy planter, legislator, and brigadier general in the Texas Militia, manumitted his slave mistress, Adeline, and moved her and their children from his Austin County plantation to a home in Houston. Like Kit Patton, slave-owning men often made extensive efforts in their wills to provide specially for their mistresses or mulatto children. William Bracken of Jackson County, for example, executed a final testament recognizing three mulatto children who were to share his estate equally. While these testamentary devices certainly contradicted economic and social precepts fundamental to the slave system, Texas courts usually enforced them.[38]

It appears men who owned numerous slaves had an easier time maintaining relations with their bonded mistresses than those who had eschewed bondage and actually married them. Noah Smithwick, for example, documented the growing plight of John Webber and his wife, Puss, in the 1840s. According to him, "After the Indians had been driven back, so that there was comparative safety on Webber's prairie, a new lot of people came . . . and they at once set to work to drive Webber out." These newcomers in actuality were immigrants from the Deep South who resented Webber's racially mixed marriage and were much less tolerant of it than had been his colonial white neighbors. According to Smithwick, "The bitter prejudice, coupled with a desire to get Webber's land and improvements, became so threatening that I counseled him to sell out and take his family to Mexico, where there was not distinction of color." It appears John and Puss saw the wisdom in Smithwick's advice. In 1851, they left Webber's Prairie, and two years later John bought several leagues of land north of the Rio Grande downstream from Hidalgo. While Webber fled to Mexico during the Confederate occupation of the Rio Grande Valley, he returned thereafter to live with Puss at their home, Webber's Ranch, until he died in July 1882. "Aunt Puss," as she came to be known around Hidalgo, died in 1891.[39]

The post-independence ban on matrimony between blacks and whites occurred in step with the development of law placing blacks at the bottom of a racial-caste hierarchy. The 1836 constitution and various statutes passed subsequently denied free blacks citizenship and thus a legal basis for them to protect their preexisting land titles. The 1836 constitution, in fact, empowered white settlers to seize forcibly the lands of free African-Americans. Denial of citizenship to free blacks also made them ineligible to obtain new land grants.[40]

Other laws adopted in the early years of the republic singled out free blacks for persecution to eliminate their presence altogether. After independence in 1836, Anglo-Texans grew intolerant of free African-Americans, and legislation to meet these exigencies quickly followed. New statutory law subjected African-Americans to unusually harsh punishments for criminal offenses Anglo-Texans associated with efforts to liberate slaves and for other conduct that more directly challenged slavery and white supremacy. An act passed in December 1837, for example, subjected both free blacks and slaves to "stripes not exceeding one hundred nor less than twenty-five" if they used abusive language toward or threatened any white person. The same legislation subjected free blacks to enslavement if they aided slaves in escaping.[41] Constitutional provisions and statutes worked to slow further manumission, coerced slaves who had been freed after independence to leave the republic, and prohibited free blacks from immigrating. This new regime, not surprisingly, ensured that free blacks remained a limited group in contrast to the growing slave population.[42]

The ideological basis for subjugating free African-Americans also undergirded the institutionalization of slavery in the new republic. The concept of Anglo-Saxonism emerging after 1836 bolstered the collective identity of the growing southern white majority and encouraged the dispossession and oppression of free blacks. Once embodied in law, this concept disqualified them from equal status with whites or political participation in the new republic. More important, however, it provided the critical ideological basis for the constitutional establishment of hereditary slavery after Texas independence on 2 March 1836. For Anglo-Texans, the pseudoscientific principle of inherent racial superiority reconciled republican self-rule with the imposition of human bondage on ever-larger numbers of blacks now conceptualized as inherently inferior. Anglo-Saxonism thus allowed Texas slave owners committed to the ideal of republican government to place its enslaved population permanently on the lowest rungs of a racial-caste structure without having to face squarely either the inconsistency or hypocrisy of this policy.[43]

As the racial-caste system hardened, the situation of free black women who had lived with white men for years became more precarious. In February 1836, for example, Adam Smith purchased Margaret Guess, began living with her, and informed his Houston neighbors she was free. Until Adam died in 1846, he and Margaret maintained a mutually consensual and relatively egalitarian relationship. During that time, furthermore, Margaret owned and operated a boardinghouse while raising Puss, a slave girl she had purchased. In early 1848, Margaret sued the administrator of Smith's estate to recover possession of the boardinghouse, the ten-acre lot upon which it was situated, and the little girl. The trial court, however, decided that Margaret was a slave, not entitled to sue or own property, and that she was, herself, part of Smith's estate. In the 1851 decision of *Guess v. Lubbock,* the Texas Supreme Court overturned the verdict. Writing for the court, Justice Abner Lipscomb noted that Smith had lived with Margaret as his wife. More important, the court maintained the jury should have at least considered that Smith's repeated declarations indicating she was not a slave established a presumption that he had freed her before independence. The ruling also validated informal manumissions rendered before then, regardless of 1836 Texas constitutional provisions limiting the practice and earlier Mexican manumission rules requiring written proof or an oral declaration before five witnesses. The holding certainly provided a measure of protection for a number of remaining free blacks. But when white men were no longer around to vouch in open court for the freedom and property rights of their black consorts, these women were particularly vulnerable to juries less inclined than ever to give them the benefit of the doubt.[44]

Even black women with impeccable freedom credentials faced increased difficulties maintaining relationships with white men. Zilpha Husk, for example, had been manumitted in Autauga County, Alabama, in November 1837. She moved to Houston in 1838 to be near her daughter Emily, who had been apprenticed to a man residing in Washington County. A bill approved in February 1840, however, requiring all free blacks not living in Texas before independence to leave the republic by 1 January 1842, jeopardized her residence. Over the next few years, Zilpha drew considerable attention with numerous petitions to the Texas Congress requesting special permission to stay. With the benefit of several proclamations that President Sam Houston issued extending the final expulsion date, Zilpha managed to avoid prosecution. The endorsements of whites and free blacks alike on her petitions, along with the support of the Harris County chief justice, Isaac N. Moreland, also bought her time. In 1849, however, Zilpha appears to have asserted herself beyond the toleration of some Houstonians. A grand jury indicted her and Edmund Mitchell, a white man, for "living in fornication." With ties to the community, Mitchell was able to obtain an acquittal. Shortly thereafter, the case against Zilpha was dropped. The message from the increasingly racist white community, however, was clear: it would no longer ignore the open cohabitation of free black women and white men as in the days of Mexican rule. Such connections would now have to be handled more discreetly.[45]

Zilpha Husk and Edmund Mitchell could not have legally married to avoid prosecution for "living in fornication" even if their Houston neighbors had been willing to tolerate it. In the summer of 1837, the Texas Congress had banned and criminalized marriage between blacks and whites. Section 9 of the Act of 5 June 1837 declared it unlawful for any people of European blood, or their descendants, to marry Africans or their descendants, whether slave or free. The new statute provided that parties to such a marriage "shall be deemed guilty of a high misdemeanor and punished as such." Rejecting multiracial Hispanic marital law, and thus "amalgamation," Texas lawmakers further reinforced the racial-caste hierarchy.[46]

Texas courts would have had serious difficulty banning or punishing marriage between blacks and whites without the 1837 legislation. Law-makers after independence were predisposed to utilize the preexisting Hispanic law governing domestic relations. Without the 1837 statute, Texas judges ruling on the validity of attempted marriages between persons of African descent and those with European ancestry could not have easily ignored Hispanic law that did recognize them. Judicial fabrication of an antimiscegenation law also would have been extremely problematic, since the common law offered no precedents for banning interracial marriage. Like many southern states that resolved the judicial dilemma of choosing between common law precedents and commitments to a free marriage market, the Texas Congress resorted to explicit legislation to ban matrimony of whites and blacks.[47]

The 1837 statute worked to limit the growth of the free black population. The act certainly prevented white women from marrying black men. It worked with more effectiveness, however, to prevent Anglo-Texan men from marrying slave women, a much more common occurrence earlier.[48] Under both Spanish and Mexican law, if a slaveholder wed his or her slave, their marriage had the effect of manumitting the slave and entitling him or her, as well as the children born of the union, to all the rights of citizenship. The 1837 act thus overturned threatening Hispanic slave law and matrimonial rules and, as a practical matter, prevented any further increase of free blacks in the new republic that might otherwise have resulted from the marriage of white men to their bonded women.[49]

The 1837 antimiscegenation statute combined with the law of slavery and bastardy to worsen substantially the situation of the mulatto children whom black women had with white men. Spanish civil law permitted a man to legitimate a child born out of wedlock by marrying the mother of the child. The Texas Congress perpetuated this principle in behalf of colonial couples who had failed to have their bond marriages solemnized, but it was otherwise abandoned. This step and the 1837 ban of marriage between blacks and whites thus denied a white man the power to legitimate a child he had with a free black consort. The absence of an affiliation procedure, furthermore, denied these women the power to impose financial responsibility for their children on the white men who fathered them. By denying slaves the right to marry their masters and thus acquire their freedom, the 1837 statute made the child of a bondwoman by her owner irretrievably a bastard and a slave. Quite clearly, the new regime eliminated important incentives slave women had under Mexican law to form relationships with their white male owners and to have children with them.[50]

Land ownership patterns and the Hispanic matrimonial regime in post-independence Texas made a law banning white-black marriage a prime goal for Anglo-Texan legislators. With marital freedom, a free black woman in most southern states could have asserted matrimonial rights to the property of any white man she might marry, while a mulatto child resulting from such a relationship could have made claims to patrimonial inheritance. Southern legislators, in fact, designed anti-miscegenation laws to forestall these results.[51] This basic legal possibility also existed in post-independence Texas. The new leadership was much more motivated to object to marriage between whites and blacks than were legislators in the more settled South, however, since most Anglo-Texan men acquired unusually large amounts of land and Spanish matrimonial rules provided a wife half of all property she and her husband acquired after marriage.[52] Multiracialism in the Mexican period, furthermore, had established mores tolerating Anglo-Texan men who lived with and sometimes married slave women and black mistresses. As did Adam Smith and Margaret Guess, numerous mixed couples continued to cohabit as husband and wife after independence. The shortage of white women and settlement exigencies that strongly promoted pair-bonding still pressured Anglo-Texan men to marry these women. These conditions also continued to encourage white men to marry black women they met after independence, free or bonded, especially if they had African ancestry not readily apparent.[53]

The 1837 statute rendered nugatory marriage between blacks and whites and thus preserved white family property. Like most southern antimiscegenation acts, section 9 of the 1837 law held null and void a marriage between a person of European extraction and a person of African ancestry. Free black or manumitted slaves who actually exchanged wedding vows with whites thus had no matrimonial rights whatsoever, including those to community property. By the same token, children born of attempted marriages between blacks and whites could assert no legal claims to patrimonial inheritance.[54]

That Texas legislators designed section 9 of the 1837 act to exclude black consorts and their mulatto children from white family membership is evident on the face of the statute. The Act of 5 June 1837 was, in actuality, a general marriage statute. It made matrimony more accessible and regularized marriage procedures. Various sections of the act permitted prospective validation of extralegal marriages performed in Mexican Texas and provided for the legitimation of children resulting from them. Other sections declared certain kinds of marriages invalid, such as those between underage parties. Given the ban on marriage between blacks and whites set forth in section 9, the act worked almost exclusively to clarify de jure white kinship and family property rights. By the same token, section 9 denied blacks legal membership in white families. In practical terms, it also denied to black women who exchanged marriage vows with Anglo-Texan men matrimonial property rights and to any mulatto children resulting from such relationships any patrimonial inheritance.[55]

After Texas courts recognized informal marriage, the ban on unions between blacks and whites became even more important for protecting white family property. The Texas Supreme Court adopted common law marriage in 1847, holding that cohabitation and repute as husband and wife gave rise to the inference of a valid marriage. Litigants usually utilized this principle when men died and left behind women and children with whom they had lived for extended periods of time. Anglo-Texan men and black women who had cohabited for years quite often satisfied a number of the circumstantial evidentiary requirements for common law marriage; this was particularly true for those who had paired off in Mexican Texas when matrimony between blacks and whites was legal. By the same token, judicial recognition of these unions would have established marital property rights for black female consorts and inheritance rights for their mulatto children. Some of these women might well have succeeded with claims of this kind without the 1837 statute. The legislation, in fact, served to protect white family property from estate claims grounded in common law marriage principles that former slave mistresses and their mulatto children made in a number of probate cases rising to the Texas Supreme Court after emancipation.[56]

Lawmakers stiffened the law of miscegenation late in the antebellum period to reinforce Anglo-Texan families and their property rights. In the late 1850s, many southern states refashioned their criminal statutes in response to the growing antislavery movement. These initiatives usually entailed more rigorous slave codes and race control measures, including legislation designed to keep the races sexually divided. Texas legislators fell in line on 12 February 1858, with an act that established more severe penalties for inciting insurrection, illegal transportation of slaves, stealing or "enticing" them, and aiding, harboring, or concealing escaped slaves. The act also revised the 1837 ban on marriage between blacks and whites to make this offense a felony and defined what persons fell within the proscription. According to the statute, no "white person" could legally "marry a Negro, or person of mixed blood, descended from Negro ancestry, to the third generation inclusive. . . ." The octoroon provision certainly reveals the curious legal calculus involved in the arbitrary binary construction of racial categories in a rapidly expanding slave state. The explicit definition, however, worked quite well to dispel confusion about the racial credentials required for women and men to marry one another legally. It also defined which men and women could produce legitimate heirs. Like their counterparts in other southern states, Texas legislators undoubtedly designed the rule to prevent free blacks and slaves from fomenting dissent among nonslaveholding whites by cultivating sexual ties with them. The 1858 Texas measure, however, also worked to firm up Anglo-Texan family membership and property rights the unusually extensive relationships of white men and black women continued to threaten.[57]

Antimiscegenation law in post-independence Texas undoubtedly made it more difficult for white men to marry black women. The ordeal of David L. Wood, at least, would suggest so. He moved to Texas from Illinois in the late 1830s, settled in Fort Bend County, and garnered considerable publicity by establishing the Richmond *Telescope,* one of the earliest newspapers in the republic. In 1839, local leaders selected him to sit on a committee to discuss building a railroad through the county. Within the next year or so, he married the cultivated daughter of well-to-do William Primm. His rising fortunes, however, collapsed abruptly in 1841 when a Fayette County grand jury indicted him for miscegenation. It seems that David's new bride was white in appearance, but Primm revealed at trial that both his daughter and her mother were slaves. David maintained publicly that he had no prior knowledge of his bride's ancestry, and he petitioned Congress to place him "beyond the reach of any future attempts against his private peace and happiness by passing an act to legalize his marriage, lest he should be driven by the spirit of persecution to seek a home with his wife in a foreign land."[58] The legislators were not persuaded. Records indicate that David and his wife indeed soon left the republic.[59]

The rise and fall of David Wood at least highlights the pitfalls awaiting careless grooms in post-independence Texas. The inquisition Wood faced before Fayette County authorities in 1841 certainly shows the difficulty of discerning African ancestry, even when not so remote, and the travails awaiting a man who neglected to investigate the lineage of his prospective wife. It also suggests that men with public roles had to be particularly careful about maintaining racial decorum in a polity seeking to reinforce its commitment to white supremacy and the institution of slavery. By the same token, the case also demonstrates just how much race relations had changed since Texas won its independence from Mexico only six years earlier.

On the other hand, the Wood case demonstrates how female slave concubinage generated intimacy between blacks and whites in defiance of marital restrictions designed to bolster white supremacy. Anglo-Texan men who actually cared about their slave children frequently made efforts to provide for them and improve their situation; William Primm did so by concealing from David Wood the heritage of his daughter and her slave status. Powerful parental emotions thus sometimes encouraged slaveholding men to introduce their mulatto children into Anglo-Texan society through marriage across the color line. Whether they did so with the cooperation of prospective brides and grooms or through deception, they ran up against rules designed to undergird the slave system. In theory, these men had to tolerate the way the law stigmatized the children they had with bondwomen. In a relatively lawless frontier society where female slave concubinage was unusually frequent, and where women were in short supply, the efforts of slaveholders to flout this precept worked with increased force to encourage illicit marriage between blacks and whites.

The law of miscegenation, however, worked quite well to protect female slave concubinage. While David Wood certainly paid the price for his matrimonial choice, prosecutions for marriage between blacks and whites after independence were relatively infrequent in contrast to the number of relationships men commonly maintained with slave women. In actuality, the 1837 antimiscegenation act permitted such connections, since it neglected to penalize sexual relations between blacks and whites in any form. This omission would have made perfect sense to men like William Primm and Kit Patton. Other legislation relevant to female slave concubinage suggests that Texas authorities continued through most of the antebellum period to concern themselves little with owners who kept slave mistresses. Texas legislators refrained from penalizing simple fornication. And while an 1836 statute aimed at the general population made it a misdemeanor to "live in fornication," not until the 1858 revision of the Texas miscegenation law did legislators make it a felony for blacks and whites to do so.[60] Even if constables or sheriffs had actually wanted to enforce the socially discordant measure, the frontier situation made prosecution of those who kept slave mistresses extremely problematic. These women usually shared rooms with their "bachelor" owners or lived in cabins nearby. This assignment of quarters, however, differed little from those typical and perfectly appropriate for slave domestics. Given the cloaking effect of living arrangements on frontier homesteads, their isolation, and the travel difficulties the relatively few law enforcement officials inevitably faced, white men easily maintained their slave mistresses with little fear of prosecution. This was especially so when these men owned large estates, held more than a few slaves, and thus enjoyed political power and social influence. Post-independence "miscegenation" law was thus quite compatible with the sexual imperatives of Anglo-Texan racial dominance.

The Texas antimiscegenation statutes were also consistent with the transracial sexual double standard. It seems quite likely the struggle for survival, isolation, and more intense interpersonal relations on frontier farms encouraged white women sometimes to take slave men as clandestine lovers. The absence of a sanction against sex between blacks and whites or simple fornication involving women and men of any race, in fact, allowed for trysts of this kind. As in the Mexican period, however, sustained and open relationships involving white women and black men were extraordinarily rare after independence. Anglo-Texans reserved virulent condemnation for white women who took black men as partners.[61] To a large degree, this sentiment stemmed from white racism that intensified sexual norms already more strict for women than men. While the keen competition among Anglo-Texan men for scarce marriageable women reduced the number of unaccompanied women at liberty to cultivate cross-racial relationships, it also further strengthened the taboo. The threat of ostracism for white women and their children resulting from relationships with black men was undoubtedly a powerful deterrent. Given that urban settings usually generated the relatively few cohabitative relationships of this kind, the criminal penalty for "living in fornication" and the 1858 law punishing blacks and whites who did so provided practical tools for authorities to intervene. For black men who dared to cross the color line flagrantly, however, "Judge Lynch" was in constant readiness to provide a swift and permanent remedy.[62]

By 1860, Anglo-Texan lawmakers had constructed a regulatory regime for cross-racial intimacy far removed from that under which Rachel Bartlett and Kit Patton initially formed their relationship. Their union was a rather common by-product of the fluid social situation existing in Mexican Texas. Most young men like Kit Patton immigrating from the more settled South viewed slave women as appropriate sexual partners. Hispanic mores accepting cohabitation of men with their bonded women and Mexican law permitting marriage between them easily allowed for such involvements. Kit's relationship developed, furthermore, amid a multiracial subculture in which Mexicans, Indians, free blacks, and escaped slaves from Louisiana intermingled with arriving white immigrants with virtually no institutional oversight. The individualism of many early settlers, the struggle for survival, a shortage of white women, and minimal social constraints also worked to encourage liaisons similar to that of Rachel and Kit.

To some extent, the hardening attitude of the Patton family toward Kit's relationship reflected the rise of Anglo-Texan dominance. In the years following independence from Mexico, pioneer conditions continued to promote sexual relationships between white men and their slave women. An ethos of "manly independence" among southern immigrants further encouraged them. The establishment of a new slave system after 1836, however, intensified the Anglo-Texan drive for racial hegemony. White supremacy impulses grew especially powerful in places like Brazoria County where the slave population rapidly became more voluminous and concentrated than in other areas of the state.

Notwithstanding the animus of the Patton clan, the kind of relationship Kit had with Rachel was not that unusual or particularly reprehensible to most Anglo-Texans. The actions the Pattons took against Rachel and Kit in 1854 were certainly not inevitable. Only after twenty years had passed, and after the Patton family had come to perceive themselves and Kit as members of the slaveholding elite, did they grow resentful enough toward Rachel to destroy her relationship with him. The rather nefarious and mercenary designs of Charles Patton also appear to have played a decisive role in having his older brother declared incompetent and transported. The calamitous result of Kit's conflict with his family over Rachel was, in fact, anomalous within the Texas slaveholding order. Few white men who kept slave mistresses had to concern themselves with nearby and well-organized families, much less with those as unscrupulous and ruthless as Kit Patton's. Through the antebellum period, most Texas whites tolerated female slave concubinage.

The Patton dispute also indicates how legal rules about interracial relationships after independence from Mexico worked to reinforce white hegemony. The intervention of the Pattons certainly shows that Anglo-Texans sometimes relied on local courts to protect family wealth regardless of primitive institutional arrangements. The wrangle over Kit Patton's estate also suggests how post-independence law banning marriage between persons of African ancestry and those of European extraction protected Anglo-Texan family property against claims that black female consorts and their mulatto children might otherwise have asserted. By the same token, it indicates just how critical antimiscegenation law was in a state where most settling men acquired extensive amounts of arable land of which wives usually acquired coequal ownership under the Hispanic matrimonial property regime. That post-independence law did not prohibit or penalize sex between blacks and whites and proscribed "living in fornication with a Negro" only on the eve of the Civil War, however, merely reflects that Texas lawmakers were ordinarily willing to tolerate "eccentric" men who kept slave mistresses. These measures also indicate how mores and gender constructs alone were adequate to discourage white women from establishing sexual relationships with black men.

The sexual relations of whites and blacks in antebellum Texas comported with white hegemony from the earliest days of colonization. Stressful living conditions, Hispanic culture, and Mexican law certainly predisposed white frontiersmen to cohabit with and sometimes marry free black and slave women. Immigrant southerners in Mexican Texas, however, only tolerated these relationships and thus marginalized them. A new lower-southern majority thereafter powerfully reinforced white hegemony and a more brutal form of bondage. Frontier conditions, however, continued to promote unusually extensive sexual interaction of Anglo-Texan men and their slave women. This included both sexual exploitation of the women and cohabitation with them in relatively stable domestic arrangements.

Post-independence law reinforced more restrictive mores concerning sex between blacks and whites, but only to the extent necessary to ensure Anglo-Texan racial dominance. In a radical reversal of Hispanic rules, post-independence lawmakers banned marriage between blacks and whites. New statutes thwarted Mexican customs permitting white men to marry free black and slave women, nullified such unions, and thus protected white family property. On the other hand, the law permitted Anglo-Texan men sexual relationships with their female slaves, while combining with social mores to deter similar involvements among white women and black men.

FOUR

Turbulent Prairie Homes

Marital Formalities

AND

Institutional Disarray

Bold and free-spirited Texas frontiersmen made the best of things in a primitive situation—often in ways helping little to improve communal order. Raised in a Virginia slave-owning family, young Branch T. Archer studied medicine in Philadelphia, commanded a cavalry regiment in the War of 1812, and then returned home to serve several terms in the legislature. Having thus established himself, he married Eloisa Clark in the 1820s and had six children with her. After the successful politician and war veteran killed one of his cousins in a duel, however, he left Eloisa and their children in 1831 and headed for Texas. In the next few years, he assumed an instrumental role in the developing rebellion against Mexican authority, ultimately rising to numerous important offices in the government of the new Republic of Texas. Settling in the small port town of

Velasco, the "Old Roman" mixed an intermittent medical practice with forays against recalcitrant Mexicans and Indians, politics, gambling, and drinking. Eloisa and some of the children had followed Archer to Texas, but his relations with them slowly deteriorated.[1]

In his last twenty years, Archer's creative profanity, volatile personality, and impulsiveness made him a local legend. A prime candidate in his time for the title of most talented practitioner of the popular frontier art of swearing, Archer often asserted that he actually meant to honor God through his lack of verbal inhibitions.[2] Indicative of this renowned colloquial eloquence was his written invitation to a kinsman to visit him in Texas, maintaining the two could enjoy a steady diet of fish, fowl, and whiskey and "live like . . . fighting cocks." Archer never ceased to enjoy an unfettered existence. As late as 1854, the seventy-four-year-old patriot commented to a relative, "[M]y nature is restless" and "[A]ction for its own sake, regardless of outcome . . . is necessary to my happiness."[3] When he died on 23 April 1856, in Brazoria, he had been cohabiting for several years with Sarah Groce Wharton, the wealthy widow of his friend and fellow founder of the Texas Republic, William H. Wharton. By that time, however, his wife and five of his six children had either died, abandoned him, or been deserted by him.[4]

Early Texas certainly offered a refuge for men and women from the more established South seeking to leave their troubles behind. Arrivals like Branch T. Archer, however, concerned themselves very little with how their "frolics" and unrestrained behavior threatened the strategic colonization aims of Mexican leaders. Initially at least, most immigrants found little wrong with a virtually unregulated polity offering extensive tracts of land to couples willing to face the rigors of the frontier. To most settlers, the arrival of self-absorbed and impetuous men like Archer seemed an inevitable by-product of a liberating milieu. By the same token, most of them believed that the social disorder and family instability resulting from the obstreperous conduct of adventurers like Archer were a small price to pay for prosperity. But very likely only settlers with a reflective bent considered how male unruliness combined with land-grant policy, Hispanic matrimonial law, and stressful living conditions to generate sexual mores and domestic arrangements that residents in the more settled South might well have considered at least rather unusual.

The attractiveness of Texas as a place for beleaguered southerners to start over stemmed initially from the immigration policies of Mexican leaders. After independence from Spain, they sought to establish a society in their northernmost province comprising their own citizens and naturalized Anglo-American settlers. Fearing spontaneous immigration from the United States, the new government resorted to land-grant policy as the most likely mechanism to absorb immigrants from *Norteamérica* into a rapidly developed population loyal to Mexico and Hispanic in culture.[5] Various enactments through to the early 1830s used sizable land grants to induce settlement of Mexicans, Europeans, and Anglo-Americans. Immigrants who swore allegiance to Mexico and converted to Catholicism were qualified. The Imperial Colonization Law of 1823 and the 1825 Texas-Coahuila Colonization Law provided extraordinarily large amounts of land to *empresarios* who settled and distributed tracts to immigrating families, as well as offering land directly to individual families. Each head of a family engaged in ranching could receive a *sitio* of pastureland, or 4,428 acres, for $30. Families engaged in farming were entitled to no less than a *labor*, or 177 acres, at a cost of $2.50 for nonirrigated tracts and $3.50 for those that were irrigated. Most family heads claimed they both ranched and farmed and thus qualified for a *sitio* and a *labor*, amounting usually to about 4,605 acres. The government, furthermore, accepted payment in multiyear installments, beginning no later than the fourth year.[6]

The terms under which the Mexican government offered settlers land provided an excellent new start for indebted spouses from the more settled South. Mexican colonization rules qualifying a married man for an estate four times the size of that available to a single man were well framed to promote the immigration and settlement of families. The acquisition of inexpensive and rich arable land in Texas, with payment long delayed, seemed to provide an excellent solution to the problems of the large number of southern men and women heavily in debt as a result of the Panic of 1819. Whether immigrating as spouses or marrying after their arrival, southern couples commonly believed with reasonable industry they might amass great wealth together in a few years.[7]

After obtaining independence from Mexico, Texas remained a prime destination for southerners wanting to start over. Under the new headright system and various colonization contracts, the Republic of Texas provided land to single immigrant men and even larger amounts to those who were married. After statehood, various preemption and homestead legislation provided inexpensive land for sale to new settlers, both women and men. Given the pragmatic benefits of family settlement, indebted southern spouses and their children continued to immigrate and newly arriving men and women married to take advantage of the land program.[8]

An innovative law of debt made immigration to Mexican Texas even more attractive to southern couples. An 1829 Mexican colonization decree recodified Castilian debt exemption principles, relevant only to chattels, and extended them to sovereign grants of land. Under this original homestead exemption rule, creditors could not seize for the payment of debt the lands colonists received from the Mexican government, their "implements of husbandry," or the "tools of their trade or machines." The new rule also prohibited a suit to seize granted land to satisfy a debt for twelve years after a colonist received it. Under pressure from United States banks and the Jackson administration, the Mexican government repealed the decree in 1831. Southern men and women, however, continued to pour into Texas both to escape debt and to acquire land they believed exempt from seizure. In the State of Coahuila and Texas, furthermore, officials generally saw to it that creditors did not lay claim to new homesteads.[9]

The law of debt continued to lure southerners after Texas became independent from Mexico. In response to the Panic of 1837, the Texas Congress enacted a homestead exemption law in January 1839. Perpetuating Hispanic principles, it provided "every head of family" could exclude from financial judgment or execution his homestead, basic household furnishings, and the "tools, apparatus, and books belonging to the trade or profession of any citizen." An 1840 reenactment made all land acquired from the Mexican government or from the Republic of Texas exempt from seizure for the payment of debts contracted before immigrants settled. Enshrined and expanded in the 1845 state constitution, the homestead exemption rule worked powerfully to draw large numbers of unfortunates, which the 1837 depression continued to generate in the more settled South for years thereafter. According to David Courtwright, Texas became so notorious as a refuge for debtors that a Gone to Texas sign hung on an abandoned farmhouse or cabin door was universally understood as a kiss-off to creditors and sheriffs.[10]

The special protection that homestead exemption law offered heads of families, nonetheless, made marriage the most economical and effective way for absconding southerners to deal with the challenges of settlement and to achieve prosperity.[11]

The civil law of Spain, rather than the English common law, governed the property relations of spouses settling in Texas. Immigrant southerners were subject to the Hispanic matrimonial property regime set forth in the medieval Castilian code *Las Siete Partidas*. Embodied in Mexican law and then adopted after Texas independence with some modifications, the Hispanic community property system ensured that husband and wife shared equally the gains of marriage. The Spanish definition of community property included the assets either a husband or wife acquired during their marriage. With some exceptions, property each owned before marriage remained separate. Excluded from the community was property acquired by gift or inheritance, as well as the property either spouse gave the other. Also excluded were purchases made with the proceeds from the sale of separate property and the natural appreciation of it. Upon the death of one of the parties, the survivor was entitled to the deceased's half of the community estate unless there were children or other descendants who stood to inherit a part of it.[12]

The community property system made the land policy particularly appealing to immigrant women. It gave them rights to coequal ownership of the property that marital efforts produced, including the land their husbands received from the government. Certainly this regime comported with the republican idealism emergent in the United States during the early nineteenth century, which posited more egalitarian marriage. It was also more equitable than the law governing married women in the common law states of the more settled South.[13] Texas immigrants, however, recognized the propriety of the Spanish law in the immediate situation. In the words of Joseph W. McKnight, the Hispanic marital property regime "empowered the wife to become co-owner of wealth acquired during marriage, to own separate property, and comported with the realities of frontier conditions under which both spouses stood together against natural and human forces." To pioneering spouses, the appeal of the community property system stemmed primarily from its functionality and fairness.[14]

Frontier conditions made marriage critical for successful homesteading. In addition to laying the foundation for an enlarged land grant—until statehood at least—marriage also facilitated the birth and rearing of children. Both sons and daughters provided a valuable labor force on farms and ranches, especially for parents in the predominant yeoman class. Ecological circumstances further pressured Anglo-Texan spouses and their children into intensely cooperative relationships. Basic material resources and creature comforts were scarce. The wilderness environment and Native Americans who violently resisted white encroachment frequently posed threats to the physical safety and security of settlers. Marriage and close family relationships thus greatly enhanced chances for survival and successful farming and ranching. Immigrant couples were also frequently cut off from the material and emotional support of their extended families. This isolation further increased the necessity for mutual aid among spouses, especially to ensure the protection and rearing of their children. In this context, nuclear-family households became the critical foundation blocks for Texas frontier society, in contrast to the more extended family organization in the more settled southern states.[15]

The stresses of settlement usually generated enduring marriages and families. Myriad testimonials suggest a singular attachment developed among pioneering spouses and their children in early Texas. The mutual commitments and esteem of family members increased considerably as they dealt successfully with daunting challenges. The tenacious cooperative efforts of early homesteaders and the staying power of their families, in fact, figured strongly in first-hand accounts of early Texas into the late nineteenth century. In his 1893 address to the Daughters of the Republic, for example, veteran pioneer John Lockhart epitomized the veneration that Anglo-Texans held for the determination of their forbears:

If ever names and families should be perpetuated it is the names of your ancestors who bore the brunt of the early settlement of this glorious state. . . . You have no doubt heard much concerning the deprivations and sacrifices they were called upon to undergo, but this hearsay is nothing in comparison with the reality. One must witness it as they did to justly appreciate it.[16]

Lockhart's linkage of families and the state was not accidental. Especially after independence from Mexico, notions of a distinctive polity emergent in Texas further reinforced frontier households. Settling men and women frequently idealized Texas as a safe haven for the "downtrodden millions of the earth." In particular, they prized the extraordinary opportunity Texas provided to escape the thralldom of debt, achieve self-sufficiency, and enjoy economically upward mobility. Leaders after 1836 certainly encouraged the values of "Texian" culture: resilience, courage, and equality. Anglo-Texan homesteaders, however, usually focused on how these ideals had translated into gains for their struggling families and promised both security and liberty for their descendants. Texas patriotism thus intertwined with devotion to kith and kin, and settling men commonly praised women who perpetuated these beliefs in their children.[17]

As much as institutional disarray and aberrant immigrant mores, however, the primitive conditions that early settlers faced often destabilized their families. Typical living arrangements for colonists in Mexican Texas were rudimentary at best. Homes were usually crudely and hurriedly built cabins made of roughly hewn logs and timber. Caroline von Hinueber, who immigrated from Germany with her family, wrote of their domicile for the first three years:

> [We lived in] a miserable hut, covered with straw and having six sides, which were made out of moss. The roof was by no means waterproof, and we often held an umbrella over our bed when it rained at night, while the cows came and ate the moss. . . . My father tried to build a chimney and fireplace out of logs and clay, but we were afraid to light the fire because of the extreme combustibility of our dwelling. So we had to shiver.[18]

Settlers also suffered acute material privations. Shortages of cash made it all but impossible to purchase domestic commodities and amenities, which were rare in any case. Early colonizers had difficulties obtaining adequate stocks of domestic animals, and many could only provide a meager fare for the table by hunting wild game.[19]

Homesteaders continued to face extreme hardship after independence. Texas remained a primitive farming society to the end of the antebellum period. As late as 1850, 96 percent of Texans lived in remote rural areas. While new towns like Gonzales, Velasco, Houston, and

Galveston grew steadily, even the largest towns lacked the comforts and amenities of the more settled South. For town dwellers and farmers alike, money was in short supply and a rudimentary barter economy prevailed. On the typical homestead, work hours were long and the labor tiresome and often tedious. Whether plowing or planting, scalding and butchering a hog, hauling dry goods from the nearest town, or tending herds, the work was constant for children, women, and men. While makeshift cabins continued to provide shelter for new arrivals, the farmhouses of even established settlers offered few conveniences. Hand-hewn and mud-chunked, with a gabled clapboard roof and dirt floor, they proved oppressively hot in the summer, drafty and cold in the winter. Sickness and death were commonplace; diseases such as malaria, yellow fever, and cholera routinely reaped their grim harvests. To make matters worse, Anglo-Texans, particularly along the line of settlement, waged brutal war against the Comanche and Kiowa. In the 1850s, this strife dealt death and misery to both Native Americans and whites as never before. While the Texas Rangers and United States Army organized the more extensive campaigns after statehood, homesteading families routinely battled their relentless foe.[20]

From the earliest days, isolation made life hard for immigrants. Because of the unusually large size of landholdings, Anglo-Texan settlers resided great distances from one another. The entertainment of chance visitors and occasional visits to neighbors, who were often thirty or forty miles distant, offered the only break from the monotony of their lives. Such trips were not easy to arrange, since there were virtually no roads. The wide dispersal of settlements, furthermore, discouraged the formation of church communities, schools, or political meetings that might have provided meaningful social contacts. The absence of adequate systems of communication, books, or newspapers intensified feelings of isolation. Conflict with hostile groups of Indians, particularly in extremely secluded locales, intensified the sense of desperation and insecurity.[21]

Poorly developed transportation systems and scattered settlement continued to reinforce the sense of isolation through to the Civil War. Roads that were developed in the last several decades of the antebellum period were often little more than rude wagon ruts or hoof tracks. Ferries were ill attended and costly to use. Bridges were almost nonexistent. Settlers could navigate the major rivers of East Texas only four or five months of the year, and even then for little more than thirty miles inland. While a few schools and Protestant churches appeared, they remained inaccessible to most homesteaders. Notwithstanding the great difficulties and dangers of travel, Anglo-Texan settlers occasionally trekked many miles by foot, ox-drawn wagon, or horseback to experience a break from the strains of their day-to-day existence. Especially worth the effort were weddings, funerals, public hangings, the speechmaking of politicians at county seats, and the social interaction available at camp meetings.[22]

The demands of homesteading placed tremendous strains on Anglo-Texan women. Given their more constant residence on farms and ranches, women especially felt the loss of friends and loved ones and the impact of loneliness. This was particularly true for some of the first generation of women who were unaccustomed to harsh conditions and the efforts that pioneer farming and survival required. Men frequently separated themselves from their wives and children for days and weeks on end to work distant farmlands, tend livestock or drive cattle to market, expand farming and ranching operations, hunt and fish, or travel to various towns to obtain provisions and do business. Working at jobs for cash while "proving up" their homesteads, chasing Native Americans with the local militia, and fighting Mexicans also kept husbands and fathers away from homesteads. Many settling women endured these separations under extraordinarily difficult circumstances. They routinely engaged in strenuous farm labor amid the anxieties of building adequate homes for their children. These efforts inevitably took their toll on the affections of partners and severely taxed the most compatible marriages.[23] According to one elderly female settler in 1827, Texas was "a heaven for men and dogs, but a hell for women and oxen."[24]

To a large degree, the ethos of male violence that worked to destabilize families in antebellum Texas stemmed simply from the social disorganization of a wilderness milieu. Immigrant men from the upper South brought with them a heritage of feuding, which predisposed them to settle private quarrels without the assistance of legal authorities. Mexican alcaldes, furthermore, often encouraged this kind of traditional justice. To some extent, maintaining order through personal violence served the settlers quite well in a province notable for its lack of effective law enforcement. Feuding in the early 1840s among regulators and moderators along the Sabine River over land titles, horse thievery, and slave stealing, however, revealed the problems stemming from the rule of "Judge Lynch." The turmoil and bloodshed resulting from customary backwoods governance became so disruptive that President Sam Houston finally had to send troops in to restore some semblance of civilization among the "redlanders." The danger that hostile Indians, Mexican troops, bandits, and wild animals posed to settlers only compounded the dilemma of unregulated self-help, since even law-abiding citizens applauded displays of courage and thus violence in the face of these threats.[25]

The disorderly behavior of many men in the first cohort of immigrants, however, appears to have had origins other than frontier social disorganization. A substantial number of arriving men were predisposed simply to discount their moral obligations to the public and other individuals. The reports of early settlers and leaders attest to the waywardness, irresponsibility, and rebelliousness of immigrant men often best characterized as antisocial misfits. In 1829, for example, Stephen F. Austin complained openly about the behavior of the men in his colony, noting their propensity for drunkenness, rowdyism, vagabondage, senseless public brawling, and abuse, as well as slandering him, members of the *ayuntamiento,* and the alcalde. Austin summed up the situation in 1829: "I had two difficult tasks to perform here, one to manage the government and the other to manage the settlers, of these, the latter was by far the most difficult."[26] Regardless of his efforts to keep men of "bad character" out of the colony, many of those who settled there were in fact maladjusted ne'er-do-wells who immigrated to escape indebtedness and punishment in the United States for serious crimes.[27]

The majority of men migrating to the southwestern frontier beginning in the 1830s brought with them a new set of social values that was unlikely to improve family cohesion. This ethos strongly emphasized an individualism, competitiveness, and willingness to take risks quite commensurate with the ideals of Jacksonian democracy and laissez faire capitalism. What "real" southern men wanted, however, was to live a defiantly unconstrained life free from the interference of traditional extended families that predominated in the more settled southern states to the east. By the same token, this ideal emphasized the fulfillment of a man's personal goals at the expense of his obligations to his family.[28]

Since Texas was situated on the westernmost edge of the southern frontier, it constituted a haven for seekers of the new masculinity. While Joan Cashin has identified quite well the defiant gender ideal of westering men from the seaboard South, it appears those who ended up in Texas expressed it in a singular form. Alexander Campbell, writing of Texas in 1840, alluded to this development: "There is a kind of manly independence among them here . . . you do not see in the United States."[29] The penchant of Branch T. Archer for alcohol, gaming, and physical conflict certainly did not make him unique in the emerging Lone Star State.

Many of the men who flooded Texas after independence, indeed, proved unusually adept at masculine behavior inimical to good social order and the stability of families. A significant segment of the immigrant male population in the 1840s and 1850s, by many accounts, was riffraff: adventurers, gamblers, and criminals prone to flout the norms of civilized society.[30] But even the undisciplined behavior of settling men without particularly disreputable backgrounds often shocked travelers. As the notoriety of Branch Archer might indicate, the distinctive modulations of language alone generated notable adverse commentary. Charles Hooten, the English author, whose Texas experiences left him misanthropic, wrote of the oaths typical of male settlers:

> [They] were of a character so entirely new and diabolical, that one would be apt to imagine the genius of Depravity herself had tasked her utmost powers to produce them for the especial use of the rising State.[31]

Slander consistently worried and perplexed responsible officials, as did drunkenness, public disorderliness, and gambling. While dueling was relatively uncommon until the end of the antebellum period (and usually the reserve of ambitious politicians), fistfights, stabbings, shootings, murders, and even the brutal practical jokes men perpetrated on one another routinely dismayed newcomers.[32]

Male brutality was not restricted to the public realm but also was a part of family life. According to Betsy Downey, private violence was a "characteristic of the American frontier that has long been buried 'in a dark, hidden place' in the nation's memory."[33] Domestic violence in the expanding West was rooted in traditional ideas about the superiority of men in a society where they customarily expected service and deference from their wives and children. This conception included the right of a man to dominate the members of his family, control them, and physically coerce them.[34] These attitudes, however, manifested themselves in unique ways on the frontier. Many of the men who drifted west were ill-equipped emotionally to deal with the stresses of responsible adult life even in normal social circumstances. The hardships, frustration, isolation, and often poverty that pioneer settlement entailed particularly exacerbated the tendency among these men to dominate and mistreat their wives and children.[35]

Some Anglo-Texan men certainly inflicted emotional abuse and violence on their wives and children. Recent historical scholarship has emphasized how the presence of women and the institution of marriage worked to stem male violence in the frontier West. While undoubtedly true, more than a few homesteading women in antebellum Texas quite likely would not have agreed entirely with this conclusion. All of the social and ecological conditions generating domestic violence throughout the western frontier were certainly at work in Texas, just as large numbers of immigrant men often had personalities making it difficult for them to cope well with stress. As a consequence, it was not uncommon for Anglo-Texan men to inspire fear in their homes with drunkenness, harsh words, intimidation, and rough handling of their wives and children. The case of Margaret C. Henry is illustrative. After finally withdrawing from her marriage and joining the utopian Woman's Commonwealth of Belton, she recalled that once she protested to her husband, John, because he sold a sick mule to an unsuspecting customer. Her husband promptly flew into a rage, physically assaulted her, and broke her arm. Numerous women from Bell County complained that through the 1840s and 1850s their husbands frequently brutalized them to maintain their predominance and ventilate their frustrations.[36]

Anglo-Texan women, however, did not always tolerate the violence of their husbands, as did some of the Bell County women. In 1838, for example, Susanna Wilkerson Dickinson of Harrisburg divorced her husband, John Williams, because he had regularly beaten both her and a four-year-old daughter she had by a previous husband.[37] Margaret Wright of Victoria divorced her extremely vicious husband, John, in the early 1850s after he attacked and killed her son by a prior marriage. Elizabeth Nogees of Jefferson County sued her husband Jacques for divorce later in the decade after he had beaten her nearly to death with a three-foot-long "meat stick" and regularly threatened her with physical chastisement.[38]

Economic pressures after independence prompted some Anglo-Texan men to mismanage household finances and abandon home. The severe deterioration of economic conditions in Texas during the late

1830s and early 1840s pushed a number of provisional and unstable marriages to the breaking point. After the Panic of 1837, with its attendant contraction of credit and widespread indebtedness, an increasing number of men misappropriated the property of their spouses. The financial ineptitude of some husbands and unrestrained "manly independence" frequently led to the total demise of marriages and households. At the 1845 constitutional convention, delegate John Hemphill was not alone when he expressed serious concern about the growing number of men who "deserted and beggared their wives" after squandering their estates to pay debts resulting from irresponsible speculation and gambling.[39]

More than a few Anglo-Texan men involved themselves in extramarital affairs. The necessity for extended travel and long periods of absence afforded most settling men regular opportunities to engage in sexual liaisons. Marriage does not appear to have always limited their encounters with members of the opposite sex. It seems a substantial number of Anglo-Texan men consorted adulterously with single and married Anglo women when possible as well as with prostitutes of varying ancestry in frontier bawdy houses. In wilderness regions and in Hispanic areas, Indian wives and Tejano mistresses were also available for those who were particularly energetic.[40]

The creative entrepreneurship of some Anglo-Texan women at times encouraged infidelity in male settlers. From the earliest days of Texas settlement, numerous women cashed in on the shortage of marriageable females by operating a variety of businesses that catered to the needs of unaccompanied men. In growing towns especially, immigrant women ran businesses such as restaurants, laundries, taverns, and inns. Some women adapted their inns to provide sexual services to boarders and local men, whether they were married or not. In addition to the notorious madams of La Grange was Pamelia Mann, who ran public houses at Washington-on-the-Brazos in 1836 and later in Houston. Sarah Bowman established more open and notorious operations in Corpus Christi during the Mexican War and later at El Paso during the Gold Rush. Other women, however, operated boardinghouses that provided only dances and concerts for their male clients. Eminent men and common frontiersmen alike much appreciated the women who provided such cultural amenities. Jane Long, who operated a hotel in Brazoria during the early 1830s and later at Richmond, received special praise for her efforts in this regard, as did Angelina Eberly, who ran boardinghouses in Austin and Port Lavaca during the 1840s.[41]

Lawmakers after independence from Mexico, however, were accomplices in the expanding sex business. They refrained from imposing penalties on simple fornication or prostitution through to at least 1860. Only in 1857, furthermore, did the Texas legislature take any steps at all to rein in the bawdy houses. A statute passed in that year imposed a fine of not less than one hundred dollars nor more than five hundred dollars on those found guilty of owning and operating "disorderly houses." It seems, however, that legislators went out of their way to protect female sex workers. No statutes were adopted penalizing the prostitutes themselves or their clients. In 1841 the Texas Congress explicitly denied men who allowed their wives to engage in the sex trade the right to divorce them for adultery. Like most men in the polity, Texas lawmakers generally accepted female sex-for-hire and did not view it as a social problem.[42]

Slave-owning husbands, however, did not always need to travel to town for illicit female variety. A tacit understanding existed among slave owners in the more developed southern states that the occasional forays of a husband into the quarters were to be expected. There was, however, an understood limit to this activity. If a man's affair became blatant enough to embarrass publicly his wife or family, or if there appeared to be a danger of the relationship developing into something more serious than the periodic sexual tryst, most slave owners agreed it had to be stopped permanently. Married men in Texas sexually exploited their slave women more frequently and openly than did their counterparts in the more settled South. In circumstances encouraging an unusual amount of familiarity among owners and slaves, Anglo-Texan men had sexual relations with bondwomen that clearly violated traditional southern mores. These men involved themselves less clandestinely with slave women than their forefathers, even at the expense of their marital relationships and white families. Extramarital affairs among Anglo-Texan men and slave women, furthermore, frequently did not remain family secrets.[43]

The infidelity and unruliness of Anglo-Texan men encouraged female adultery. Across time and cultures, a number of situations have led women to be unfaithful to their husbands. Typical inducements have included the desire for sexual variety, satisfaction of attention and intimacy needs, the impulse to feel attractive, the urge to experience excitement or danger, and the determination to exact revenge on a faithless husband. These prompts have spurred infidelity when women have been financially independent and thus less intimidated by divorce, and when women have been married to neglectful husbands absent for long periods of time. They have especially encouraged unfaithfulness when social disorganization has resulted in flagging commitment to cultural ideals and religious beliefs that discouraged adultery. Clandestine sexual variety has also worked to provide women and their children with additional resources, as well as a kind of insurance policy against the death of a husband or his desertion. In essence, the self-absorption and irresponsibility of many Anglo-Texan husbands in a disorganized pioneer society was a virtual prescription for female adultery.[44]

The sexual adventurousness of Anglo-Texan men undoubtedly presented the greatest threat to the fidelity of married women. Women were valuable assets for husbands and often virtually indispensable for survival and prosperity. Because of the shortage of women, Anglo-Texan men competed even more vigorously for the practical benefits, child-bearing capacities, and companionship of mates than in societies where a more balanced sex ratio prevailed. The sexual promiscuity of many of the Anglo-Texan men bereft of regular female company compounded the threat. In these circumstances, married men had more reason to be concerned about female adultery than if women were abundant and competition for them less keen. The disorganization and lawlessness of the frontier magnified the danger further, since they reduced social constraints and further encouraged sexual interlopers.[45] The comments of one old Texan to Frederick Law Olmstead attest to this distinctive frontier phenomenon:

> If your life . . . would be of the slightest use to any one, you might be sure he would take it, and it was safe only as you were in constant readiness to defend it. Horses and wives were of as little account as umbrellas in more advanced states. Everybody appropriated everything that suited him. Justice descended into the body of Judge Lynch, sleeping when he slept, and when he woke having down right and left for exercise and pas-time.[46]

The frontier situation certainly created ample opportunities for Anglo-Texan women to commit adultery. Whether to satisfy intimacy needs or exact revenge on a philandering husband, some unhappy women undoubtedly took advantage of the surplus of willing male sexual partners when unsatisfactory mates were neglectful or abusive. Marriages that were based on practicality and opportunism almost certainly made this step seem less morally reprehensible for many women than if they had built their marriages on deep emotional commitment and romantic ideals. The extended absences of inattentive husbands, furthermore, made extramarital trysts easy to arrange.[47]

Survival and the quest for prosperity also encouraged Anglo-Texan women to replace unsatisfactory husbands with new ones. Given the pragmatic benefits of a spouse in pioneer circumstances, women with unfit mates and overburdened with work certainly had serious reservations about severing their marriages. This reticence was even more pronounced when a woman had infant children in her charge and was thus hampered in her ability to survive independently. A large number of unaccompanied men, however, were eager to find wives to qualify for family-size land grants, enlarge their own estates, or help them work at developing homesteads. Abandonment of an unsuitable husband, the establishment of a more workable relationship with an ambitious man, and ultimately remarriage to him provided women a means of escaping an intolerable union and acquiring a half interest in a new and potentially more profitable one. The disorganization and lack of public surveillance on the frontier, furthermore, reduced the notoriety attendant on informal coupling and uncoupling. The financial independence that community property law provided to most divorcing women lent even greater force to these inducements.[48]

Some married women, however, cultivated new relationships before terminating old unions. In May 1835, for example, James M. Berryman, a physician in San Felipe de Austin, squared off with local hotel owner Robert A. Stephenson in a contest over the affections of the latter's wife. Stephenson prevailed, placing a musket ball through Berryman's heart. Bystanders discovered on his body a lock of Mrs. Stephenson's hair in an envelope containing a letter from her naming a "place of assignation" where the two were to have met after her husband had been eliminated. Stephenson included the bloodied lock in a letter to his wife shortly thereafter, pointing out to her that it had not provided Berryman with a very effective shield. It would seem, however, that Mrs. Stephenson had hedged her bet. According to Mary Austin Holley, who arrived on the scene shortly thereafter, "The deceitful woman had written back to her husband to kill Berryman for the injury done to her name, or she would never live with him again. What now will be her position—all destroyed—all lost? Woman—when bad—how bad!"[49]

The pattern of wife abandonment, however, sometimes left women little choice but to take new partners. As was the case across the expanding frontier, men commonly deserted their wives in early Texas by simply departing on apparently harmless travels and then never returning. Homesteading women quite naturally believed long-absent and unheard-from husbands had abandoned them entirely. The temptation for a woman in this predicament to form a new relationship when the arduousness of farming and ranching imposed intolerable burdens upon her was often overwhelming. Such a relationship provided her with companionship, physical protection, and a working partner to aid in her own survival and that of her children and to ensure the viability of her farm or ranch.[50]

Maladapted land-grant policy, beginning in Mexican Texas, exacerbated marital instability. National and state colonization rules did not establish a harmonious and racially integrated Hispanic community in Texas, as planned. Land allocation rules induced instead the immigration of highly individualistic men and women, mostly from the more settled South. Mexican law requiring land commissioners to grant new tracts without vacancies between them encouraged men to marry quickly and carelessly, in order to obtain larger, cohesive family-sized allotments.[51] The policy of granting larger amounts of land to family heads encouraged men poorly equipped for responsible domestic life to immigrate hastily with their families, or to immigrate and then marry with equal precipitation. In tandem with the community property system and homestead exemption rules, land-grant law spurred the settlement of indebted couples on the brink of financial disaster and precariously formed marriages based primarily on opportunism. These unions were particularly susceptible to the inherent stresses of homesteading, including those stemming from the isolation which land-grant law itself produced, as well as the frequent unruliness and sexual promiscuity of Anglo-Texan men. Mexican policy thus intensified pressures that undermined relationships in any case.

Poorly conceived Mexican land-grant rules also encouraged bigamy. Offers of unusually large tracts of inexpensive land made Texas a migratory society almost from the beginning. Land distribution rules generating widely dispersed settlement, furthermore, provided not only a refuge for immigrants who were deserting failed marriages but also the personal liberty and anonymity to remarry without bothering to obtain legal divorces. Since Mexican authorities granted land and thus prosperity more generously to families, women and men who abandoned failed marriages frequently concealed the existence of still undivorced spouses when they remarried. Anglo-Texan settlers thus often established bigamous marriages in response to extremely attractive economic incentives, rather than in consideration of the long-term consequences for themselves and others. Regardless of their profitability, these unions were nonbinding, adulterous, and subject to criminal prosecution and dissolution.[52]

Colonial rules about marriage and divorce further generated illicit sexual relationships. The Mexican government required all citizens to marry only before a Catholic priest. Neither the government nor the Catholic Church, however, sent enough clerics to the State of Coahuila and Texas to effectuate this policy. Consequently, many Anglo-Texans simply cohabited out of wedlock. The Mexican ban on absolute divorce created further problems. Mexican law embodied Catholic doctrine, which held marriage as a lifelong, permanent arrangement. As received and developed under the civil law of New Spain and then perpetuated in the Republic of Mexico after 1821, the canon law of the Roman Catholic Church recognized only two forms of marital dissolution: divorce *a vinculo* and divorce *a mensa et thoro*, with the latter often referred to as "separation from bed and board." The church could grant a divorce *a vinculo*, or absolute divorce, only in the most unusual circumstances, such as apostasy to Judaism or Islam. In essence, divorce for postmarital causes was a virtual impossibility. Anglo-Texan women and men, however, were accustomed to much more provisional conceptions of marriage. Those who desired to terminate unsatisfactory unions and establish new ones were left with little choice but to remarry bigamously or cohabit in adultery, with the children that resulted inevitably illegitimate.[53]

National policy on religion in colonial Texas worked in other ways to generate marital breakdown and extralegal sexual connections. According to one settler, the Catholic leadership made "no efforts to secure forcible subscription to the tenets of that church. Every man was free to follow the bent of his own inclination in that respect." Anglo-American immigrants could thus easily claim to embrace Catholicism just long enough to obtain land. Even this ruse was unnecessary after

1834, when the legislature of the State of Coahuila and Texas abrogated the test of Catholicism. While most Anglo-Texans had little interest in organized worship, maintenance of Catholicism as the state religion through much of the colonial period undermined the efforts of the few devout Texans to form viable Protestant congregations. Dispersed settlement further retarded the establishment of Protestant churches. Without priests, ministers, religious institutions, extended families, or an organized social structure to bolster precariously formed marriages, Anglo-Texans were particularly vulnerable to the frontier stresses undermining them. In this context, illicit coupling and uncoupling proceeded with little impediment.[54]

Post-independence land-grant rules continued to generate tenuous marriages. The policy of granting larger amounts of land to family heads, at least through the years of the republic, encouraged men poorly equipped for responsible home life to immigrate impulsively with their families or to immigrate and then marry with equal rashness. Preemption and land-grant law after statehood worked similarly. In tandem with the adopted community property regime and revitalized homestead exemption rules, land-grant rules persisted in spurring the settlement of an unusually large number of indebted couples and precariously formed marriages rooted in expedience. The isolation of farms and ranches that the land-grant program continued to generate compounded the stresses at work on these marriages.[55]

Dysfunctional governance under Anglo-Texan rule continued to promote illicit relationships. While post-independence law permitted marriage before Protestant ministers and secular authorities, both the administrative apparatus and officials necessary for formal marriage were often inaccessible to homesteaders. Many settlers thus simply cohabited and claimed to be married. The Texas Congress expanded grounds for absolute divorce beginning in 1837. But inadequate transportation, a poorly organized judicial system, and the expense and delay of litigation made divorce an unattractive option to couples with unsatisfactory unions. Legal marriage required a single trip to a minister, justice of the peace, or county court house. A legal divorce, however, required hiring a lawyer and often making multiple trips to court. Faced with that prospect, Anglo-Texans who were determined to terminate their marriages often did so informally. This method was especially common among immigrants who had simply left spouses behind in other polities. For individuals who ended their unions informally and desired to obtain once more the benefits of marriage, bigamy—and thus living in adultery—was the practical alternative. Illegitimate children, however, were a common consequence.[56]

Organized religion in post-independence Texas was ineffectual in shoring up precarious marriages. Scattered congregations of Baptists, Methodists, and Presbyterians certainly began to coalesce in growing towns in the 1840s and 1850s. But the isolation of homesteads and the dearth of churches before the Civil War hardly worked to reinforce Anglo-Texan relationships under stress. Pastoral guidance and viable church communities were still lacking. With considerable input from concerned women, some church congregations actually attempted to impose discipline on their male members who drank, fought, and stole. They also sanctioned both women and men who fornicated and lived in adultery. Given the weakness of organized religion, however, male unruliness and the capricious mating habits of many men and women endured.[57]

The unusually expansive sexual license that settlers enjoyed certainly met with resistance. Anglo-Texan men nurtured a particularly strong antipathy toward those who inveigled their wives into adultery. They commonly perceived such conduct as a highly reprehensible usurpation of their marital prerogatives and a supreme insult. Husbands also undoubtedly objected to female unchastity because of their concern that it might impose a "spurious issue" on them. Increasing concerns about property rights in the United States in the early nineteenth century made adulterine bastardy more reprehensible than ever before. In Texas, as in most jurisdictions of the United States, illegitimate children resulting from such unions almost always stood to inherit family estates. The threat to family assets that "baseborn" children presented to men in frontier Texas, however, was greater than in the more settled states of the nation, since most Texas women and men acquired title to unusually large amounts of land. Anglo-Texan men undoubtedly also viewed the philandering of a wife as a step toward abandonment, which meant the loss of a valuable working partner and female companionship in a demographic situation in which a replacement was difficult to find.[58]

Racism quite likely generated the most intense animus among Anglo-Texan men toward female adultery. Immigrant men from the South viewed the infidelity of a wife with a bondmen as one of the most opprobrious marital offenses. The more intimate and familiar relationships of owners and slaves on frontier farms in Texas, however, are likely to have tempted some married white women into involving themselves sexually with male slaves. The racism of Anglo-Texan women, as well as their apprehension of social censure and outraged spouses, almost certainly limited this kind of activity. Even so, their husbands could not have easily dismissed the enhanced possibility of it.[59]

A few women objected vigorously to the brazen adultery of their husbands with slave women. Most Anglo-Texan women were in close proximity to the affairs their husbands arranged with bonded females. They were thus much more aware of them than they were of liaisons that occurred away from their homesteads. The racism of white women generated an especially strong resentment of male infidelity when it occurred with female slaves. In the 1850s, however, it was the flagrant philandering of Anglo-Texan husbands with slave women that compelled a number of wives to register strong public condemnation of the practice. Mary Pridgen of Harrison County, for example, sued her husband, Wiley, for divorce because he had committed adultery with no less than five of his slave women between 1845 and 1850. It does not appear the Creek heritage of Rebecca Hagerty induced her to tolerate marital infidelity. She sued her husband, Spire, for divorce in 1853 for having fathered two children by a slave he had carried on with openly for years. Amid particularly rancorous divorce litigation, Pink Cartwright accused her husband, Williford, of having maintained one of his slaves virtually as a mistress.[60]

On the other hand, the attractive sanctuary that Texas lawmakers established and the marital dilemmas they inadvertently created led to more tolerant attitudes toward illicit sexual relationships. In the 1875 Texas Supreme Court decision of *Lewis v. Ames,* Chief Justice Owen Roberts commented on the situation and the attitudes it induced among the inhabitants:

> Texas being then [during the Mexican period] and afterwards a place of refuge for unfortunates, persons came here and lived as husband and wife, leaving behind a living husband or wife; and persons lived here together as husband and wife having in this country a living husband and wife. . . . Society in the country was not sufficiently organized (the mass of people being sparsely scattered over the country and strangers to each other) to frown on these irregularities . . . as might have been done in older countries.[61]

While often ignoring the errancy of immigrating women, jurists continued to take note of the disordered situation late in the nineteenth century. The complicated marital career of Jonathon Routh demonstrates this concretely. In 1845, he abandoned Elizabeth, his second wife, in Illinois and moved to Texas. Without divorcing her, he married Nancy Thompson in Fannin County in 1852, living with her until his death in 1864. In the 1882 decision of *Routh v. Routh*, Justice P. J. Walker of the Commission of Appeals explained the socioeconomic circumstances dictating recognition of Nancy's marriage:

> It is not a matter of surprise that, in the early settlement of Texas, cases like the present should have occurred. The great efforts to induce settlement brought people from almost every state in the Union and many portions of Europe together in this new country. That some men should have taken advantage of the occasion to rid themselves of unhappy domestic ties, and that others should have become indifferent to former obligations, is natural. The unmarried women of the new population being innocent of a knowledge of these circumstances, entered into marriages in good faith, and throughout a life-time were good and faithful wives and mothers. Such was the case with Nancy Thompson. . . .[62]

As Chief Justice Roberts indicated in *Lewis v. Ames*, most antebellum Texans had fairly realistic attitudes about women who neglected marital formalities or traditional sexual decorum. Harris County resident Pamelia Mann, for example, was prosecuted for "living in fornication" in the late 1830s shortly after the death of her third husband, Marshall. It appears she had begun living with her future fourth spouse, a man named Brown, before bothering to marry him ceremonially. No conviction resulted, however, as jurors took into account the informal marriage customs that had flourished in Texas since the Mexican period. Notwithstanding her notoriety for the fornication prosecution, and for charges of larceny, assault, and forgery, the Houston community continued to accept her. The attendants at the wedding of her son, Flourney Nimrod Hunt, included President Sam Houston as best man, with Ashbel Smith and other luminaries assisting. In 1857, Peter Bellows successfully divorced Susanna Wilkerson Dickinson, also of Houston, charging her with both adultery and prostitution. Even so, she remained a local favorite and continued to receive praise for her well-known heroics at the Alamo and for her work in assisting cholera victims. She ultimately took a fifth and final husband, prospering merchant Joseph William Hannig.[63]

The continuing social acceptance of Pamelia Mann and Susanna Dickinson and the ease with which they remarried lend credence to the conclusion that the frontier situation encouraged men to take female adultery in stride. The shortage of marriageable women and toleration of informal coupling and uncoupling, bigamy, and adultery worked to make women who deviated from customary sexual mores less reprehensible. The same demographic and ecological situation that made female adultery objectionable to Anglo-Texan men, furthermore, encouraged them to abide it. The infidelity of a woman certainly threatened her husband with the loss of a valuable mate. Given the difficulties of finding a replacement, however, rejection of a sexually wayward wife hardly left a man in a better situation, practically speaking. For men eager to sustain their homesteads, the least troublesome and most sensible solution was to reconcile with dissatisfied wives and take steps to make their marriages more secure.

In essence, frontier social dynamics encouraged Anglo-Texan men to adopt conceptions of women that deviated substantially from those commonly found in the rest of the South. White men in the more settled southern states idealized their women as especially chaste, pure, and loyal. They placed white women on a pedestal and demanded male respect for their wives' superior moral station. According to this theory, southern men resolved the threat that their own promiscuity posed to the chastity of wives by shielding them behind an elaborate southern code of chivalry which demanded extremely virtuous behavior.[64] Immigrant men in Texas were certainly familiar with southern views of female propriety. These romantic notions, however, withered in the frontier environment.[65] To survive and prosper amid the intense competition for scarce marriageable women, men had to adopt much more pragmatic attitudes toward female unchastity than in the more civilized and better organized southern states.

By the same token, Anglo-Texan women modified their traditional conceptions of masculinity. Since the great majority of immigrant women had southern origins, most of them were ready through acculturation to permit married men more sexual latitude than men ordinarily allowed wives. These women were also familiar with the customary expectation that they should ignore at least the discreet adulterous liaisons of their husbands with slave women.[66] Also, the very commonplaceness of cohabitation out of wedlock, adultery, and bigamy on the frontier softened adverse judgments among Anglo-Texan women about illicit sex. By the same token, the exigencies of survival and successful homesteading placed great pressures on them to endure male infidelity. Quite likely, this was more difficult for some women than others. For those who had seen frontier travail reduce their marital affections or had married opportunistically in the first place, however, the unfaithfulness of a husband might well have been only a minor irritant. In any case, as long as husbands made solid contributions to the success of family ventures, rejecting them for occasional trysts quite likely was not worth the trouble. For men who carried their sexual liberty too far, however, wives could rest assured that replacements were readily available.

          Relatively egalitarian Anglo-Texan marriage norms, geared for the accumulation of land and economic independence, were grounded in Hispanic matrimonial law that allocated power to manage marital estates. Under that regime, a husband in residence ordinarily had prerogatives regarding the disposition of marital property superior to those of his wife. As at common law, the Spanish regime required a man both to provide for and attend to the well-being of his wife and children. Presupposing a responsible husband, the law provided a man with expansive power to control marital property. Under the law, he could manage, encumber, and alienate community property. He could control, but not alienate, certain segments of his wife's separate property. The contract of a woman involving her separate property, furthermore, generally needed the approval of her husband. The Texas Congress adopted the Hispanic community property system statutorily in 1840. With some modifications, the act appropriated all of the essential principles of the pre-existing regime, including superior powers of marital property control for husbands.[67]

The adopted matrimonial regime, however, empowered a wife to manage marital estates independently in well-defined circumstances. The Hispanic civil law did not merge the legal identity of a woman with that of her husband, as in the common law. There were also important exceptions to the powers vested in a husband that were intimately related to the separate legal identity of his wife. These included her coequal and independent property interests and her inherent power to contract. A man could not dispose of his wife's dowry, and a woman maintained control of her "paraphernalia" after marriage. Should a man fail to take action to protect the community property, his wife could legally do so. If a man neglected to provide his wife with essentials, or "necessaries," she could enter into contracts drawing on her own separate property, that of her husband, or the community estate to provide them for herself and her children. If a man neglected or refused to consent to a contract involving the separate property of his wife, she could obtain authorization from the court to effect it. If a contract worked to her benefit or that of her children, it was valid regardless of whether her husband had approved it. Most important, however, a woman could control, convey, and encumber the community property and her separate property if her husband consented or if he was absent from the home for an extended period of time.[68]

Without expansive family enterprises, opportunities for most Tejanas to work outside the home and utilize their powers of marital property management were severely limited. A stagnant and underdeveloped economy prevailed in Hispanic areas of Texas through the antebellum period. With small-scale subsistence farming or wages from day labor providing the livelihood for most Tejano families, Tejanas found their occupational opportunities commensurately circumscribed. They generally assumed the responsibility for cultivating garden plots to provide the household with vegetables and fruit. Their labor also included washing, cooking, sewing, spinning and weaving, and the manufacture of other household items from available raw materials. While a few wealthy Tejanas helped manage farms and ranches, the great majority of Hispanic women had few occasions to make use of their legal powers.[69]

The allocation of power in the Tejano family further restricted women to domestic work. Despite certain liberalizing tendencies on the frontier that might have improved the economic opportunities of Hispanic women and their status, Tejano family culture remained thoroughly masculine in orientation. Tejano family norms were basically of European derivation, featuring a patriarchal dynamic growing out of a Spanish tradition developed long before 1800. Such families were usually subject to the dictates of a domineering male head of household. Husbands and fathers believed strongly in the subordination of women and thus substantially restricted the activities of women. While

Tejano men dominated business and politics, Tejanas developed roles connected entirely to home and family. As a consequence, many of them, it appears, often functioned as virtual domestic servants for their husbands.[70]

Gender dynamics at work in Tejano households worked to reinforce a limited role for wives. Close-knit Hispanic families frequently exhibited a degree of harmony and mutual cooperation that favorably impressed some Anglo observers.[71] The practical control of the home that many Tejano women acquired, however, gave them a degree of authority that often generated conflict with husbands determined to maintain their dominance. The overall effect of this discordance of gender ideals and reality, however, was to alienate spouses and bolster the rigid allotment of marital responsibilities which relegated Tejano women to domestic work only. In the view of Robert C. Hunt, Tejano marriages typically exhibited "strong and often manifest . . . hostility, distance, and little sharing of information."[72]

Tejano mores placed marital property management almost exclusively in the hands of husbands. Family norms combined with Hispanic law and enduring customs that deterred divorce to maintain households and thus a system of intergenerational property control comporting with patriarchal hegemony. Husbands traditionally assumed exclusive responsibility for making decisions affecting marital property and the relationship of the family to the larger economy and society. Most Tejano husbands resided more or less continuously with their families on relatively small subsistence farms and assumed day-to-day responsibility for household finances and business decisions. The community property system thus provided them exclusive and indisputable control over the disposition of both separate and community property.[73]

With different internal dynamics, Anglo-Texan families experienced the law differently. The clearing and development of unusually large parcels of land required Anglo-Texan women to function independently as homestead managers much more frequently than did Tejano wives. Men regularly spent long periods of time away from their homes. During these extended absences, they almost always left their wives in charge. Thousands of early Anglo women routinely managed family property alone while their husbands were away, blending their skills and labor with that of their sons and daughters to make farms and ranches flourish. They also assumed the task of rearing young children and protecting their homesteads from intrusions with equal self-reliance.[74]

While women who managed homesteads had widely variable impressions of their experiences, most of them fulfilled their expanded roles with great competence. First-generation southern women settling in frontier Texas from comfortable middle-class and more affluent backgrounds undoubtedly felt the impact of rough conditions to a greater extent than did immigrant southern women raised in yeoman families or women who grew up on the Texas frontier. For newly arriving daughters of planters, merchants, and professionals, inexperience with farming and ranching tasks and the strains of frontier survival intensified the sense of isolation and loneliness which the separation from their extended families induced in any case. It is undoubtedly true that some first-generation immigrant women from comfortable backgrounds and those otherwise unprepared for pioneer life gave up and returned home or languished into early graves. The great majority, however, ultimately adapted to the frontier environment, became self-reliant, and made their family farms and ranches thrive despite their fears, insecurities, and sense of alienation.[75]

Anglo-Texan women also had important independent roles as owners and managers of family businesses in growing towns after 1840. While the great majority of Anglo-Texans lived in dispersed rural settlements, small towns provided a distinct milieu for Texas women to wield considerable economic influence and power. As on rural homesteads, Anglo-Texan women living in early towns often managed family property while their husbands were away on business. Utilizing homemaking skills at first, and then acting in partnership with their husbands, an unusually high percentage of town-dwelling women staked out ownership interests in lucrative commercial ventures and took control of them. On the so-called urban frontier, women ran schools, dressmaking and millinery shops, confectionaries, laundries, bakeries, restaurants, and dry goods stores. Women who resided in towns also taught music in their homes, made extra cash by producing needlework, edited and wrote newspapers, and operated livery and sales stables. More adventurous and sociable women, it seems, owned and operated boardinghouses and hotels with particular ingenuity. In these businesses, married women frequently managed cash and handled accounts, correspondence, banking transactions, and deliveries while their husbands traveled to obtain new customers and arrange for business expansion. Such activities were also common for widowed women. Up to the Civil War, as many as 15 to 25 percent of Texas women living in towns engaged in work of this kind.[76]

The independent family role of Anglo-Texan women often required them to function in ways traditionally reserved for men. Settlement exigencies fostered an ethos of rugged individualism that encouraged Anglo-Texan women to be strong, ambitious, and self-reliant. In their efforts to ensure the efficient operation and profitability of homesteads, these women undoubtedly crossed into a traditional male sphere. In the frontier situation, consequently, no clearly delineated female realm or ethos of domesticity emerged as in the urbanizing North. This regular participation in "men's work," furthermore, diverged significantly from the routine of Tejanas and white women residing in the more settled southern states.[77]

The Hispanic matrimonial property regime amply equipped Anglo-Texan women to operate family enterprises independently. Frontier exigencies activated legal powers of marital property management and control that lay dormant in the case of most Tejanas. In the absence of a husband, or with his consent, Anglo-Texan women had full legal authority to control, protect, and convey both their own separate estates and community property to promote family ventures.

The statutory qualifications of a woman's legal power to control marital property did not reduce its utility in the frontier situation. A creditor accustomed to modern economic relations and an urban society certainly might have been skeptical about the contracts that Anglo-Texan women routinely sealed to operate their family farms, ranches, and businesses; after all, a dishonest husband could have denied that he had consented or claimed that he had not actually been absent from home, thus making their enforcement problematic. Most Anglo-Texan men, however, admired and respected the independent contributions and business efforts of their wives and had every reason to support them. In the small frontier villages where women usually made purchases or arranged sales, furthermore, people knew one another well. By the same token, merchants and factors had relationships with homesteading women and men that depended more on personal trust and shared values than on law or the courts. While some spouses might well have abused the law, creditors usually had confidence in their dealings with women whom they knew were working hard and honestly to make family ventures thrive. Married women had both the right and the power to buy, sell, and make contracts in the circumstances the law provided.[78]

That Texas policymakers intended for the Hispanic regime that they adopted to provide Anglo-Texan women with the power to run family enterprises and to profit from them is well established. Legislators, constitutional delegates, and jurists after independence from Mexico and through to the Civil War supported the community property system because of its utility. They consistently recognized that the adopted Spanish law meshed well with the reality of frontier settlement, which required women to be active and effective partners with their husbands. They also routinely noted the fairness of the Hispanic system in rewarding married women for their contributions and sacrifices.[79]

The Hispanic regime, in fact, motivated Anglo-Texan women to make strenuous efforts to ensure the success of family enterprises. Anglo-Texan women had a vested interest in family lands and often in slaves, as well as in the success of farming, ranching, and business operations. This was much more often the case than in the common law states of the more settled South, where the income deriving from the use of marital property fell into the hands of husbands exclusively. Under the Texas law, however, although women stood to make substantial profits from successful homesteading, they also risked standing liable for farms and ranches that failed. For all of these reasons, the economic incentive to make family ventures successful was strong among most Anglo-Texan women.[80]

Particularly after independence from Mexico, rapid frontier expansion reinforced the economic position of settling women in lucrative marital enterprises. The land most Anglo-Texans acquired after 1836 derived from state-sponsored dispossession of indigenous and Mexican peoples. Southern immigrants then utilized violence, warfare, and legal chicanery to despoil Native Americans and Mexicans of their land, held by the latter under old Spanish and Mexican land patents, and by the former since prehistory. New policies rooted in Anglo-Saxonism no longer required white immigrants to cooperate and settle with indigenous populations or share available lands with them. Anglo-Texan women and men who embarked upon this process of land acquisition embraced an ethnocentric mentality that energized their dispossession of indigenous peoples and Mexicans; they rationalized their conquest with tenets of free-market capitalism, democracy, Christianity, and manifest destiny. Legislators and jurists, furthermore, repeatedly upheld the coequal ownership of Anglo-Texan women because of the instrumental role they played in acquiring, defending, and developing their new homesteads. Community property law and white supremacy policies that subjugated and dispossessed Tejanos, Native Americans, and free blacks thus placed Anglo-Texan husbands and wives securely in the upper echelon of the racial-caste structure.[81]

In many cases, Anglo-Texan women elevated their fortunes, status, and power through the exploitation of slaves. Anglo-Texans acquired land in the context of the rapid expansion of the cotton-growing and slave-labor system previously established in the more settled southern states from which most of them came. By virtue of community property law, Anglo-Texan women acquired legal title to slaves much more often than did married women in the more settled South. According to Randolph Campbell, widespread slaveholding among white women gave many of them positions of economic power far greater than those held by most men in the state. By the end of the antebellum period, extensive ownership of slaves solidified the position of approximately 30 percent of Anglo-Texan women with their husbands within the highest tier of the dominant racial caste.[82]

At the expense of those they dispossessed and exploited, Anglo-Texan marital venturers were able to cultivate much more reciprocal relationships than spouses further east. Most women and men settling in frontier Texas did not romanticize their marriages as did urban spouses in the North or those attuned to liberalizing trends in the more civilized South.[83] Many Anglo-Texan men and women undoubtedly cherished and revered one another. But whether they immigrated initially as wife and husband or married after their arrival, settling spouses maintained marriages geared for survival, conquest, and mutual profit. Anglo-Texans, furthermore, usually maintained their unions regardless of the settlement stresses that eroded marital affections, the destabilizing effects of "manly independence," and the unusually lax sexual mores that the frontier situation produced. Given the coequal ownership interests and self-reliant roles of both men and women in family enterprises, their marriages were more practical than those of spouses further east. The increased mutuality of these relationships, furthermore, stemmed from necessity rather than companionate ideals. Under these circumstances, Anglo-Texan men were neither predisposed nor able to subject their wives to the patriarchal despotism that white women in the more settled southern states frequently endured.

The adventures of Branch T. Archer indicate a number of important influences in the development of distinctive family mores in frontier Texas. The immigration of men like Archer certainly complicated the goal of Mexican leaders to provide a colonial bulwark against Anglo-American encroachment. The government had intended to draw immigrants who would establish a traditional, Hispanic society of free-holding family farmers loyal to Mexico. An unexpectedly large number of unaccompanied, adventurous, and individualistic men like Archer, however, flooded Texas after 1823. Men of this ilk helped little to promote either family settlement or communal order, much less widespread devotion to Mexican political authority.

Archer's life also reveals how the self-absorbed behavior of immigrant men from the more settled South destabilized frontier families. Men like Archer certainly enjoyed the benefits of a loosely organized society that accepted all comers regardless of their past misfortunes. As refugees from personal travail and frequently fugitives from justice, however, they often displayed a reduced capacity or willingness to maintain obligations not only to authority, but also to society and other individuals. These men strongly embraced the emerging southern ethos of "manly independence." Within an atomized and virtually unregulated society, however, multitudes of Anglo-Texan men cultivated their distinctive gender role with especial vigor. They displayed a rampant individualism that found its most typical expression in zealous participation in warfare, personal violence, drinking, gambling, swearing, sexual promiscuity, and a pronounced disregard of marital and family obligations.

The basic conflict between "manly independence" and the exigencies of homesteading, however, is also implicit in Archer's escapades. Mexican law and Anglo-Texan policies after 1836 granted land in larger amounts to married couples, inducing many debt-ridden immigrant women and men to marry primarily for survival and pecuniary gain. While difficult frontier conditions placed considerable strains on tenuous marriages forged in this circumstance, they also made family unity much more desirable to those who homesteaded than to the relatively few town-dwellers like Archer. Both wives and husbands assumed independent roles to survive in a wilderness environment and prosper, while the labor of children made family farming and ranching ventures even more profitable. With the aid of adaptable Hispanic matrimonial rules, settling women and men thus situated themselves as marital enterprisers in the racial-caste elite, usually at the expense of the darker-skinned peoples they despoiled and subjugated. This was so even if men of Branch T. Archer's persuasion did, from time to time, indulge the emergent masculine ethos to excess and thus place additional stresses on their families.

The separation of Archer from Eloisa Clark and his cohabitation with the widow of his compatriot indicate some of the more problematic aspects of pioneer courtship and marriage. In most respects, his neglecting to divorce Eloisa after the two had separated, as well as his decision to live out of wedlock with Sarah Groce Wharton to the end of his golden years, simply reflected frontier mores and the unusually uninhibited sex drive characteristic of Anglo-Texan men. While this alone often generated an unusual amount of extramarital sex in the frontier situation, stressful conditions, the imperatives of settlement, and the absence of public restraints in a disorganized frontier society encouraged Anglo-Texan women and men to couple and uncouple with little regard for marital formalities. Institutional disarray, however, often left Anglo-Texans little choice but to marry bigamously and cohabit in adultery. While apparently not the case with Archer, these innovative customs of conjugal self-help often seriously deranged marital property and inheritance rights and thus further eroded family cohesion.

Through the antebellum period, frontier conditions and the law generated distinctive family norms for Anglo-Texans. Generous land distribution and homestead exemption rules spurred a massive migration of southerners and family settlement. Immigration policies, however, often produced tenuous, opportunistic marriages, while stressful conditions worked to undermine them. Land-grant rules, the law of marriage and divorce, and institutional disarray combined with the unruliness and sexual promiscuity of radically independent men to generate informal coupling and uncoupling, bigamy, and adultery. Consequently, settling Texans developed relatively tolerant attitudes about illicit sex and marital infidelity. The Hispanic community property regime, however, gave wives coequal ownership of new homesteads and powers of marital property management to make unusually autonomous contributions to family enterprises. In tandem with white supremacy policies and related land allocation rules, this body of domestic relations law permitted Anglo-Texan women and men to establish themselves as conjugal joint venturers in the dominant racial caste.

FIVE

Slip-knot Marriages

and

Patchwork Nests

The Household Redefined

iven the capricious mating habits of many immigrants, authorities in Mexican Texas were disinclined to deal with marriage as traditional law and custom prescribed. Having recently arrived in Gonzales, Frederick Roe was fortunate to strike up a relationship with a young woman like Sarah Grogan. Not only were attractive single women hard to come by in the fall of 1832, but crude living conditions, rising tensions with indigenous Mexicans, and even talk of revolt among the Anglo-Texan colonists made courtship difficult. Sarah found the adventurous young man appealing, however, and he seemed entirely capable of obtaining for them a *sitio* and settling down. With no priest in the vicinity to marry them ceremonially, Sarah and Frederick utilized the local custom of "marriage by bond." They signed the contract obligating them to marry in November 1832 and filed it with the alcalde. When Frederick took no real steps toward establishing a new homestead, Sarah became disenchanted with the pact. In the spring of 1833, the two went their separate ways. No one gave much thought to the unsolemnized marriage bond.[1]

Sarah soon began a serious relationship with William Sowell, who had immigrated to Texas with his family much earlier. His father, John Sowell, had received a league of rich bottomland along the Guadalupe River from *empresario* Green De Witt. Quite satisfied with Sarah, William soon began to talk with her about tying the knot. The two agreed, however, that they should live with William's family for a short time, until they were ready to homestead independently.[2]

It seems Sarah had reasons entirely her own for slowing down plans with William to break new ground. Shortly after moving in with the Sowells, it became apparent she was with child. Given the rapidity of her switch from Frederick to William, even Sarah Grogan might have had some doubt as to which of the two men had actually impregnated her. The Sowells, however, didn't make an issue of her special condition. When Sarah gave birth to a baby girl around Christmas in 1833, any lingering doubts the Sowells might have had quickly disappeared. More than ever, William's brothers and parents seemed to accept Sarah and appeared to enjoy the bright addition to the household. They began speaking openly of Sarah as William's wife and named the baby girl Rachael after his mother, the matriarch of the family.[3]

William and Sarah finally got around to formalizing their union just in time for disaster to strike. With Rachael just beginning to walk, Sarah tracked down Frederick Roe and asked him to release her from their marriage bond. Little concerned about her new situation, he agreed, but only for a price. Having fallen seriously ill and eager to finalize the matter, William paid Frederick the bond forfeiture penalty to release Sarah from the contract. Now free from the troublesome obligation, Sarah and William executed their own nuptial bond a few days later, on 1 June 1834. William hardly had the energy to celebrate—he grew much more ill and died without having been able to have the bond solemnized before a priest. Unfortunately for the Sowells, and particularly for Sarah and baby Rachael, William's own father expired from illness a few weeks later.[4]

Without the support of her husband, Sarah saw her position in the family and that of her daughter deteriorate as William's brothers and widowed mother became engulfed in the disposition of John Sowell's vast estate. Working constantly to obtain for themselves as much of their deceased father's property as possible, the brothers wrangled for years with the administrator over unsettled estate debts. They ultimately procured court decrees granting them equal portions of Sowell's community share available to them as heirs. After remarrying George Nichols, and long before probate closed, William's mother sold off her half interest in the estate in 1845 to extricate herself from the tedious litigation.[5] Through it all, however, neither the newly organized Guadalupe County Court nor any of the Sowell brothers made any effort to set aside whatever portion young Rachael might have had coming to her as William's heir. Much less did they recognize any inheritance rights Sarah Grogan might have had as his lawful widow. Thus ignored, and with William's mother having remarried, Sarah and her daughter drifted away from the Sowell clan and had to fend for themselves.[6]

Having grown vexed through the years over the disposition of her deceased first husband's estate, Rachael Nichols reopened the case to set things right. The aging matriarch sued to reclaim and enlarge her community share of the property she had owned with John. In so doing, however, she also facilitated the belated inheritance claim her namesake had filed after having come of age in 1851 and taken a husband named Turner. At trial, those who had purchased land from the Sowell brothers attacked the legitimacy of Rachael Turner and thus her right to inherit. They argued that evidence relevant to Sarah Grogan's cohabitation with Frederick Roe years earlier clearly made Rachael his child rather than William's. They also maintained that an 1836 statute retroactively validating unsolemnized bond marriages had fixed Sarah and Frederick irrevocably as husband and wife. The two thus could not have simply canceled the marriage bond as if it were just any other kind of contract. Finally, they argued that similar legislation passed in 1837 only legitimated children born to couples after they had executed their marriage bonds. In the view of the appellants, Sarah's second bond marriage to William Sowell was thus bigamous and invalid, and Rachael Turner was a bastard incapable of inheriting.[7]

The Texas Supreme Court recognized the legitimacy of Rachael Turner and her inheritance. In the 1855 decision of *Nichols v. Stewart*, the high court upheld the verdict of the trial jury, stating that Sarah and Frederick had the right in 1833 to cancel their unsolemnized marriage bond on their own initiative. That Mexican law virtually prohibited divorce in those days was of no consequence. The court discounted entirely the arguments casting doubt on the paternity of William Sowell, even ignoring substantial evidence that made them quite plausible. The court maintained that the 1836 legislation validated Sarah and William's unsolemnized bond marriage. Furthermore, it invoked Hispanic bastardy law to interpret expansively the 1837 statute, ruling that it legitimated Rachael Turner and other children born to parents even before they sealed their marriage bonds. Justice Abner Lipscomb, who wrote the opinion, added in dictum that even if there had been no post-independence legislation on the subject, William and Sarah's union would have been valid. According to Lipscomb, "At the time . . . these bonds were entered into, there was no means of solemnizing matrimony . . . and parties were driven back to the primitive elements, constituting the married state; and this, no doubt, was the mutual consent of the parties."[8]

Like Justice Lipscomb, few settlers in antebellum Texas would have condemned Sarah Grogan for the informality with which she formed and severed her relationship with Frederick. That she and William had not actually been married would not have occurred to most homesteaders. From the earliest times, Anglo-Texans understood the difficulties of adhering to matrimonial formalities in a disordered polity. As the adoption of marriage by bond might indicate, legislators and jurists eager to clarify family property rights in land could hardly afford to insist on strict adherence to traditional marriage and divorce procedures or conventional sexual decorum. On the other hand, it seems unlikely Texas lawmakers ever gave much thought to how their own land-grant rules actually encouraged the immigration of unruly settlers and the informal coupling and uncoupling that threatened family stability and property rights in the first place. As indicated in the ruling of *Nichols v. Stewart,* however, they could not afford to ignore the very real threat to social order that resulted inadvertently from their energetic promotion of rapid frontier development.

The unsuccessful attempts of local leaders to rectify the precarious state of marriage in Mexican Texas began with a direct assault on the problem of informal cohabitation. The ease with which Sarah Grogan entered and exited her relationship with Frederick Roe was certainly not unusual. Anglo-Texan leaders through the colonial period were quite cognizant of the fluid mating habits among immigrants. In the beginning at least, local lawmakers felt compelled to respond with rules to thwart the informal cohabitation which the shortage of priests had stimulated. As primary lawgiver in the colonies, Stephen F. Austin set about establishing his "Criminal Regulations" on 22 January 1824. Article 9 provided that "living publicly with a woman as man and wife without first being lawfully united by the bonds of matrimony is a gross violation of the laws of this nation, and a high misdemeanor." The punishment was a fine of not less than one hundred nor more than five hundred dollars; authorities could also condemn those convicted to "hard labor on public works until the superior government of the province decides the case." The article, however, was not to take effect until sixty days after the arrival of a priest who could perform legal marriages.[9] In this way, Austin took steps to eliminate the objectionable behavior, but also made an allowance for the difficulties that the requirement of a ceremonial marriage before a Catholic cleric posed to widely dispersed settlers in a province where travel was difficult and dangerous.

Austin adopted bond marriage to deal more aggressively with the problem of extralegal sexual relationships. In 1824 he introduced contractual matrimony as a temporary expedient to create at least respectable unions in the absence of priests capable of performing ceremonial marriages. In theory, Catholic clerics who arrived in the colonies later would solemnize the unions. He specifically intended marriage by bond, however, to work in tandem with the new law proscribing cohabitation out of wedlock. In essence, Austin sought to discourage illicit relationships and to provide an effective, albeit makeshift, means to create more valid ones.[10]

The early Texas marriage bond formally expressed the intention of a couple to be united as lawful spouses. Sometimes at festive weddings, but often at more attenuated gatherings, the bride and groom signed a written agreement containing the traditional marriage vows. The signing ceremony usually took place before the alcalde or *comisario* (town commissioner) in the presence of witnesses attesting to the bond. As William Sowell came to know only too well, the contract also obligated the parties to pay a penalty should either of them refuse to solemnize the union. The forfeiture penalty was as little as $2,000 in some cases and as much as $60,000 in others.[11]

From the beginning, the attitudes of the Anglos toward Catholic priests did not promise successful implementation of bond marriages.

The xenophobia of settlers, usually raised in the Protestant South, created little enthusiasm to cooperate with the clerics. Colonists also resented the priests because of the condescension and hypocrisy they perceived to be common among the men in black. Anglo-Texan settlers typically believed the Catholic Church used religion to control and enslave the Mexican peasantry, while extracting money from them for sacramental rites. By the same token, the Anglos held the view that educated and relatively liberal Catholic ecclesiastics looked down on the ignorant and superstitious populace they were accustomed to exploiting, while holding little faith in their own doctrines.[12]

The skepticism of many of the immigrants toward doctrinaire religion of any kind further made the priests suspect. While most immigrants refrained from speaking publicly about religion in adherence to their nominal profession of Catholicism, some settlers were undoubtedly devout Protestants. Many, however, simply viewed dogmatic religion in any form and the contentiousness among the sectarians as a threat to the colonial venture. A good many of the settlers were quite skeptical about the abuses of evangelical religion, viewing camp ministers who sang, shouted, fell into trances, and railed about fire and brimstone as men on the make, shiftless idlers who sponged off of hard-working homesteaders.[13] According to C. L. Douglas, many of the preachers did not escape the "contamination of vice" that primitive conditions generated. In his estimation,."the ministers of the gospel themselves, who came out as missionaries . . . proved greater adepts in villainy than those from whom they had learned their original lessons."[14]

The priest who finally arrived in the colonies to provide the sacrament of matrimony for the Anglos, unfortunately, fulfilled the settlers' expectations. Father Michael Muldoon circulated ceremoniously through the towns of East Texas in 1831 and 1832. In the words of Noah Smithwick, "Padre Muldoon was a bigoted old Irishman with an unlimited capacity for drink . . . an important personage . . . he being the only authorized agent of Cupid east of San Antonio."[15] Henry Smith, who became alcalde of the jurisdiction of Brazoria after 1827, wrote of the visitor, "He wore a wig or was white headed from age—grave gentlemanly and prepossessing in his appearance and manners at first interview, but proved to be as vain vulgar and very a scamp as ever disgraced the colony."[16]

Father Muldoon soon announced troublesome plans to rectify the lax marital habits of the Anglos. While being careful not to burden the settlers with mass, the padre made it clear he had come to redeem them from their waywardness. He immediately issued an edict forbidding provisional marriages, which created considerable dismay among the colonists. His insistence that all settlers married by bond appear before him to have their unions solemnized generated an equal amount of consternation and proved quite inconvenient to homesteaders scattered over a district several hundred miles in extent.[17] The way the reverend actually proceeded in his marriage campaign did little to improve the situation. According to Smithwick, "The father made a tour of the colonies occasionally when in need of funds, tying the nuptial knot and pocketing the fees therefor, $25 being the modest sum demanded for his services."[18]

Under the circumstances, Father Muldoon did not have great success in his matrimonial efforts. Most of the colonists received him as a kind of necessary evil, while ignoring his dictates. Occasionally, however, they organized sumptuous banquets to spoof his proffered ceremonies and "make a wholesale business and frolic of it."[19] These gatherings, however, usually featured "barbecu" and "all the necessary exhilarating libations."[20]

While many of the colonists appear to have enjoyed themselves at the mass marriages, some of the more thoughtful observers found them disagreeable or at least a bit odd. Mary Austin Holley recorded how strange it was to see young couples with "blooming families" submitting to the padre's "infallible decree, that no other form of marriage was sanctioned by high heaven."[21] Smith observed that compliance with the padre's demands "seemed to carry with it a kind of acknowledgment of both, error and crime."[22] He also described the multifarious impression a handful of marriage bond supplicants made on him at one of the gala events:

> The scene take it all in all, was truly ludicrous in the extreme. Most of them had children and some five and six. To see brides on the floor, and while the marriage rites are performing, with the bosoms open and little children sucking at the breast, and others in a situation realy too delicate to mention, appeared to me more like a burlesque of marriage than a marriage in fact. It was a fine scene for a painter and afforded much for amusement, and much for serious and sober reflection.[23]

Regardless of their efficacy, colonial bond nuptials certainly comported with contractual notions of marriage familiar to the Anglos. The bond procedure was entirely consistent with the republican notion, current then in the United States, that marriage was a simple, private agreement. By the same token, it deemphasized the traditional precept that marriage was also a public act subject to official oversight and regulation for the maintenance of social order.[24]

The introduction of marriage by bond, however, derived primarily from the distinctive social-legal situation prevailing in Mexican Texas. Marriage became almost solely a private contract there because southern immigrants could not rely on Protestant ministers or secular authorities to effect legal marriages. Even had the law recognized such unions, ministers and government officials were usually inaccessible to most colonists. Bond marriage thus stemmed from the impulse at work among local leaders to adjust marital practices to the isolation of the settlers and the institutional disarray present within the colonies.

Bond marriage also worked to achieve the larger goal of promoting the orderly distribution of land to families. Austin and other political chiefs who adopted marriage by bond were quite conscious that the legal mechanism empowered immigrating women and men to qualify for family-sized grants the Mexican government offered. Colonial proprietors understood full well that large numbers of couples utilized the procedure almost exclusively to achieve this end. Indeed, Anglo-Texan leaders designed the bond as much to help immigrating women and men achieve their economic objectives as they did to maintain public morals.[25]

Many Anglo-Texans also utilized marriage bonds in an inventive manner to circumvent Mexican divorce law. According to Smithwick, because of the infrequency with which priests visited the colonies to solemnize contractual marriages, the settlers began to view the bond as "combining in itself the essential features of both marriage and divorce."[26] If a contracting couple wished to dissolve their union, they simply discarded, ignored, or purposely misplaced the document. To this extent, the flexibility of the device was extremely compatible with the sexual habits of Anglo-Texans and their conception of marriage.[27] Henry Smith described the not uncommon practice:

Many couples . . . not finding the marriage state to possess all the alluring charms which they had figured in their fond imaginations have taken advantage of this slip [k]not plan—sought the bond, and by mutual consent committed it to the flames—returned to the world as young as ever and free as the air.[28]

The number of couples who viewed marriage by bond as simply a license to cohabit, "lost" their bond agreements, or otherwise purposely neglected to solemnize them was quite large.[29]

Settlers with troublesome legal marriages utilized the bond in an equally inventive manner. The near impossibility of divorce under Mexican law was particularly onerous to the immigrants who had left undivorced spouses behind. Men and women who had managed to marry ceremonially in Texas but desired to terminate those unions also felt the pinch of the restrictive law. To obtain the maximum benefit of the land-grant policy, some Anglo-Texan women and men in these situations exploited the flexibility of the marriage bond to circumvent the divorce ban and the criminal penalty for bigamy. They simply created semilegal marriages by bond and purposely left them unsolemnized. Such arrangements provided them the basis for obtaining enlarged land grants, as well as the means to terminate easily unsatisfactory relationships and move on if necessary.[30]

The rudimentary organization of the State of Coahuila and Texas ultimately undercut official efforts to reduce the number of extralegal sexual relationships. The casual attitude of the Sowell family toward the illicit cohabitation of Sarah and William indicates the ineffectiveness, if not speciousness, of criminal laws punishing cohabitation out of wedlock in a disorganized frontier society. The court system and law enforcement agencies in Mexican Texas were poorly situated and ineffectual. Language barriers and differences in governmental background between Mexican and Anglo-Texan officials, the dearth of roads, and inadequate means of communication allowed the Anglos to be extremely self-governing, if not lawless. Stressful conditions and the unruliness of immigrants, furthermore, were much beyond the control of local officials. For these reasons, Austin and other political leaders who had passed laws to regulate sexual activity showed much less capacity or even interest in enforcing them. Anglo-Texan men and women continued to form and dissolve their unions on their own initiative, and illicit cohabitation continued.[31]

To a large extent, however, the failure of colonial leaders to limit cohabitation out of wedlock originated with the Mexican government.

Local leaders were virtually powerless to alter Mexican law that contributed to Anglo-Texan marital instability. As long as the central government and that of the State of Coahuila and Texas recognized only ceremonial marriage before Catholic clerics, local rules designed to thwart cohabitation out of wedlock and makeshift means to create cognizable unions could address the problem of illicit relationships with only minimal success. This was especially so given the whimsical coupling of many immigrant settlers and the provisional marital conceptions to which most of them adhered. The virtual ban on absolute divorce, furthermore, almost ensured that Anglo policymakers would be ineffective in deterring immigrants from abusing bond agreements to dissolve unsatisfactory unions, cohabit in adultery, or remarry bigamously.

Post-independence lawmakers working diligently to rectify sexual disorder dealt with a polity in which the maintenance of nuclear families was critical for the well-being of society. In the more settled areas of the Old South, extended kinship networks provided the basic components of the white social structure. Immigrant women and men in Texas, however, almost always left their extended families behind. As in the earliest years of settlement, the nuclear family was the fundamental unit of Anglo-Texan society for at least the remainder of the antebellum period. Massive immigration from the more settled South after independence, however, produced family dislocations, transience, and social turmoil on a much larger scale than before. Official maintenance of isolated and vulnerable families in this increasingly chaotic milieu thus became an institutional imperative.[32]

During the struggle for independence, legislators began fashioning a law of matrimony better suited to most Texans. The Consultation, a revolutionary body, passed legislation on 22 January 1836 granting clerics of any denomination, judges, alcaldes, and *comisarios* the power to celebrate the rite of marriage.[33] The general marriage act of 5 June 1837 similarly made legal matrimony much more accessible to settlers than in the Mexican period. The new rules empowered government officials, Protestant ministers, and Catholic priests to perform legal marriages. These measures certainly reflected a republican commitment to freedom of religion and a Texas constitutional provision guaranteeing this, as well as a consensus that matrimony was basically a private, secular agreement. The 1837 act also worked to rectify the unduly restrictive Mexican religion and marriage policy that had produced unusually frequent illicit cohabitation and thus more bastard children than was the case in more settled areas.[34]

After statehood, lawmakers adopted common law marriage to legitimate the informal unions of many settlers. The Texas Supreme Court took this step in 1847 with its decision in *Tarpley v. Poage's Administrator.* That ruling held that a man and a woman were legal spouses if they had agreed to marry or if they cohabited and were reputed to be husband and wife in a community. This doctrine certainly reflected secular and contractual conceptualizations about matrimony rooted in republican idealism.[35] On the other hand, the new rule clearly had jurisprudential antecedents in the peculiar circumstances of Texas. Justice Lipscomb in *Nichols v. Stewart,* for example, maintained that the "mutual consent" of Sarah Grogan and William Sowell to marry had validated their union because of "primitive elements" making ceremonial marriage impossible. It thus seems the high court viewed frontier social disorganization and colonial bond practice as important sources of Texas common law marriage.[36] In any case, legal matrimony based simply on the declarations of cohabiting couples or "habit and repute" legitimated the informal relationships of homesteaders, which continued to arise voluminously because of the inaccessibility of clerics and secular officials who could perform weddings.[37]

Common law marriage rules also worked with post-independence criminal law to transform cohabitative relationships into valid unions. That post-independence lawmakers omitted to penalize simple fornication certainly allowed for the sexual adventurousness of Anglo-Texan men. But criminal legislation in 1836 and in 1857 punishing men and women who "lived in fornication" encouraged cohabiting couples to marry ceremonially.[38] These statutes also prompted those who cohabited for mere pleasure or convenience to behave as if they were married or at least to tell neighbors they were. After the adoption of common law marriage, this behavior made such men and women actual spouses in both the eyes of society and the law. By the same token, common law marriage principles permitted cohabiting couples with bona fide intentions to avoid prosecution with similar, but more sincere, declarations or conduct. In any case, the combined rules worked further to transform the large number of informal relationships into more binding unions, while ensuring legitimacy and thus inheritance for the children resulting from them.

Leaders in post-independence Texas greatly expanded grounds for divorce. With legislation in 1837, the Texas Congress made absolute divorce much more available than did the Hispanic law. The new divorce statute enumerated no specific grounds. According to Chief Justice John Hemphill in the 1857 decision of *Sharman v. Sharman*, however, the "changed condition" of the new republic required that its courts at least have the power under the statute to render divorce decrees for causes similar to those in the various jurisdictions of the United States. The new divorce policy was certainly in accord with republican contractual conceptions of marriage. On the other hand, the statute allowed for the provisional matrimonial notions of Anglo-Texans and a viable exit from the discordant marital relations that pioneer conditions often produced.[39]

An 1841 act established a substantive law of divorce well tailored to frontier society. On 6 January 1841, the Texas Congress passed comprehensive legislation authorizing courts to grant decrees of absolute divorce on specific grounds. Categorically speaking, they were similar to those found typically in the divorce statutes of many jurisdictions of the United States, including those in the more settled South. The act permitted Texas trial courts to render divorce decrees for cruelty, abandonment, and adultery. In a polity where isolation, primitive living conditions, and the sexual promiscuity and unruliness of Anglo-Texan men placed unusually great stresses on many relationships, these grounds provided an effective means to dissolve unions for the most common forms of marital breakdown. They also permitted men and women to sever intolerable unions, remarry legitimately, and establish legally cognizable families.[40]

Amid the fight for independence and in the year following, Texas legislators took steps to legitimate extralegal colonial marriages and the children born of them. In the 1875 decision of *Lewis v. Ames*, Chief Justice Owen Roberts summed up the situation:

> There were . . . persons living together under agreements, whether written or unwritten, to terminate at the pleasure of either party. . . . Those marriages . . . were of such pressing consideration and consequence as to demand the attention of the Anglo-

Americans even in the very first initiatory stages of their assumption of superior power in Texas.[41]

Members of the Consultation thus passed legislation in 1836 permitting ministers or secular officials to validate unions based on properly filed marriage bonds. The Act of 5 June 1837 empowered couples who had taken at least this step to appear before authorized officials within six months to validate their marriages. It also legitimated children born to couples who took corrective action or who had been cohabiting when one of the parties had died.[42]

The problem of illicit colonial marriages remained unsolved, however, and required a more workable measure. Father Muldoon probably would not have been surprised to learn that relatively few Anglo-Texans traveled to justices of the peace and ministers to have their colonial bond marriages validated. With more power to deal with the problem than the reverend, Texas legislators decided to spare them the trouble. The Act of 5 February 1841 automatically recognized all irregular and unsolemnized bond marriages, thus legitimating the children resulting from such relationships. Language set forth in the provision expressed its overriding purpose:

> Public policy and the interest of families require a legislative action on the subject . . . of the many persons [who] heretofore . . . had, for the want of some person legally qualified to celebrate the rites of matrimony, resorted to the practice of marrying by bond . . . [or had] been married by various officers of justice not authorized to celebrate such marriages.[43]

The 1841 statute, along with the 1836 and 1837 legislation, finally provided something resembling a comprehensive remedy to the extensive problems that a dysfunctional Mexican marriage policy and the twelve-year experiment with matrimony by bond had produced.

In the fifteen years following independence, Texas legislators implemented rules specifically designed to include illegitimate children within families. As Justice Roberts noted in *Lewis v. Ames,* many settlers had cohabited in Mexican Texas with only the simple unwritten understanding that they were spouses. While common law marriage after 1847 certainly provided a plausible means to legitimate children born to many cohabiting parents, legislators realized that some couples might take advantage of a formal corrective. Perpetuating the same principle of Hispanic law upon which the high court had relied in *Nichols*, Texas leaders passed statutes in 1840 and 1848 providing the means for unwed parents to marry formally and thus legitimate their children. These statutes also legitimated children born of various kinds of unlawful marriage. In the 1852 decision of *Hartwell v. Jackson*, the Texas Supreme Court liberally construed the 1840 and 1848 statutes specifically to bring children resulting from bigamous marriages within their scope.[44]

Post-independence bastardy legislation also protected the children of single mothers. Generous land-grant policies, community property principles, the success of family ventures, and equal inheritance for sons and daughters commonly provided young, unmarried women in Texas with wealth more substantial than that which their counterparts in the more settled South acquired. Utilizing a traditional Hispanic rule of succession unknown in the common law, the Texas Congress passed legislation in 1840 allowing children born out of wedlock to inherit property from their mothers. The omission of legislators to adopt a paternity procedure certainly shielded sexually promiscuous Anglo-Texan men from financial responsibility for the children they fathered carelessly. That the 1840 legislation empowered illegitimate children to inherit often substantial property from their mothers, however, also helps explain the lapse. Since the law developed in Texas was, generally speaking, extraordinarily attentive to the plight of illegitimate children, the omission of legislators to adopt an affiliation procedure certainly cannot be emblematic of unconcern for such children. The 1840 act was certainly consistent with the enlightened republican law of bastardy; it also provided, with singular effectiveness, for the out-of-wedlock children who were produced in unusually large numbers through informal coupling and uncoupling.[45]

Texas courts utilized common law marriage to provide property rights for women when their mates died and inheritance for their children in this situation. The flexible Scottish law doctrine of "habit and repute" furnished Texas courts disposing of estate claims with broad discretion to validate informal unions retroactively. The imposition of marital status in this situation was frequently done at the expense of strict consideration of whether cohabiting women and men had actually intended to marry or consented to do so. Other United States jurisdictions in the first half of the nineteenth century certainly resorted to common law marriage and liberalized evidentiary rules to provide inheritance for "baseborn" children in keeping with republican idealism. In Texas, however, the rules usually protected the property interests of women surviving their partners and ensured patrimony for their out-of-wedlock children in a disorganized society in which formal marriage was impeded.[46]

Social pressures encouraging legal innovation to validate bigamous marriages placed Texas jurists squarely at odds with mainstream opinion and law in the United States. Most women and men in the United States before the Civil War viewed strict monogamy as essential for social efficacy in a rapidly expanding and transforming nation. According to Michael Grossberg, judges and legislators saw polygamy, and thus bigamous marriage, as inimical to republican family ideals. Lawmakers and social critics alike denounced bigamy as immoral and heathenish. The practices of Mormons, other radical utopian groups, and even Native Americans further intensified these sentiments. Civic leaders also argued that bigamy was hostile to democracy because it threatened to introduce patriarchy, elitism, and despotism. Reflecting a male sexist bias and more than a few patriarchal presuppositions, these commentators maintained that only the wealthiest men would be able to afford multiple wives if the law permitted polygamy. Legal opposition to bigamy thus grew in intensity, and almost every jurisdiction in the United States made bigamy a serious crime. Some humanitarian lawmakers, equally committed to republicanism, worked along the margins to soften the strict common law rule making bigamous marriages null and void in order to protect the innocent children resulting from these unions. The great majority, however, reinforced the old doctrines.[47]

Lawmakers in Texas had little choice but to deal with the ongoing predicament that bigamy presented there. As the ruling in *Nichols v. Stewart* indicates, they were predisposed to be lenient toward bigamists, even to the extent of decriminalizing bigamy through the republic and most of the antebellum statehood period. By the same token, civil courts focused on these unions in probate cases with notable frequency. An extraordinarily large number of civil bigamy and related estate settlement appeals challenging established common law bigamy and bastardy doctrine came before the Texas Supreme Court from 1845 to 1860. The high courts of fewer than half a dozen states ruled on such challenges, with civil litigation of this type working its way up to the state supreme court level most often in Texas. Bigamous marriages leaving family membership and property rights in disarray, in fact, plagued probate and estate adjudication late into the nineteenth century.[48]

Judicial adoption and modification of Spanish putative marriage principles substantially eased the strict common law relevant to bigamy. In the 1846 decision of *Smith v. Smith,* which dealt with the bigamous marriage of John W. Smith and María Delgado, the Texas Supreme Court held that traditional Spanish putative marriage rules were applicable in Texas until 1840. Under these principles, an innocent woman deceived into wedding a man with an undissolved marriage enjoyed a valid union as long as the deception lasted, giving her community property rights and legitimating the children that resulted from the relationship. Dictum in *Smith,* furthermore, indicated a novel presumption sustaining a putative marriage even when a wife discovered the existence of her husband's undivorced spouse.[49] Based on this dictum, the 1858 Texas Supreme Court ruling in *Carroll v. Carroll* established an expansive "presumption of divorce" to validate the union of a woman who knowingly wed a man with an undissolved marriage. This presumption certainly altered preexisting Hispanic law relevant to bigamy and marital dissolution. More important, the presumption and putative marriage rules provided courts with the means to uphold the marriages of women to immigrant men who had left their undivorced wives behind.[50]

The Texas Supreme Court also built on Anglo-American legal principles after statehood to legitimate bigamous marriages and the children born of them. To accomplish this goal, the high court developed a distinctive evidentiary rule in the 1848 decision of *Yates v. Houston* and the 1856 ruling in *Lockhart v. White.* The fully formulated principle maintained that persons who remarried without having first legally divorced were presumed to have done so innocently and in the good faith belief that their spouse had died. In other words, the "presumption of innocence" of a remarrying husband or wife, with no knowledge of the continuing life of an absent, undivorced spouse, prevailed over the presumption of the continuing life of that spouse, even when the period between separation and remarriage was briefer than a year.[51] Like the presumption set forth in *Carroll,* this one was entirely at odds with traditional law punishing bigamy as highly reprehensible and making bigamous marriages null and void. It was also more protective of big-amists than the few Enoch Arden laws of some United States juris-dictions. Those rules usually worked to validate only the much less reprehensible remarriage of a woman with a husband who had dis-appeared and been unheard from for seven years.[52] The presumption of innocence was also eminently functional in a disorganized society that attracted an extraordinarily large number of runaway spouses often looking to remarry.

The 1848 decision of *Yates v. Houston* also allowed courts to utilize common law marriage principles to legitimate the informal relation-ships of women who homesteaded with men whose marriages were undissolved. In *Yates,* the Texas Supreme Court dealt with the problem of whether Tabitha Kinkaid owned a community share in the land she had worked since the early 1820s in Austin's colony with John Jiams, her cohabitant. The problem was that John had not bothered to di-vorce his Ohio wife, Mary Haslett, before making his new Texas home with Tabitha.[53] Looking first to the Mexican law, the court held that land the government granted to a husband was community property. Of equal importance, it ruled that granted lands were also the well-deserved reward for husbands and wives who had actually engaged in "settling up the wild and uncultivated wastes of a new country." While Mary had not laid claim to the community property in question, the court relied on both common law marriage principles and the presump-tion of innocence to find Tabitha the cognizable wife because of her pioneering efforts.[54]

The decision in *Yates* was rooted in Texas mores. Reformism among the northeastern middle class at midcentury reflected a strong belief in the essential malleability of human personality and the possibility of rehabilitation.[55] Consistent with these assumptions, the *Yates* court rec-ognized that Tabitha had been aware of John's marriage but refused to accept "the unlawful character" of her connection with him "was un-susceptible of change." According to Chief Justice Hemphill, "The judgment which would presume that erring humanity would not re-pent and reform is too harsh to have a place in any beneficent system of law, and we cannot yield or assent to such doctrine."[56] Cloaked in the language of high jurisprudence and principled reform language, Hemphill thus adopted a rule entirely consistent with Anglo-Texan attitudes and practices. Over half a century ago, William Ransom Hogan described the "democratic willingness" among early Texas settlers to accept any person regardless of his or her past record. The large number of newcomers who immigrated to escape marital problems certainly fell in the category of those "unfortunates" leaving their "hard luck" behind.[57] Given the thorough familiarity of Chief Justice Hemphill with the migratory forces at work in Texas and the social situation developing there, it seems unlikely that the suitability of rehabilitation principles for legitimating the bigamy of struggling homesteaders could have escaped him.

The high court also recognized community property rights for women who homesteaded with men who had undissolved marriages regardless of competing claims made by their legitimate wives. In 1829, David Babb of Tennessee abandoned his wife, Elizabeth, and began living with Eda Collier. In 1835 Eda immigrated to Texas with David and her son by an earlier adulterous connection. Although she knew that David was already married, Eda lived with him as his wife in the Old Red River County until he died in 1837. The land office issued a headright certificate for a square league to his heirs in 1838. Eda successfully claimed a community interest in the *sitio* as his surviving spouse. Elizabeth filed suit in Collin County Court years later to claim the same parcel as David's legitimate widow. In the 1858 decision of *Babb v. Carroll*, however, the Texas Supreme Court recognized title in Eda. Writing for the court, Chief Justice Hemphill maintained that common law marriage rules had validated her relationship with David. The court thus upheld the community property rights of a reputed wife against the rival claim of an abandoned legal wife. For support, Hemphill simply alluded to *Yates* and its progeny.[58]

In *Carroll v. Carroll*, the Texas Supreme Court revealed again its eagerness to reward deserving women who homesteaded in bigamous marriages. In that case, both Susan and Nathaniel Carroll of Navarro County had undissolved marriages before remarrying ceremonially in Texas. The *Carroll* court ultimately innovated the presumption of divorce to uphold the marriage. Even so, on its own initiative, the court raised and seriously entertained the inventive notion that Susan might have based her claim to a community share in Nathaniel's estate as a wife in fact rather than as a legal one. Chief Justice Hemphill elaborated the point:

> I have not considered the strong claim which the defendant Susan, independently of her rights as a lawful wife, might have

urged to a community share of the property. She was his [Na-thaniel's] wife *de facto*. By her labors and toils she contributed to the accumulation of the estate. At the time of her marriage they were in a state of indigence; the property not amounting to more than one hundred and fifty dollars. Their gains were the result of their joint industry, thrift and economy, and she is reasonably entitled to a share of the proceeds.[59]

The willingness of the justices to consider this unorthodox rationale certainly revealed their determination to protect women in Susan's position. The solicitude of the court, however, indicated an equitable theory far ahead of its time. Only in the 1980s did some Texas courts of civil appeals begin to recognize the claims of de facto wives.[60]

Legitimating statutes and judicially developed rules worked fundamentally to stabilize families in frontier circumstances that undermined them. The new Texas law relevant to bigamous marriage and illegitimacy certainly seems to have reflected a national "republican family" trend toward protecting innocent "baseborn" children and softening the harsh common-law doctrine bastardizing children born of unlawful marriages.[61] Legitimating statutes and judicial rules in Texas, however, stemmed initially from the official resolve to validate unsolemnized Mexican bond marriages that had secured extensive land grants and laid the foundation for prospering homesteads. As a practical matter, Texas bigamy and bastardy law bound together large numbers of informal families and particularly ensured inheritance for children resulting from the merely cohabitative unions that dispersed settlement and institutional disarray had generated. It also worked well to improve the chances that homesteading women would receive the fruits of their labors. In essence, the impetus of bigamy and bastardy policy in Texas stemmed essentially from the determination of lawmakers to square legal family membership and property rights with frontier social reality.

The rulings of the Texas Supreme Court after statehood augured a nationwide change in bigamy and bastardy law. Frequently referring to the presumption of innocence established initially in *Yates* as the "presumption of death," the courts of many jurisdictions in the United States began to follow Texas in the last decades of the nineteenth century and early decades of the twentieth century.[62] State courts began utilizing the presumption of divorce set forth in *Smith* and *Carroll* at about the same time.[63]

The presumptions of divorce and innocence established in the Texas bigamy decisions were extraordinarily modern in conceptualization. Following Texas' lead, late-nineteenth-century courts in the United States began using the presumptions to uphold second unions regardless of whether remarrying men and women had abandoned their first spouses, how grave were the marital transgressions inducing desertion, or how long a time intervened between separation and remarriage. By ignoring the fault of the remarrying parties, they departed radically from traditional law, which condemned bigamy as morally reprehensible and punished the children, men, and women associated with it. As in Texas, the less punitive rules that emerged in many states late in the nineteenth century represented legal fictions which either misconstrued established law or otherwise strained the limits of reasonable inference. And, as in Texas, the high courts of these states designed the presumptions to forward a social policy that judges adopted a priori: the legitimation of innocent children, the maintenance of amicable marital relations in keeping with the expectations of spouses and kin, and the consolidation of marital and family property rights. Among almost all states, including Texas, this policy rooted itself variably in pragmatism, republican idealism, and capitalist free-market imperatives. In antebellum Texas, however, the policy derived from the attractiveness of the frontier to runaway spouses and the extraordinary social-legal interplay there which generated informal coupling and uncoupling and severely inhibited ceremonial marriage and formal divorce.[64]

The bigamy and bastardy rulings of the Texas Supreme Court reflect enlightened judicial innovation that discounted doctrinal continuity and mainstream social policy. As chief justice of the Texas Supreme Court from 1840 to 1858, John Hemphill is well established in Texas history as the principal early proponent of Spanish civil law, the community property system, and homestead exemption principles, and as a formidable champion of the rights of Anglo-Texan women.[65] This characterization is certainly accurate, but indicates only part of his larger purpose. Hemphill authored every major decision from 1846 to 1858 that created the judicial law of bigamy and bastardy. These unorthodox rulings worked in tandem with others he penned establishing common law marriage and modulating community property rules to generate a coordinated policy of family stabilization. This goal was ultimately more important to Hemphill and his fellow justices than adhering to mainstream Anglo-American jurisprudence, the parameters of legal reform in the United States before 1860, or the traditional Spanish civil law. The extraordinary innovation of the Hemphill court, furthermore, distinguished it from other appellate tribunals in the antebellum South, which generally employed the power of the state with cautiousness, eschewed the instrumental formulation of legal doctrines with the self-conscious aim of accommodating or stimulating social change, and expressed hostility toward the notion of judges as lawmakers.[66]

Post-independence legislators who wanted to shield the property of sacrificing frontier women from their unruly spouses began with the 1840 statute adopting the Hispanic community property system. That act maintained that if a man sold the separate property of his wife without her consent, or in any other illegal manner, she had the right to sue for it. If a husband improperly reduced her separate property, she had a legal claim on his. If a husband in residence neglected to support his wife or educate her children from the proceeds of her separate land and slaves as her fortune would justify, the law empowered her to sue her husband and obtain a court order for him to relinquish sufficient separate property to allow her to obtain "necessaries." If a husband in residence neglected to take legal action to protect the separate property of his wife, she was empowered to do so. The 1840 act also gave a spouse the power to insulate his or her separate property from the creditors of the other by way of a written premarital agreement. The act, furthermore, provided that any asset a man or woman acquired during a marriage, or possessed at the dissolution of it, was presumptively community property unless a contesting spouse could prove otherwise.[67]

Subsequent legal innovation offered additional safeguards against squandering and mismanaging husbands. Legislation in 1841 and a subsequent revision of it prescribed a "privy examination," requiring a judge or court official to ask a woman outside the presence of her husband if she actually wanted to transfer any or all of her separate estate. Extending Hispanic principles further, an 1845 constitutional provision and legislation passed in 1846 shielded the homestead from forced sale and prohibited a man from selling it without the consent of his wife;

the rule applied even if the homestead was the separate property of her husband. A different 1845 constitutional provision and subsequent statutes established a procedure for a woman to register her separate property and thus insulate it from the creditors of her husband. Building on an 1845 constitutional mandate John Hemphill supported, legislation passed in 1848 enlarged the quantum of real and personal separate property to include the "increase" of that which the spouses owned before marriage. This development certainly brought the definition of separate property in line with the pre-independence Hispanic regime. The 1848 legislation and all of the other new measures, however, shared one common policy objective: reducing the power of a man to misuse or squander the separate property of his wife or the proceeds from it.[68]

The post-independence reformulation of marital property rules dealt forthrightly with the misconduct of husbands generated by the frontier situation. The protective devices included in the Texas matrimonial law might appear to have derived from the larger mid-nineteenth-century married women's property reform movement. The 1840 act describing marital property rights, however, was less a reform than a perpetuation of selected Hispanic precepts in a piece of legislation designed otherwise to adopt virtually wholesale the Anglo-American common law. To a substantial degree, the act underscores the determination of legislators to provide more than a hundred thousand married settlers continuity in their domestic property arrangements, while preserving a regime allocating power and wealth among them in accordance with their just expectations. Many of the prophylactic rules set forth in the act and in subsequent measures through the 1840s drew on preexisting Hispanic principles. More important, these rules dealt directly with the unusually severe problems that self-indulgent and financially irresponsible Anglo-Texan men created for their families. Particularly in the half-dozen or so years following the Panic of 1837, such men misappropriated and absconded with marital property with a frequency deeply disturbing to lawmakers. Heightened attentiveness to the needs of Anglo-Texan women and children was thus, in their view, imperative to a commensurate degree. Legal safeguards adopted in 1840 and thereafter thus reduced the likelihood homesteading women would be denied the well-deserved fruits of their labors and left with their children penniless in the wilderness.[69]

While post-independence married women's property law certainly protected the interests of pioneer wives, it was only one element of a larger body of rules placing a premium on the contributions of homesteading women and dealing with frontier pressures that generated family instability. As indicated in the ruling of the high court in *Nichols v. Stewart*, Texas lawmakers had little choice but to deal pragmatically with the extralegal relationships of settling men and women like Sarah Grogan and William Sowell. Probate of John Sowell's estate and the decision in *Nichols* highlight how marriage and family property rights were inextricably woven into the economic fabric of the polity and thus of great concern to citizens, legislators, and judges. By the same token, these proceedings show that clarifying family membership and property rights on the frontier was much more important to them than traditional southern commitments to sexual decorum or adherence to established Hispanic or Anglo-American legal rules relating to courtship, sex, marriage, and child-bearing. The litigation resulting from the complicated relationships of Sarah Grogan certainly demonstrates how informal coupling in Mexican Texas generated makeshift remedies that worked with only marginal effectiveness. The protracted dispute over John Sowell's estate, however, shows how marital self-help among Anglo-Texans continued to leave family membership and inheritance confused long after independence from Mexico. The *Nichols* decision thus indicates the vital necessity for post-independence law to deal with this continuing problem.

Much of the distinctive, forward-looking Texas family law was an attempt to deal with pioneer life and the inadvertently destructive governmental policy. Through the antebellum period, institutional disarray, stressful living conditions, and land policy encouraged Anglo-Texans to couple and uncouple with marked informality. Local leaders in the colonial period punished cohabitation out of wedlock and implemented marriage by bond to promote at least some order on sexual interaction and land distribution. Domestic relations law after independence dealt more aggressively with the problem. Lawmakers made ceremonial marriage more accessible and divorce easier, thus validating relationships and reducing the adverse impact of their demise on family property rights. Pragmatic innovations legitimated informal unions, bigamous marriages, and the children resulting from such connections.

Texas law thus redefined the family to suit extraordinary frontier circumstances, while clarifying the property rights of its members. It also thwarted the efforts of self-indulgent and irresponsible Anglo-Texan men to deny wives the rewards of their strenuous settlement efforts. What the law aided and abetted in destroying with one hand, it tried to mend with the other.

SIX

Iniquitous Partners

Wanton Husbands

AND

Delinquent Wives

Social disorder in early Texas produced unusual forms of marital misconduct and equally distinctive official responses. Having recently become a widower, and with his infant daughter, Eliza, in need of a mother, Sherwood Dover of Kentucky decided to find a new wife. After convincing a spirited young acquaintance named Frances to marry him in 1833, Sherwood began laying plans with her to establish their home in Texas. Regardless of the growing political turmoil in the Mexican province, they both appreciated the exceptional opportunities there to acquire cheap land and get ahead quickly. In the spring of 1834, the couple arrived in Gonzales. Harsh living conditions and a particularly virulent cholera epidemic, however, made life unexpectedly difficult. With many of the Anglo immigrants eager to settle matters with the Mexican government once and for all, the turbulent situation hardly comported with the fresh start

Frances had envisioned back in Kentucky.[1] Sherwood involved himself in the growing rebellion. The rigors of everyday life and the burden of caring for Eliza, especially with Sherwood frequently absent, soon made the arrangement intolerable to Frances. Early in 1835, the fond addresses of newly arrived and much more attentive Joseph Martin proved irresistible to her. Before the year was over, Frances had left Sherwood and Eliza and taken up with him. Unable to obtain a divorce under Mexican law, and with no grounds for one even under Anglo-American rules, she had little choice but to live with Joseph out of wedlock. Given the often extralegal relationships of colonial men and women, local officials concerned themselves little with Frances and Joseph's adulterous cohabitation, especially in the turmoil of revolution.[2]

The decision of Sherwood Dover to go to war proved a fateful one for his young daughter and errant wife. More involved than ever with the revolt, Sherwood had little time to straighten things out with Frances. He placed Eliza in the care of his friend Jonathan Burleson and joined a Gonzales unit of the new Texas "Army of the People." After helping repulse a small contingent of Mexican troops in early October, Sherwood and the rest of the Gonzales volunteers marched on San Antonio to engage General Cós and his reinforcements. Sherwood, however, didn't see much action. He was shot dead in a skirmish with Mexican soldiers outside San Antonio in late November, just days before the main invasion of the town. But his death immediately made life less complicated for Frances and soon much more secure for her. Sherwood's demise freed her to marry Joseph, which she did sometime in 1838. By virtue of the marriage, furthermore, Joseph obtained a headright to a family-sized allotment comprising a square league and a *labor*. While these developments left Eliza an orphan, the little girl's situation was not as bad as it might have been. As her new legal guardian, Jonathan Burleson obtained for Eliza a headright to a *sitio*, which the Texas Congress made available to all heirs of soldiers killed in the war. Thus provided for, Eliza grew to womanhood with Burleson and his wife, while Frances made her home with Joseph through the years of the republic and early statehood.[3]

Eliza had not seen the last of Frances. Jonathan Burleson placed Eliza in possession of her inheritance when she came of age around 1850. The headright she inherited from her father included 4,605 acres of fertile, cotton-growing blackland in the San Gabriel River basin. Eliza thus appeared well endowed when she married William Owens at the Burleson home in 1851. A plot her long-lost stepmother hatched shortly thereafter, however, threatened plans Eliza had made to homestead it with her husband. After the death of Joseph Martin, Frances had sold her community share of the land he had acquired for them and taken William Wheat as her third spouse. Frances soon joined with Wheat to file suit in Williamson County District Court, claiming she had been the wife of Sherwood Dover at his death in 1835 and thus his lawful widow when the headright certificate was issued in behalf of his heirs. In essence, Frances laid claim to a one-half community share in the huge San Gabriel tract then in the possession of Eliza and William Owens.[4]

The scheme didn't pan out. Eliza and her husband prevailed at trial, regardless of evidence irrefutably establishing that Frances had been married to Sherwood at his death. The Texas Supreme Court sustained the decision. With Chief Justice John Hemphill writing the opinion, the court resorted to Hispanic law, holding that a wife who abandoned her husband forfeited her right in the gains subsequently acquired and that one who committed adultery, in any case, lost all of her community property. Hemphill, however, was careful to point out "the many exceptions under which a wife would be exempt from the punishment imposed by the laws," including the mistreatment of a husband that drove her to infidelity, his disposition to forgive her adultery, and situations "such as made the act of the woman virtually one of innocence."[5] The chief justice also emphasized that no loss of the ganancial estate was justified for abandonment if a husband had ejected his wife from the home or otherwise forced her to leave with cruel treatment.[6] In the view of the court, however, none of these circumstances excused Frances. The relevant Spanish law, applicable in Texas until 1840, thus warranted a forfeiture of her community interest. In further support of its ruling, the court invoked a principle developed in its own decisions, holding that only women who were actively engaged with their husbands in cultivating granted lands were entitled to a community share in them. Because Frances had deserted Sherwood and Eliza and "lived in open and flagrant adultery" with another, she had not been "part of a family . . . and thus entitled to such lands as were due to Dover at the time of his death."[7]

To some extent, the ruling of the Texas Supreme Court in *Wheat v. Owens* simply vindicated a patriot who had paid the ultimate price for Texas independence. Frances cultivated her illicit relationship with

Joseph while her husband risked and lost his life for the successful revolutionary cause. It seems unlikely that in 1855 a trial jury, any more than the members of the high court, would have approached dispassionately Frances's attempt to acquire half of the land compensating Sherwood's heirs for his sacrifice, particularly at the expense of the stepdaughter she had left in the lurch and helped to orphan. Given that Frances had profited handsomely from marriage to Joseph, the equities cried out with even greater force.

On the other hand, Anglo-Texans were not ordinarily inclined to condemn women who responded to settlement stresses by abandoning one partner to start over with another. Indeed, frontier pressures that continued in Texas through to the end of the antebellum period often encouraged men and women to involve themselves in an array of extralegal sexual relationships. Common folk understood, however, that divorce for adultery or any other cause portended disaster for farming and ranching families. Few settlers would have taxed themselves to comprehend the arcane discussion of Hispanic adultery law that Chief Justice Hemphill belabored in *Wheat v. Owens*. But Hemphill's judicial brethren were undoubtedly aware that his carefully measured opinion took into account the capricious coupling and uncoupling of settlers, while forwarding the larger policy of safeguarding the interests of hardworking pioneer wives and reinforcing Anglo-Texan families.

Progressive divorce rules devised by post-independence lawmakers to assist homesteading women included an unusually expansive cruelty standard. Section 3 of the 1841 divorce act empowered trial courts to dissolve a marriage when a spouse was guilty of "excesses, cruel treatment, or outrages" against the other so as to "render their being together insupportable." The 1848 Texas Supreme Court decision of *Sheffield v. Sheffield* adopted a cruelty definition from Louisiana civil law, relevant only to separation from bed and board, that specified acts of physical violence, behavior creating apprehension thereof, or outrageous conduct and verbal abuse. Between 1851 and 1857, the high court construed various English ecclesiastical court definitions, also dealing only with legal separation, to broaden the standard and make it particularly serviceable to women. Behaviors specifically interdicted in independent rulings included the rudeness and incivility of a man toward his wife, unfounded charges of unchastity against her, his physical assault of children a wife had by a former marriage, habitual drunkenness that disqualified a man from fulfilling his marital obligations, and battery of a wife or verbal abuse portending future acts of violence against her.[8]

The Texas cruelty standard was among the most liberal found in the antebellum South. Most southern states before the Civil War retained the traditional English criterion for cruelty, which required a showing of severe physical brutality. Aside from Texas, only the statutes of North Carolina, Tennessee, Arkansas, and Louisiana legislated against "excesses" or "personal indignities" rendering cohabitation "intolerable." Judges in these states used their discretion unsparingly and modified the traditional definition of cruelty to include verbal abuse, threats, insults, and imputations of immorality. Except for the other frontier state of Arkansas, however, the Texas standard was the most expansive and solicitous of women.[9]

The broadened definition of cruelty reflected judicial consideration of social conditions compelling heightened attentiveness to homesteading women. The Texas Supreme Court certainly did not believe that women in the polity deserved increased protection because they were more sensitive than their counterparts in the more settled South. Texas women were not known for their special delicacy, and rough conditions compelled even the relatively small number of refined immigrant women from comfortable middle-class and more affluent backgrounds to harden themselves. The high court was acutely aware of the difficulties that settlement imposed on women regardless of their origins. Judicial elaboration of the cruelty definition addressed the most common forms of frontier wife abuse. The strenuous and often dangerous efforts of pioneering women consistently induced Texas courts to address their needs. The expansive cruelty ground thus comported with the belief that mistreatment of isolated and sacrificing homesteading women was simply too unjust to tolerate.[10]

Judicial interpretation of the abandonment ground also indicates a special effort to assist frontier women. Section 2 of the 1841 act empowered courts to render a divorce in favor of a husband or wife when either had voluntarily left the "bed and board" of the other for three years with the intention to abandon. In the 1853 decision of *Hare v. Hare*, the Texas Supreme Court established rigorous standards of pleading and proof, requiring clear evidence that a husband seeking a divorce for abandonment had not, in fact, immigrated to Texas while leaving his reluctant wife behind. In two other cases, however, the high court elaborated a different rule. It permitted juries to presume the intent of a husband to abandon even if his wife could only show that he had ventured from home and then failed to communicate with her again. Given the frequency with which Anglo-Texan men deserted their wives by simply failing to return from seemingly harmless travels, the evidentiary presumption was quite functional. The rule also empowered forsaken women to remarry more quickly and thus acquire a new working partner.[11]

Innovative judicial interpretation of the abandonment ground provided additional relief for women having to deal with intractable husbands. In the 1857 decision of *Camp v. Camp*, the Texas Supreme Court held that drunkenness so continuous and debilitating as to disqualify a man from performing his family obligations, or any other conduct amounting to actionable cruelty, justified his wife in separating from him and obtaining a divorce after three years. By the end of the nineteenth century, jurists had come to refer to the principle set forth in *Camp* as "constructive desertion." Before 1860, however, only four other southern high courts had adopted this judicially manufactured artifice.[12] Given the extraordinarily expansive definition of cruelty in Texas, however, *Camp* held that an unusually broad array of physical and verbal abuse empowered a wife to withdraw quickly from an intolerable situation and expeditiously obtain a more suitable working partner.[13] As the Texas Supreme Court indicated in *Wheat v. Owens*, furthermore, the law did not deny a woman her community interest when her husband forced her from home and she cohabited with a new mate.[14]

The Hispanic matrimonial regime generated divorce rules for property division unusually favorable to Anglo-Texan women. In the more settled southern states, divorce left most women propertyless and destitute under established common law principles, especially if they were at fault. As a matter of good public policy, many southern judges agreed a divorced woman should receive a rudimentary "maintenance" out of the property of her former husband when possible.[15] Texas courts almost always awarded a divorcing woman her community share and all of her separate property.[16] They usually did so even if she was the marital culprit and her transgression had been adultery.[17] In some cases, women received more than half of the community estate when there were equities to be adjusted or when there were children to take into account. Courts adopted the policy of granting a 50 percent allotment, or an even larger one, neither to forestall such women from turning to vice and crime because of economic disabilities nor to provide a rudimentary form of public assistance. Trial judges and appellate justices alike simply considered such awards the just compensation for hardworking and sacrificing pioneer women.[18]

Widespread property holding among Anglo-Texan women dictated alimony rules much different from those found in the states of the more settled South. In eighteenth-century English law, courts ordered men who separated from their wives to pay alimony, since they continued in their ownership and exclusive control of marital property. United States courts in the early nineteenth century provided permanent alimony even in the case of absolute divorce, but usually only if the man was the offender. By the mid-nineteenth century, many states awarded at least some alimony to a divorced woman even if she was at fault. During the first half of the nineteenth century, southern courts tracked this liberalizing trend to some extent. Antebellum Texas law was radically different — it provided no permanent alimony. This unusual omission, however, derived from official recognition that land policy and the Hispanic matrimonial regime had helped to generate a society in which most divorcing women were quite capable of handling their own affairs, owned substantial amounts of land and other property, and did not need the ongoing support of their former husbands.[19]

Land-grant policy and Hispanic matrimonial law also worked with progressive divorce rules to give Anglo-Texan women unusually good chances of retaining custody of their children. During the first half of the nineteenth century, republican idealism, transforming conceptions of women, and new theories of child development undercut the traditional right of divorcing men to custody of their children. While the economic power of men and morals of both parents continued to be important considerations, legislatures and courts in many United States jurisdictions began to award custody of children to divorced women by emphasizing their supposed innate nurturing capacities and the best interests of the child. To some extent, all these changes occurred within the antebellum South. The persistence of patriarchal authority and a social system based on extended families, however, hindered equal custody rights for divorcing women in many southern states. The 1841 Texas divorce statute, however, mandated equal custody rights for women. As in the more liberal jurisdictions of the more settled South,

Texas jurists emphasized the best interests of the child and gave full consideration to the perceived special nurturing abilities of mothers. Widespread property holding and economic effectiveness among Anglo-Texan women following divorce, however, substantially increased their chances to retain custody.[20]

Women took advantage of the new divorce law much more often than men. Chief Justice John Hemphill authored almost all of the divorce decisions of the Texas Supreme Court before the Civil War. Blending English ecclesiastical court principles, the common law of the United States, and French and Spanish civil law doctrines, they clearly bear the mark of a jurist strongly committed to the welfare of women. Out of the fifteen Texas Supreme Court divorce appeals arising from 1841 to 1860, women initiated ten, or 66 percent, of them.[21] Women petitioners significantly outnumbered men at the trial level. In the Eleventh District Court of Harris County, for example, all but one of the divorce plaintiffs in 1845 were women.[22] In 1860 women in and around Houston filed twice as many divorce suits than did men.[23] Of the five divorce decrees rendered in that year, three stemmed from suits women initiated.[24]

Expanded divorce grounds, however, did not quickly generate a large volume of divorce litigation. As the data for Harris County in 1845 and 1860 suggest, Anglo-Texans strapped with bad marriages did not rush to divorce courts. The practical benefits of marriage to homesteaders and the inaccessibility of courts usually made divorce undesirable. Particularly in isolated areas, many Texans undoubtedly terminated intolerable marriages by simply moving on. The disorganization and transiency of antebellum Texas society, furthermore, facilitated this approach.

That the Texas Supreme Court remained strongly committed to maintaining marriages is evident in its 1848 decision of *Sheffield v. Sheffield*. That case dealt with the divorce appeal of Lydia Sheffield of Gonzales County, whose husband James had successfully utilized the unusually broad cruelty ground. While he had also charged Lydia with clandestine adultery, her verifiable misdeeds in a marriage of less than two years turned out to be little more than "a gadding disposition," "sulkiness," and a habit of addressing James in "an angry, insulting, and aggravating manner." The high court overturned the decree, and Chief Justice Hemphill explained the policy rationale undergirding the decision:

While full effect is to be given to the statute, it should be remembered that . . . the prospect of easy separation foments the most frivolous quarrels and disgusts into deadly animosities. . . . [T]here should not be such looseness of exposition as would defeat the beneficial objects of the marriage institution, and sunder its bonds with almost as much facility as if it were a state of concubinage, dependent alone on the will of the parties.[25]

Hemphill emphasized the object of matrimony involved not only the "mutual comfort and happiness of the parties" but "the benefit of their common offspring . . . and the moral order, security, and tranquility of civilized society."[26]

Sheffield indicates lawmakers had no intention of permitting Anglo-Texan men and women to misuse the expanded cruelty ground as they had marriage by bond. The 1841 divorce act required that trial courts only render divorce decrees when there was "full and satisfactory evidence independent of the confession or admission of either party. . . ." The act also required trial judges to deny a divorce when a plaintiff had encouraged adultery in his or her spouse simply to provide the basis for a decree.[27] In the 1858 decision of *Moore v. Moore*, the Texas Supreme Court empowered judges to overturn juries that awarded divorces when the only evidence supporting a complaint of cruelty was the mutually consistent testimony of both parties.[28] The high court was thus on the lookout for collusive divorce, as had been the Texas Congress when it implemented explicit divorce grounds initially.

In the 1852 decision of *Nogees v. Nogees*, the high court built a "sliding scale" into the divorce cruelty standard, further delimiting its use. According to Chief Justice Hemphill, "Among persons of coarse habits . . . [blows] may pass for very little more than rudeness of language or manner. They might occasion no apprehension and be productive of but slight unhappiness." Perpetuating a class-oriented principle developed in the English ecclesiastical courts, *Nogees* thus established that an occasional blow between some Texas spouses might or might not provide grounds for divorce.[29]

The malleable standard certainly did not require a woman to tolerate the brutality of a husband. Some southern jurists might well have adopted it to offer heightened protection to the supposedly delicate women of the planter elite, while requiring common women to tolerate the violence of their husbands.[30] Few historians familiar with the record of Chief Justice John Hemphill, however, could easily accept the proposition that he was insensitive to the plight of battered women. The extraordinarily broad definition of cruelty he worked to establish included, as a baseline standard, the physical mistreatment of a wife. The court adopted this criterion regardless of the common law rule, not yet defunct in many jurisdictions in the United States, that gave a husband the privilege of "chastising" his wife. In the *Nogees* opinion itself, Chief Justice Hemphill vigorously deplored the "ancient privilege" which Jacques Nogees invoked to justify the severe and repeated beatings he administered to his wife, Elizabeth. Hemphill's opinion set the Texas Supreme Court apart from the majority of southern high courts, which either remained silent on the issue or upheld common law wife "chastisement," at least through to the Civil War. The 1857 Texas penal code, furthermore, denied a husband the traditional prerogative. Men who struck their wives were subject to prosecution for assault and battery.[31]

In actuality, the cruelty standard had to take into account the not inconsiderable unruliness of some rather aggressive wives. Texas women undoubtedly suffered much more from the physical mistreatment of their spouses than did men. But that the *Nogees* court designed the sliding scale with both women and men in mind is patent on the face of the decision. It certainly was not unheard of for some wives to object vigorously to the more intolerable forms of "manly independence." Caroline Rice of Liberty County was one such woman. After having put up with the "dissipated character and habitual intoxication" of her husband Edward for years, she apparently reached the breaking point in June 1856. While Edward was confined to bed "very feeble from the effects of a severe spell of illness," Caroline began threatening him with a knife. In his divorce petition, Edward described the onslaught following shortly thereafter:

> She came into . . . [the] room with a stick, locked the door after her, and commenced beating your petitioner in such a cruel . . . manner that he believes she would have killed him had it not have been for the timely interposition of one of his neighbors, for whom he had dispatched a little negro.[32]

Edward further alleged some time later in the month of June that Caroline "took a hatchet and ran after your petitioner through the house and yard, threatening to split his skull open with it." After cataloging additional "cruelties, outrages, and excesses," he prayed for a divorce because life with Caroline had become "unbearable."[33]

As the divorce of Edward and Caroline might indicate, Texas cruelty doctrine had to allow for an extraordinarily violent society. It is undoubtedly true some women and men immigrating to the polity had been raised to expect brutality in the home more than others. By the same token, rapid settlement threw together immigrant men and women from different regions of the South, some of whom were from traditional yeoman communities and others who came of age in more refined circumstances. Men and women with very different socialization thus frequently paired off on homesteads in a loosely organized society lacking extended families, church congregations, public surveillance, or effective law enforcement to moderate the conflict that sometimes occurred between partners with different acculturation about marital relations. Hemphill and the rest of the justices, furthermore, confronted the issue of wife beating in a setting that often eroded the affection of spouses and intensified strife among those predisposed to violence. For the cruelty standard to function, it had to be flexible enough to deal with the impact of harsh conditions on an unusually broad array of settlers and domestic situations.

The cruelty sliding scale worked to maintain workable marriages among men and women who engaged in relatively rough forms of marital strife. Whether a single blow amounted to actionable cruelty, furthermore, was not an issue for judges but for juries, whom the law allowed unusually broad discretion to assess the circumstances and temperaments of the parties. As a practical matter, the rule permitted jurors to consider the dispositions of litigants they often knew quite well. By the same token, it permitted them to determine whether the cruelty complained of had actually made the marriage "insupportable," the chances of reform on the part of the offending spouse, and the likelihood of reconciliation.[34] More important, the variable standard helped maintain marriages capable of enduring in a society where nuclear family cohesion was critical for the very survival and well-being of women, children, and men.

The principle of cruelty condonation worked further to fortify marriages. In the 1851 decision of *Wright v. Wright*, the Texas Supreme Court expanded the statutory divorce defense of "condonation," applicable only to suits involving adultery, making it available to a husband guilty of cruelty. Once a woman forgave her husband for a particular mistreatment, she could not use that misconduct as a basis for divorce.[35] It might be argued the rule reflected a peculiarly southern patriarchal attempt to impose female submissiveness.[36] The *Wright* court, however, held that a woman who condoned the cruelty of her husband could utilize forgiven transgressions to support a new suit should he abuse her again.[37] The condonation rule certainly comported with the belief, common among frontier women, that it was primarily their obligation and mostly in their power to maintain marriages.[38] On the other hand, the rule made it easier for a woman to divorce a forgiven husband who renewed his mistreatment. Given the great value of a working partner on homesteads, the rule also provided women with a potent point of leverage to induce their spouses to straighten up. In actuality, the precept worked to achieve its purported purpose, that is, to reinforce reconciliation.[39] This policy, furthermore, assumed unusual importance in a primitive setting where family cohesion was critical.

The cruelty condonation principle also took into account practical incentives encouraging women to reconcile rather than divorce. Under property division rules, a Texas woman who divorced more often than not was awarded title to at least half of the farm or ranch she had usually worked hard to establish. But in some cases the courts effectively denied a woman possession of her lands when they awarded improvements to her husband. And if the courts sold the land, the woman was left with little more than a handful of cash rather than possession and enjoyment of the farm or ranch. Thus, although an Anglo-Texan woman usually exited marriage with a community share of lands and sometimes slaves, practical considerations and her emotional investment in the homestead often compelled her to consider reconciliation. The cruelty condonation rule took these strong economic pressures and personal considerations into account. It also allowed for the risks women faced when they sought to maintain their marriages with particularly self-indulgent and recalcitrant husbands.

Post-independence law permitting husbands more sexual liberty than wives was unusually tolerant of both male and female infidelity. Deviating substantially from mainstream Anglo-American and traditional Hispanic law, the 1841 Texas divorce statute imposed liability upon women for a single instance of adultery, but only upon men for abandonment of their wives and adulterous cohabitation.[40] In his 1901 treatise regarding the law of married women in Texas, Ocie Speer expressed considerable dismay at the dual standard, which had remained on the books. While reflecting a more modern sensibility regarding gender equality, as well as late-nineteenth-century male idealization of Texas womanhood, his assessment highlights the peculiarity of the rule:

> A single act of indiscretion upon the part of the weaker vessel exposes her to the loss of her husband and family; his, however often repeated, unless accompanied as well by the additional sin of abandonment, is not matrimonial sin in the eye of the law. By whose authority is this distinction made?—this premium upon marital licentiousness; this mandate to pure wives to embrace adulterous husbands![41]

Speer omitted, however, to comment on the distinctiveness of the criminal law relevant to infidelity before the Civil War. A statute implemented in 1836 proscribed only "living in adultery." The penalty was a fine not less than one hundred nor more than a thousand dollars. An 1857 revision of the sanction explicitly maintained that a single act of adultery was not punishable.[42] The new rules certainly constituted a radical departure from that of the preexisting Mexican regime, which heavily fined or banished a man guilty of a single act of infidelity and subjected a similarly offending woman to seclusion in a monastery.[43] The post-independence law was also lenient in the case of both men and women relative to that of most other jurisdictions in the United States, which usually punished a solitary instance of infidelity.[44] Anglo-Texan criminal law thus extended to men an expansive prerogative to engage in extramarital sex, while laying down a stricter standard for women that was still less rigorous than those for women in most other southern states.

Several Texas Supreme Court rulings in the 1850s indicated the law might permit a woman to divorce a husband for having sexual relations with his female slave. Dicta in Chief Justice Hemphill's opinions in the 1851 decision of *Wright v. Wright* and the 1857 decision of *Sharman v. Sharman* cited English ecclesiastical authority holding that a husband who attempted to "debauch servant women" was guilty of actionable cruelty. In the view of the high court, the adultery of a man with his female servants was "inconsistent with the matrimonial relation and its duties, obligations, and affections."[45]

The 1857 decision of *Cartwright v. Cartwright* empowered a woman to divorce her husband for cohabiting with his female slave. That case dealt with Williford and Pink Cartwright of Montgomery County. They married in 1834, obtained a *sitio,* and developed a successful cotton-growing operation with the use of slave labor. Pink, however, divorced Williford in August 1853. She based her successful suit on allegations that he had falsely accused her of infidelity, denied the paternity of her child, and moved out of the house to live in a cabin with his bondwoman Jane, whom he had purchased before marrying Pink. The high court upheld the divorce, finding Williford guilty of cruelty in numerous respects. Chief Justice Hemphill, writing for the court, reserved choice commentary for the way Williford had conducted himself with Jane:

> Without scrutinizing or discussing, in detail, the repulsive features in the facts of the case, it will be sufficient to say . . . there was . . . so much cruelty . . . in his obstinately persisting continuously to live in a Negro house with his Negro woman. . . .[46]

The *Cartwright* court, however, declined to impose divorce liability on men who indulged in sexual relations with their slave women. Hemphill was careful to avoid characterizing the involvement of Williford with Jane as adultery, nor did he refer to her once as a slave. He made no reference to his dicta in *Wright* or *Sharman.* While strenuously condemning Williford's cohabitation with Jane in her cabin, Hemphill refrained from inferring that this involved sexual relations between them. According to him, "[T]here may have been no improper intimacy between them, as however, there was, in the opinion of the jury. . . ." With this tortured circumlocution, the court managed to draw no conclusions suggesting that the sexual relations of a married man with his slave woman amounted to actionable cruelty. Regardless of a newly enacted penal code provision holding a married person who cohabited with a member of the opposite sex presumptively guilty of criminal infidelity, the court did not find a husband residing exclusively with his slave woman liable for divorce on the ground of abandonment and living in adultery.[47]

Cartwright also reversed long-standing Hispanic community property principles to deny Pink an ownership interest in Jane's children. While Williford certainly challenged the divorce decree, he also attacked the decision of the trial court for awarding Pink a community interest in the four children to whom Jane had given birth since he had purchased her. Neither the lower court nor the Texas Supreme Court actually decided whether Williford had fathered them. Even so, the appeal clearly involved the right of a divorcing woman to acquire ownership, and thus possession, of the children her husband had with a slave mistress. By the same token, it addressed the possibility that a wife might impose her retribution on them. With Hemphill writing voluminously on this point, the court discounted traditional Hispanic law making the children of separately owned slave women part of the community estate. By characterizing Jane's children as the "increase" of separate property, rather than the "fruit" of it, the court provided that the children would remain exclusively the property of Williford.[48] This holding prevented Pink from having her way with them.

The ruling in *Cartwright* was entirely consistent with the policy of protecting slave mistresses and their children from the retribution of aggrieved wives announced a year earlier in *Hagerty v. Harwell*. In 1848, Rebecca Hagerty sued her husband Spire for divorce in Harrison County Court, alleging his adultery with a slave women in whom they had a community interest. During the pendency of the action, however, he conveyed the female slave in question and her two children to his sister, Delilah Harwell. After Spire died in 1849, before the trial court could rule on the divorce, Rebecca appealed a decree validating the transfer. She claimed it had been done fraudulently in violation of her ownership rights. Justice Abner Lipscomb, however, explained the decision of the high court to uphold the conveyance:

It is making the only mitigation of the [adultery] . . . that is left to the [husband] . . . and it is natural that he should trust the mother and her children, in such cases, to the kindness of his own sister, rather than leave them to the injured and infuriated wife, who would possibly, yea, probably, inflict severity, cruelty, and hardship on them, when the offender was beyond the reach of her angry passions.[49]

Cartwright suggests that the concern of the high court for the needs of Anglo-Texan women ultimately yielded to the imperatives of the slave order. That decision came amid the growing debate over abolitionism and the ascendance of the militant states' rights wing of the Texas Democratic party. Beginning in 1857, these "fire-eaters" began seriously discussing secession, while agitating to reinforce the slave system and race control with new criminal law. Chief Justice Hemphill, born and raised in South Carolina, and having come of age during the Nullification Crisis, was a dedicated member of the staunch proslavery faction.[50] While his opinion in *Cartwright* certainly exposed husbands who cohabited with their bondwomen to divorce liability, it did not place men at risk of divorce for otherwise sexually involving themselves with their female slaves. Such a holding would have been politically disastrous in the circumstances, since it would have implicitly castigated an abuse abolitionists had stridently condemned for years. A ruling of that kind also would have jeopardized far too many marriages. Abandoning earlier dicta to the contrary, Hemphill carefully preserved the long-standing sexual privileges of slave-owning men with their female chattel. His *Cartwright* opinion, furthermore, provided a jurisprudential shield for married men who cohabited with their slave women against the new 1858 penal code provision punishing "[e]very white person who shall live in adultery . . . with a Negro, or person . . . descending from Negro ancestry to the third generation inclusive."[51]

Criminal law further reinforced the sexual double standard. In England and in almost all the jurisdictions of the United States, the killing by a husband of his adulterous wife or her paramour was murder. Reviving a medieval precept set forth in *Las Siete Partidas,* the Texas legislature included a rule of justifiable homicide in the 1857 penal code permitting husbands to kill men they caught having adulterous relations with their wives. The provision, however, did not grant a like prerogative to women who discovered their husbands indulging their "manly independence" with members of the opposite sex.[52]

Texas law also placed limits on the power of men to impose chastity on their wives. A companion penal code provision to that establishing the adultery rule of justifiable homicide denied men the right to kill or even harm their wives when they caught them being "taken in adultery."[53] Further, dicta in at least four Texas Supreme Court decisions handed down in the 1850s invoked English ecclesiastical precepts holding that a man who maliciously and groundlessly charged his wife with unchastity was guilty of actionable mistreatment and thus subject to divorce. The belligerence of Williford Cartwright, however, provided the impetus for the high court to expand the legal definition of cruelty to this unusual extent.[54]

Defenses set forth in section 12 of the 1841 divorce act, all of which were relevant only to infidelity, substantially qualified the right of a man to dissolve his marriage to an unfaithful wife. The defense of recrimination shielded from divorce an adulterous woman who could demonstrate that her husband was similarly guilty. While the statute almost necessarily disallowed the defense of connivance to men, a wife guilty of simple infidelity could avert a divorce judgment if she could show her husband had entrapped her. The defense of condonation permitted a woman to avoid divorce liability if she could show her husband had forgiven her unchastity. Successful invocation of these defenses, furthermore, established a perpetual bar against a subsequent divorce suit based on the excused transgression.[55]

In the 1855 decision of *Simons v. Simons*, the Texas Supreme Court worked inventively to limit the availability of divorce to men suspecting their wives of infidelity. In late March 1854, Paul Simons of Walker County sued his wife, Elizabeth, for divorce on the heels of the sexual adventure she had while he was away on business that month. Mrs. Gray, owner of a local boardinghouse, testified Elizabeth had rented one of her rooms and been "too thick" there several nights with Cartwright Logan. Nancy Blackburn attested that Elizabeth had not "kept herself in her place as she ought" with Cartwright when the three had shared an evening at the Simons home. Cartwright himself admitted on the stand that he had slept with Elizabeth at Mrs. Gray's boardinghouse.[56] While the trial jury had little trouble awarding Paul a divorce, Elizabeth succeeded in having the verdict reversed on appeal. Chief Justice Hemphill acknowledged standard Anglo-American divorce law accepting the testimony of a woman's paramour, or *particeps criminis*, but this was not to be the rule in Texas.[57] In his view, a man who had sexual relations with a married woman was too often tempted to commit perjury to protect himself and "the guilty fair one." He also emphasized the potential for slander of innocent women:

> We are disposed to question the propriety and policy of the rule. . . . If we were certain that such witness would be only called on when there was in truth guilt it might well be allowed them to swear. . . . But we have reason to believe that such testimony would be often offered when there had been no guilt committed.[58]

The court thus established an unusual rule excluding altogether the testimony of the *particeps criminis*. The precept certainly protected the reputations of women who had remained faithful. It also worked to prevent suspicious and unscrupulous men from calling sham witnesses to the stand to obtain divorces when valid or conclusive evidence against their wives was unavailable.

In *Sheffield v. Sheffield*, the high court worked with equal ingenuity to disallow a woman's confession of infidelity. In addition to allegations of cruelty, the divorce suit James Sheffield brought against his wife, Lydia, alleged she had been absent from home often to engage in clandestine trysts. The evidence supporting this charge was limited to the testimony of one male witness who averred Lydia had admitted to him making "an assignation with a stranger . . . for the purpose of illicit and adulterous cohabitation." [59] According to Chief Justice Hemphill, however, general principles of divorce law required that "[p]resumptions of guilt must be raised from other circumstances, such as gross indecorums, improper familiarities, opportunities of privacy sought and indulged . . . before such confessions are admissible. . . ." In his view, furthermore, the 1841 divorce act required "full and satisfactory evidence, independent of the confession or admission of either party." The Texas Congress, however, had designed this provision simply to prevent collusion among divorce litigants.[60] Hemphill thus discounted general rules of evidence and expansively interpreted the divorce statute to exclude all testimony to the effect a female defendant had confessed adultery. Like the *Simons* rule, the holding in *Sheffield* worked quite well to prevent ruthless men suspecting adultery from manufacturing bogus evidence to divorce their wives.

Adultery law dealing with frontier social conditions and settlement pressures protected the interests of Anglo-Texan men in their homesteads and deterred them from deserting their wives. By keeping the standard the same for women as in most other jurisdictions and making only abandonment of a wife and cohabiting with another woman actionable, the divorce law of adultery accommodated the unusually extensive extramarital sexual activities of Anglo-Texan men. The dual standard protected philandering husbands from divorce liability and the loss of half their farms and ranches. By the same token, it spared them the forfeiture of female

companionship difficult to replace, the important homesteading contributions wives ordinarily provided, and the valuable labor of their
children. It also discouraged men eager to retain the benefits of marriage from permitting their affairs to amount to more than intermittent
sprees.

The divorce adultery double standard relieved abandoned wives,
while rationally allocating scarce females. Rather than punish male infidelity, the abandonment and living in adultery criterion allowed a
deserted woman to dissolve her marriage quickly and acquire a new
partner legally and expeditiously. The rule, however, also worked to
make women in short supply available for remarriage. All at once, it
addressed the plight of deserted wives, took into account the frontier
sex imbalance, and bolstered family farms and ranches.

In a similar fashion, the criminal sanction against "living in adultery"
worked to maintain homesteading families. According to nineteenth-
century legal commentator Joel Bishop, the rationale undergirding the
crime of living in adultery in most United States jurisdictions where the
rule prevailed was that "a series of [adulterous] acts, more or less continuous, and more or less open [is] . . . more or less offensive to the
public sense of decency."[61] In Texas, however, informal cohabitation
and extralegal sexual relationships were commonplace, and authorities
and settlers dealt sympathetically with these aberrations. Public decorum or extramarital sex were thus not likely the prime concerns of lawmakers when they implemented the sanction against living in adultery.
The criminal statute worked best to discourage men and women from
abandoning one another. Living in adultery necessarily entailed desertion. This was a situation that left both homesteading women and men
with onerous burdens. The 1857 version of the sanction recognized
common law marriage, thus punishing men and women who had cohabited as spouses, abandoned home, and commenced living with new
partners.[62] By the end of the period, the possibility of prosecution deterred the informal dissolution of marital relationships, whether they
had been formed ceremonially or not. Through the republic and antebellum statehood period, however, prosecution for "living in adultery"
provided deserted women and men with at least some institutional
means to reestablish marital relations.

The divorce rule making the cohabitation of a man with his slave
woman actionable cruelty promoted the viability of his wife. The *Cartwright* decision certainly refrained from characterizing the cohabitation

of Williford with Jane as abandonment and living in adultery. When he moved out of his house to live with Jane in her cabin, however, he imposed on Pink all of the practical hardships of desertion. The court clearly recognized her predicament. In fact, Chief Justice Hemphill noted particularly that Williford's cruelty entailed his "perverse neglect to furnish his wife with the necessary supplies." By the same token, he refused to allow her to contract for such purchases herself.[63] The holding in *Cartwright* thus provided women means to divorce and replace husbands whose philandering undermined their accustomed autonomous role in managing their homesteads and their efforts to thrive independently.

The unusual adultery rule of justifiable homicide worked as an effective deterrent to female infidelity. Although the prerogative of a man to kill his wife's paramour was certainly consistent with the southern ethos of male honor, this rule's primary purpose was to help husbands to cope with infidelity in a society where law enforcement and public surveillance were often nonexistent. That is, the rule of justifiable homicide discouraged male sexual intruders in the absence of a husband, based on the possibility of his unexpected and sudden return.[64]

The rule of justifiable homicide helped Anglo-Texan men secure their wives in circumstances that made divorce an ineffectual deterrent to adultery. Given Hispanic matrimonial principles, land-grant policy, and the respect Texas jurists had for homesteading women, those who were divorced for infidelity usually exited their marriages with substantial property and economic effectiveness. The threat of divorce for female adultery, therefore, restrained wives from philandering less forcefully than in other states, where divorce courts typically denied sexually delinquent women a "maintenance" or otherwise considerably reduced it. The rule of justifiable homicide thus provided a tool much more potent than divorce to discourage clandestine female adultery.

The permissible use of deadly force provided Anglo-Texan men with a way to deal with female adultery much more practical than divorce. Some men undoubtedly rejected unfaithful wives out of anger and because they felt betrayed. Given the importance of marriage for survival, others quite likely thought more pragmatically about female infidelity. Because of the inaccessibility of courts, divorce was usually a difficult and time-consuming procedure. It also left men without a working partner. In these circumstances, the prerogative of a man to use lethal violence to secure exclusive sexual relations with his wife was an effective tool with which to maintain his marriage and the efficacy of his homestead. This approach, furthermore, was consistent with frontier mores of using violence for self-help and personal justice. The adultery rule of justifiable homicide certainly indicates legislative notice of the unusual competition for women. By the same token, it reflects the high value Anglo-Texan men attached to marriageable women.

The Texas Supreme Court, in holding that groundless charges of adultery were actionable cruelty, recognized that this conduct was particularly abusive in frontier circumstances. Accusations of female infidelity were quite frequent in Texas divorce litigation.[65] Husbands routinely absent from home easily suspected adultery in a setting where men aggressively pursued relatively scarce women. Texas courts, however, respected the sacrifices of women working hard to establish homesteads in isolation and often in physical danger. Jurists, furthermore, were not oblivious to the outrage that loyal women felt when their husbands wrongly and maliciously accused them of unfaithfulness. Many falsely accused women undoubtedly forgave husbands who charged them mistakenly. The elaborated cruelty ground, however, at least gave those wrongly accused the option of terminating their marriages when reconciliation was either physically dangerous or emotionally intolerable. The innovative law developed in the unchastity cases thus protected women who were constant in the face of trying circumstances and a demographic situation which made remarriage relatively easy for them.

Exclusionist rules laid down in *Simons* and *Sheffield* protected even unfaithful women, but only in circumstances mitigating their misconduct. The precepts categorically disallowing the confession of a wife and disqualifying the testimony of a *particeps criminis* certainly safeguarded innocent women from bogus prosecution by suspicious and unscrupulous husbands. These doctrines also excluded the testimony and out-of-court averments of the best and often only witnesses when women were, in point of fact, guilty. Even so, the rules often worked in a realistic and humane way. A neglected wife who gave in to the advances of one of the many Anglo-Texan men carousing and searching the prairies for female companionship was not considered nearly as reproachable as in normal circumstances. This was especially true if her husband was unusually neglectful and she continued in her marriage. Both the *Simons* rule and the precept set forth in *Sheffield* reflected this. Women invoked the rules only when husbands attempted to use their inadvertent confessions or the testimony of a paramour to prove clandestine adultery. By the same token, the rules offered a transgressing woman protection only when she had stayed with her husband and continued with her homesteading efforts.

Evidentiary rules shielding women from divorce for adultery discounted dubious charges of infidelity to protect the vested interest many of them had in their marriage ventures. Many Anglo-Texan women accused of marital infidelity undoubtedly desired to retain possession and common ownership of the whole farm or ranch for which they had worked hard and sacrificed much to establish. Some of these women certainly wanted to maintain their marriages at least long enough to "prove up" their titles to lands, which the government granted only on the condition that homesteaders would cultivate and thus "improve" them for at least three years.[66] Evidentiary rulings in *Simons* and *Sheffield* clearly made it more difficult for men to divorce their wives for clandestine adultery. By the same token, these rules permitted especially determined female defendants to maintain their marriages and thus protect their community interest in homesteads when evidence indicating their secretive infidelity was not conclusive.

Protective evidentiary rules and the cruelty standard worked together to permit women sued speciously for infidelity to retain custody of their children with an optimal property settlement. A divorce decree entered against a woman for clandestine adultery did not threaten her community property rights. On the other hand, Texas courts were often predisposed to grant a woman who prevailed in divorce litigation and received custody of her children more than a 50 percent share of community property, some or all of the separate personalty of her husband, and income from his separate real estate. Evidentiary rules set forth in *Simons* and *Sheffield* shielding a woman from divorce liability for questionable secretive adultery permitted her to fend off a decree based on her fault. Cruelty doctrine making false charges of unchastity actionable permitted her to obtain a decree in her favor, along with custody of her children and a property settlement maximizing her ability to support them.

To some extent, the *Simons* rule also limited the power of sexual interlopers to inveigle wives and sabotage viable families. A rule disqualifying the testimony of a wife's paramour worked well to preserve marriages. A persistent frontiersman might succeed in involving himself with a lonely and neglected married woman. The rule, however, prevented unscrupulous men from securing mates by testifying in court about their trysts to destroy the marriages of otherwise devoted women. Given that Anglo-Texan men embraced the ideal of sexual prowess, for some to boast of an erotic conquest, especially under the influence of strong drink, was almost certainly a temptation.[67] The *Simons* evidentiary rule thus helped spare women guilty of clandestine adultery, and their husbands, from the unsavory publications of boastful male sexual partners. It also implied Anglo-Texan men were to keep their mouths shut about the liaisons they finagled with married women still living with their husbands and committed to them and their children.

The coupling routines of Anglo-Texans make suspect a conclusion that the divorce recrimination defense worked in a traditional way to punish spouses for their extramarital sexual breaches. According to section 12 of the Texas divorce act, a plaintiff could not obtain a divorce on the ground of adultery if he or she was similarly guilty. Section 12 also held that when a defendant successfully invoked the recrimination defense, thus showing each spouse was unfaithful, neither could obtain a divorce based on the particular infidelity of the other. The traditional basis for recrimination doctrine was the principle extending throughout the English law and equity jurisprudence forbidding "redress to one for an injury done him by another, if [he is] himself . . . in the wrong about the same thing whereof he complains." Also undergirding the rule was the presupposition that women and men who had committed adultery were unsuitable for remarriage and deserved a sentence of lifelong, mutual penance, since they had scandalized society with their immorality.[68] This logic has dubious applicability in antebellum Texas, where immigrant settlers commonly flouted the traditional sexual decorum of the more settled South by coupling and uncoupling in disregard of marriage and divorce formalities, cohabiting bigamously, and living in adultery.

In actuality, the recrimination rule worked best to repair and sustain marriages male infidelity undermined. Both women and men could certainly avail themselves of the recrimination defense. Given the much more common spontaneous adultery of Anglo-Texan men, however, invocation of the rule usually stemmed from female sexual retaliation. If a woman who had responded in kind to the adultery of her husband chose to reconcile with him, she simply invoked the defense at trial to sustain the marriage. Section 12 also denied a woman who had invoked recrimination to reconcile from using the forgiven adultery of her husband as a pretext to divorce him should she change her mind. The recrimination rule thus tolerated the illicit female sexual shenanigans which the philandering and unruliness of Anglo-Texan men often induced. It also worked to reinforce marriages that had been pulled apart by male sexual adventurousness and reconstituted by forgiving women.

The divorce connivance defense helped to preserve the marriages of men who resorted to permissible violence to discourage the adultery of their wives. As a result of the adverse practical consequences of divorce, Anglo-Texan men were left with mostly personal means to deter their wives from extramarital sexual involvements. Given the ethos of lawlessness and violence pervading the frontier, suspicious men were tempted to entrap their spouses in adultery for punitive purposes more frequently than in normal circumstances. The adultery rule of justifiable homicide facilitated this practice, but only within prescribed bounds. A statutory exception to the rule made a man liable for murder if he ensnared his wife in adultery and then killed her paramour.[69] Even so, a man who did so was still free to entrap and intimidate his wife and a sexual interloper to discourage further violations. The rule of justifiable homicide itself, however, prohibited him from physically harming her. The divorce defense of connivance, furthermore, shielded a woman from divorce liability when her husband entrapped her. The law of homicide and the connivance rule thus allowed for social conditions that induced female adultery, while also comporting with the practical considerations that deterred men from divorce. They also worked to restrain violently jealous husbands and protect wayward women. To the extent that the connivance rule served the pragmatic, tactical goals of husbands, rather than thwarting unethical schemes to lay a foundation for divorce, it deviated radically from its traditional function.[70]

That the adultery condonation defense reinforced chastity among women and punished male dishonor in keeping with Old South ideals is unlikely, given the social context of the precept. Texas wives guilty of clandestine adultery undoubtedly sought forgiveness much more often than did husbands who had deserted home and commenced living with their mistresses. It might be argued that the perpetual bar denying divorce to a man for the condoned adultery of his wife punished him, in accordance with southern ideals, because he had tolerated the misconduct and thus dishonored himself. In this conception, the rule pressured an aggrieved husband into court, since a forgiven wife's renewed adultery could not "revive" the condoned past offense for purposes of a divorce suit.[71] On the other hand, since illicit sex was commonplace, traditional southern attitudes that considered female infidelity extremely reprehensible were muted. Powerful practical incentives encouraged men to forgive and reconcile with unfaithful wives. Under the rule, furthermore, a man could divorce a wife for renewed infidelity if his forgiveness and efforts toward reconciliation proved fruitless.[72]

The condonation defense in the case of female adultery actually worked to reinforce the relationships of reconciled spouses, while protecting women whom husbands forgave. The rule certainly reflected Anglo-Texan contractual conceptions of marriage by permitting spouses to repair consensually damaged marital relations and then holding them to their resolutions. On the other hand, the perpetual bar derived from Scottish jurisprudence and embodied its basic policy goal, that is, to place reconciling spouses in the position of newlyweds as much as possible. After a man forgave the infidelity of his wife, the marriage was no less secure legally than on the day they married.[73] In Texas, however, the rule operated in a milieu that placed tremendous strains on marriages and made the marriages of reconciled spouses particularly unstable. It thus worked best to ensure that a forgiven woman did not run the risk of seeing her renewed settlement efforts wasted on, or exploited by, a husband who later used forgiven adultery as a pretext for divorce.

The law relevant to mating and childbearing that Anglo-Texans adopted to reinforce their social system assumed relatively lax sexual mores for white women. Texas lawmakers knew that female sexual activity in frontier circumstances often deviated from the norms more settled southern society prescribed for women. They consciously shaped adultery policy to deal with behavior rather than ideals. The divorce defense of connivance excused female adultery when jealous husbands encouraged it for punitive purposes. The recrimination and adultery condonation rules protected the infidelity of a woman when her husband forgave her or when both spouses committed actionable sexual transgressions. Protective evidentiary rules shielded a woman who engaged in clandestine adultery as long as she continued in her marriage and family settlement efforts. As in the case of judicially developed law and statutes ameliorating bigamy, illicit co-habitation, and bastardy, flexible divorce rules diminished traditional concerns with female sexual misconduct. While this approach dealt with frontier conditions both encouraging adultery and placing a premium on marital reconciliation, it necessarily dispensed with the southern ideal of female purity, loyalty, and chastity.

Post-independence Texas law also presupposed limits on the sexual liberty of husbands. In combination with the law of miscegenation, slavery, and justifiable homicide, the law of adultery prescribed clear parameters for the extramarital sex of Anglo-Texan men. The inter-mittent tryst of a married man with an unmarried woman or with a female slave was acceptable and not punished. The law, however, strongly discouraged the clandestine adultery of a married man with a married woman, as well as a man's abandonment of his wife and co-habitation with a mistress. These steps could result in penal conse-quences, divorce liability, or the permissible murderous retribution of an aggrieved husband. Anglo-Texan husbands, however, did not need to cohabit with available white women, female slaves, Native Ameri-can wives, Tejano mistresses, or with prostitutes of any racial descent to have occasional sexual intercourse with them. Philandering men who did not abandon their wives and set up housekeeping with other women could maintain their liaisons within the law.

The legal limitations on extramarital sex worked to augment Anglo-Texan families within a chaotic frontier social setting. By punishing a man for cohabiting with his mistress, whether free or bonded, adultery law discouraged his prolonged separation from his wife and children. It thus worked to reduce the chance that his affair would impose undue hardships upon them or threaten the operability of their homestead. By discouraging a married woman from abandoning home to cohabit with her paramour, the law similarly limited the potential for female adultery to undermine family cohesion and efficacy. Given the unusual power of common law marriage to legitimate both informal and biga-mous unions, the extramarital sex regime deterred married men and women from taking the risk of establishing relationships that had the appearance of a second marriage and thus the potential to create con-flicting claims to marital property and inheritance.

Post-independence law defining parental obligations for the chil-dren that resulted from adultery worked to shore up Anglo-Texan families and promote social order. The absence of an affiliation procedure, unusually good chances for daughters to receive a substantial inheritance, and abundant opportunities for women to marry worked to reduce demands for paternal support among unwed mothers. This was especially so when the fathers of their children were married men. These women, consequently, were usually predisposed to maintain guardianship of their children and financial responsibility for them. The mothers of adulterine bastards usually retained custody of them, while cuckolds unwittingly treated these children as their own. As in the common law of all jurisdictions of the United States, Texas marital rules required a man to assume legal responsibility for the children of his wife. Even a man who suspected he was not the father of his wife's child was required to do so unless he could prove he could not have had sexual intercourse with his wife at the time she conceived.[74] In essence, bastardy law and the uncertainty of men about paternity in any case worked usually to place illegitimate children with mothers rather than with fathers disinterested in or resentful of their progeny. Illegitimacy rules and the indeterminateness of paternity also encouraged male sexual promiscuity at the expense of faithful husbands. Even so, this not altogether sensible social-legal allocation of fathering resources worked well to preserve marriages, maintain families, and improve the chances for illegitimate children to receive optimal nurturing.

Post-independence law worked with frontier social mores to protect the property of Anglo-Texan families from interracial adultery and its procreative consequences. The intermittent sexual contacts that Anglo-Texan men had with dark-skinned prostitutes, Native American wives, or Tejano mistresses usually did not qualify as legal marriages, while the law of adultery permitted them. The law of bastardy ensured that children resulting from these involvements could not assert inheritance claims against their fathers or challenge the estates of legal wives and other white family members. The law of miscegenation, slavery, and adultery permitted married men to exploit slave women sexually. Mulatto children born of this kind of adultery, however, were illegitimate and usually remained in bondage, assuring that white family property could not be diverted to them. The law of adulterine bastardy usually made the child of a married woman legitimate. Sexual norms more restrictive for women than for men, racial prejudice, and the possibility that adultery with male slaves or other dark-complexioned men could produce children with features revealing their paternity discouraged Anglo-Texan women from having extramarital sex across the color line. While the economic disincentives of divorce weakened its power to inhibit this activity, harsher restraints included capital punishment for slave men and free men of color, the brutal retribution of slave-owning husbands, and the murderous vengeance against sexual inter-lopers that the adultery rule of justifiable homicide permitted in any case. The infidelity of Anglo-Texan men and women thus only rarely diverted their property to black or mixed-race children, free or bonded.

While the substantial social-legal barriers to cross-racial infidelity achieved a rather clear purpose, law-makers dealing with adultery involving only white women and men faced a more complex problem. As indicated in *Wheat v. Owens,* the Texas Supreme Court clearly disapproved of Frances Wheat's aban-donment of her family and adultery with Joseph Martin. Yet the mem-bers of the high court, as well as legislators, were keenly aware that the vigorous competition for the companionship of marriageable women sometimes encouraged female unfaithfulness. The care that the *Wheat* court took to emphasize the qualifications of the Hispanic adultery forfeiture rule thus reflected the leniency of Texas lawmakers toward women who engaged in relatively blameless forms of adultery. These qualifications, furthermore, substantially reinforced the broad discre-tion that post-independence divorce law gave trial judges to divide community property in a manner that was just. This was a preroga-tive they almost never used to deny sexually delinquent wives their fair share.

More important, the *Wheat* decision indicates the way post-indepen-dence leaders dealt with transgressing spouses to maintain marriages. The Hispanic matrimonial property regime and land-grant program made the adultery of both women and men extremely problematic. While lawmakers were strongly committed to reinforcing families, di-vorce and the property division attendant on it broke up homesteads, denied both women and men the full benefit of their pioneering exer-tions, and often threatened the security and survival of settlers. By tak-ing care to excuse forms of female adultery less reprehensible than in a more civilized society, however, the *Wheat* court helped to establish a policy that reduced the frequency of this undesirable outcome.

Post-independence law dealing with marital transgressors worked to accommodate the mercurial mating habits of Anglo-Texans, stabilize their families, and ensure racial hegemony for them. Texas lawmakers fashioned a law of divorce well suited to a turbulent and often violent populace. The law of marital dissolution provided special relief for sacrificing pioneer women subjected to the cruelty and neglect that stressful conditions prompted among especially impetuous husbands. On the other hand, the law of adultery prescribed a greater sexual freedom for men than for women. And rules about extramarital sex were not as strict for either women or men as they were in other jurisdictions. The divorce law of adultery and cruelty took into account the practical benefits of marriage by promoting reconciliation. It also worked with the criminal law, bastardy rules, and interracial sexual mores to maintain Anglo-Texans atop the racial-caste hierarchy they had constructed.

Conclusion

Frederick Jackson Turner argued that antebellum southerners placed an incomparable value on the liberty to compete for the "public domain" and the natural resources abundantly available in the unsettled wilds further west. Freedom from class rule and elite-dominated institutions of law that might limit this prerogative, furthermore, was fundamental to the "squatter ideal." From the perspective of settlers, government was an evil. Westering southerners regulated themselves with "extralegal, voluntary associations. . . . where settlement and society had gone in advance of the institutions and instrumentalities of organized society." Only in time did courts and legislative halls appear and, even then, only in response to the leadership of able men who had proven their worth in the struggle for survival. These men were thus especially equipped to make wise law that reinforced frontier democracy.[1]

There is certainly some merit in Turner's characterization. But Texas society from 1823 to 1860 did not develop in an institutional vacuum. While the strategic aims of Mexican policy-makers and Anglo-Texan leaders varied considerably, they consistently promoted rapid immigration with extraordinarily generous offers of real estate. The power of governments through the antebellum period to allocate land and clarify title thereto was critical in spurring the Anglo invasion and organizing settlement. As Gordon Morris Bakken has demonstrated quite convincingly, law was essential in defining and stabilizing property rights in nineteenth-century frontier regions.[2]

Regardless of institutional primitivism, the impact of law on social development in Texas was not limited to land policy. The Hispanic matrimonial property regime and an innovative law of debt created powerful additional incentives for southern immigrants eager to obtain new homesteads and start over. Settlement exigencies requiring the co-operative exertions of spouses and the sharing of profits derived from successful family ventures under community property rules, further-more, produced unusually reciprocal and egalitarian marriages among Anglo-Texans. The law thus had an influence extending far beyond those who actually involved themselves in litigation or otherwise had dealings with the legal system.

The impact of law on Anglo-Texan society, however, was not always positive. Institutional disarray and social atomization combined with male unruliness and stressful conditions to produce informal coupling and uncoupling, illicit sexual relationships, bastardy, and marital in-stability among far too many of those who responded to economic in-centives. Sexual disorder of this kind deranged family property rights in land—the socioeconomic foundation of the polity.

After independence from Mexico, Texas lawmakers dealt aggres-sively with the disruptive, rampant individualism of settlers. Legislators and the justices of the high court blended and modified Hispanic prin-ciples, common law doctrine, and English ecclesiastical precepts to accommodate distinctive frontier marital norms and sexual behavior. Along with constitutional delegates, these leaders also adopted rules that safeguarded pioneer women and children against the more exag-gerated forms of "manly independence." New legal measures also bol-stered homesteading families and their property in land. Many of these laws were extraordinarily progressive. Law supporting more equitable marital relations and reinforcing the sexual practices of settlers helped generate family mores that deviated radically from those found con-temporaneously in the more settled South and urbanizing Northeast.

For many in antebellum Texas, however, the social-legal system that developed was anything but democratic. After the Anglo war of inde-pendence, the law of domestic relations often combined with positive pronouncements regarding citizenship, land policy, Indian Removal, slavery, and miscegenation to fashion a racial-caste system. This insti-tutional scheme certainly destroyed a preexisting multiracial polity that had recognized a viable role for Native Americans, Tejanos, and blacks. It also merged with a transcultural array of gender constructs, mores, and political exigencies to facilitate and encourage cross-racial sexual relationships. These connections, and their reproductive consequences, almost always comported with Anglo-Texan supremacy.

The development of Texas society and law involved much more than the cooperative response of freedom-seeking homesteaders to harsh ecological circumstances and the unwavering guidance of sage law-givers. Legal concepts regarding real estate, contracts, marriage, illegitimacy, and inheritance arrived with immigrants to influence how they and their rudimentary institutions dealt with settlement, each other, and those they dispossessed and subjugated. To provide socio-economic coherence for a rapidly developing pioneer community, however, Anglo-Texan officials had to refashion rules about matrimony, informal cohabitation, bastardy, adultery, and bigamy to ameliorate the often aberrant mating behavior of a virtual swarm of exceedingly ambitious and ungovernable homesteaders. In essence, immigrant women and men responded vigorously to generous land-grant opportunities to achieve their self-interested economic and personal goals, but often in ways that lawmakers had neither intended nor anticipated. Texas society and law thus developed reciprocally, symbiotically, and experimentally. Viewing law as a tool for shaping social and economic change, instrumentalist justices frequently employed old doctrines selectively, creatively, and pragmatically to deal with the social dysfunctions that expansionist policies and maladapted matrimonial law had helped to create. Legislators and constitutional delegates, however, had the relative luxury of picking and choosing precepts formulated in other jurisdictions, or inventing new rules out of whole cloth, to improve the social order, an arrangement that consistently maintained Anglo-Texan families on top.

Notes

INTRODUCTION

1. *Lewis v. Ames,* 44 Tex. 323 (1875); James R. Norvell, "Lewis v. Ames— An Ancient Cause Revisited," *Southwestern Law Journal* 13(3)(summer 1959): 310; Harriet Ames, *The History of Harriet Ames* (1842), ch. 17. A typewritten manuscript of the unpublished Ames narrative is in the Texas State Archives at Austin.

2. Norvell, "An Ancient Cause Revisited," 310–14; Stephen L. Hardin, "'A Hard Lot': Texas Women in the Runaway Scrape," *East Texas Historical Journal* 29(1)(1991): 35–45.

3. C. L. Douglas, *Famous Texas Feuds* (Dallas: Turner Co., 1936), 50–57; Norvell, "An Ancient Cause Revisited," 307, 313–14.

4. Olivier Zunz, "The Synthesis of Social Change: Reflections on American Social History," in *Reliving the Past: The Worlds of Social History,* ed. Olivier Zunz (Chapel Hill: University of North Carolina Press, 1985), 53–114.

5. For a review of the scholarship through the late 1980s, see Steven Mintz, "Regulating the American Family," *Journal of Family History* 14(1989): 387–408; idem, "Children, Families, and the State: American Family Law in Historical Perspective," *Denver University Law Review* 69 (1992): 635–61.

6. Michael Grossberg, *Governing the Hearth: Law and the Family in Nineteenth-Century America* (Chapel Hill: University of North Carolina Press, 1985).

7. Peter W. Bardaglio, *Reconstructing the Household: Families, Sex, and the Law in the Nineteenth-Century South* (Chapel Hill: University of North Carolina Press, 1995).

8. *Ibid.,* xi–xiii.

9. *Ibid.,* xi–xv, 27, 106. For a Marxian version of this model, see

Eugene D. Genovese, "The Hegemonic Function of the Law," in *Roll, Jordan, Roll: The World the Slaves Made* (New York: Random House, 1974), 25–49.

10. Prominent works emphasizing patriarchy and the cult of male honor include Catherine Clinton, *The Plantation Mistress: Woman's World in the Old South* (New York: Pantheon, 1982); Bertram Wyatt-Brown, *Southern Honor: Ethics and Behavior in the Old South* (New York: Oxford University Press, 1982); and Jane Turner Censer, "'Smiling through Her Tears': Antebellum Southern Women and Divorce," *American Journal of Legal History* 25(1)(1981): 24–47. For monographs that emphasize the influence of egalitarianism and domesticity, see Jan Lewis, *The Pursuit of Happiness: Family and Values in Jefferson's Virginia* (New York: Cambridge University Press, 1983); Jane Turner Censer, *North Carolina Planters and Their Children, 1800–1860* (Baton Rouge: Louisiana State University Press, 1984); and Daniel Blake Smith, *In the Great House: Planter Family Life in Eighteenth-century Chesapeake Society.* (Ithaca: Cornell University Press, 1980).

11. Victorian Bynum, *Unruly Women: The Politics of Sexual and Social Control in the Old South* (Chapel Hill: University of North Carolina Press, 1992).

12. Suzanne Lebsock, *The Free Women of Petersburg: Status and Culture in a Southern Town, 1784–1860* (New York: Norton, 1984).

13. Joan Wallach Scott, *Gender and the Politics of History* (New York: Columbia University Press, 1988).

14. Natalie Zemon Davis, "Women's History in Transition: The European Case," *Feminist Studies* 3 (1975–76): 90; Joan Wallach Scott, *Gender and the Politics of History,* 28–50; Susan Bordo, "Feminism, Postmodernism, and Gender-Skepticism," in *Feminism/Postmodernism,* ed. Linda J. Nicholson (New York: Routledge, 1990), 133–56.

15. Joan Cashin, *A Family Venture: Men and Women on the Southern Frontier* (New York: Oxford University Press, 1991).

16. Philip Mason, *Patterns of Dominance* (New York: Oxford University Press, 1970).

17. George M. Fredrickson, *White Supremacy: A Comparative Study in American and South African History* (New York: Oxford University Press, 1982).

18. Edward Said, *Orientalism* (New York: Pantheon, 1978); Robert Young, *White Mythologies: Writing History and the West* (London: Routledge, 1990); Bart Moore-Gilbert, *Postcolonial Theory: Contexts, Practices, and Politics* (London: Verso, 1997); Ann Brooks, *Postfeminisms: Feminism, Cultural Theory and Cultural Forms* (London: Routledge, 1997).

19. Scott, *Gender and the Politics of History,* 32–33; Anthony Giddens et al., *The Polity Reader in Gender Studies* (Cambridge: Polity Press in association with Blackwell Publishers, 1994), 1–4. See also Susan B. Boyd, ed., *Challenging*

the Public/Private Divide: Feminism, Law, and Public Policy (Toronto: University of Toronto Press, 1997).

20. Kathleen M. Brown, *Good Wives, Nasty Wenches, and Anxious Patriarchs: Gender, Race, and Power in Colonial Virginia* (Chapel Hill: University of North Carolina Press, 1996); Catherine Clinton and Michelle Gillespie, eds., *The Devil's Lane: Sex and Race in the Early South* (New York: Oxford University Press, 1997).

21. Mark Tushnet, "The American Law of Slavery, 1810–1860: A Study in the Persistence of Legal Autonomy," *Law and Society Review* 10 (fall 1975): 110–86.

22. James Willard Hurst, *Law and the Conditions of Freedom in the Nineteenth-Century United States* (Madison: University of Wisconsin Press, 1956); Kermit Hall, *The Magic Mirror: Law in American History* (New York: Oxford University Press, 1989).

23. S. F. C. Milsom, *Historical Foundations of the Common Law* (London: Butterworths, 1969); Robert C. Palmer, *The Whilton Dispute, 1264–1380: A Social and Legal Study of Dispute Settlement in Medieval England* (Princeton, N.J.: Princeton University Press, 1984); idem, *The County Courts of Medieval England, 1150–1350* (Princeton, N.J.: Princeton University Press, 1986); idem, *English Common Law in the Age of the Black Death, 1348–1381: A Transformation in Governance and Law* (Chapel Hill: University of North Carolina Press, 1993); William E. Nelson and Robert C. Palmer, *Liberty and Community: Constitution and Rights in the Early American Republic* (New York: Oceana Publications, 1987). See also Robert W. Gordon, "Critical Legal Histories," *Stanford Law Review* 36 (January 1984): 57–125.

24. Lewis W. Newton and Herbert P. Gambrell, *A Social and Political History of Texas* (Dallas: Turner Co., 1935); William R. Hogan, *The Texas Republic: A Social and Economic History* (Norman: University of Oklahoma Press, 1946); Stanley Siegel, *A Political History of the Texas Republic, 1836–1845* (Austin: University of Texas Press, 1956); Mark Nackman, *A Nation within a Nation: The Rise of Texas Nationalism* (Port Washington, N.Y.: Kennikat Press, 1975); Margaret Henson, *Anglo-American Women in Texas, 1820–1850* (Boston: American Press, 1982); Florence G. Gould and Patricia Pando, *Claiming Their Land: Women Homesteaders in Texas* (El Paso: Texas Western Press, 1991); Margaret S. Henson and Deolece Parmelee, *The Cartwrights of San Augustine: Three Generations of Agrarian Entrepreneurs in Nineteenth-Century Texas* (Austin: University of Texas Press, 1993).

25. Joseph W. McKnight, "Texas Community Property Law: Conservative Attitudes, Reluctant Change," *Law and Contemporary Problems* 56(2) (spring 1993): 71–98; James W. Paulsen, "Remember the Alamo(ny)! The

Unique Texas Ban on Permanent Alimony and the Development of Community Property Law," *Law and Contemporary Problems* 56(2)(spring 1993): 7—70; Michael J. Vaughn, "The Policy of Community Property and Inter-Spousal Transaction," *Baylor Law Review* 19 (1967): 20—33.

26. Harold Schoen, "The Free Negro in the Republic of Texas," *Southwestern Historical Quarterly* 39(4)(April 1936): 292—308; 40(1)(July 1936): 26—34; 40(2)(October 1936): 85—113; 40(3)(January 1937): 169—99; 40(4)(April 1937): 267—89; 41(1)(July 1937): 83—108; Ann Patton Malone, *Women on the Texas Frontier: A Cross-Cultural Perspective* (El Paso: Texas Western Press, 1983).

27. Jane Dysart, "Mexican Women in San Antonio: The Assimilation Process, 1830—1860," *Western Historical Quarterly* 7 (October 1976): 365—75; Arnoldo De León, *They Called Them Greasers: Anglo Attitudes toward Mexicans in Texas, 1821—1900* (Austin: University of Texas Press, 1983).

CHAPTER I

1. Joseph Milton Nance, *Attack and Counterattack: The Texas-Mexican Frontier, 1842* (Austin: University of Texas Press, 1964), 304; Frederick C. Chabot, *With the Makers of San Antonio* (San Antonio: privately published, 1937; printing by Artes Gráficas), 171—74; *Smith v. Smith*, 1 Tex. 624 (1846).

2. Amelia W. Williams and Eugene C. Barker, eds., *The Writings of Sam Houston, 1813—1863*, 8 vols. (Austin: University of Texas Press, 1943), 3:278; M. L. Crimmins, "John W. Smith: The Last Messenger from the Alamo and the First Mayor of San Antonio," *Southwestern Historical Quarterly* 54 (1950—51): 344—46; James Ernest Crisp, "Anglo-Texan Attitudes toward the Mexican, 1821—1845" (Ph.D. diss., Yale University, New Haven, May 1976), 155.

3. *Smith*, 1 Tex. at 622—23; "Obituary of the Honorable John W. Smith," in *Texas National Register*, 18 January 1845.

4. *Lee v. Smith*, 18 Tex. at 143—47 (1856); *Smith*, 1 Tex. at 622.

5. In this book, a Tejana is a Mexican woman or a woman of Mexican ancestry residing in Texas.

6. U.S. Bureau of Statistics, *Statistical Abstract of the United States, 1907* (Washington, D.C.: U.S. Government Printing Office, 1907), 34; U.S. Bureau of the Census, *The Seventh Census of the United States: 1850* (Washington, D.C. Robert Armstrong, 1853), 493; Terry G. Jordan, John L. Bean, and William M. Holmes, *Texas: A Geography* (Boulder: Westview Press, 1984), 48, 89; Homer V. Kerr, "Migration to Texas, 1860—1880," *Southwestern Historical Quarterly* 70 (1966): 184—216; Terry Jordan, "Population Origins of Texas, 1850," *Geographical Review* 59 (1969): 85.

7. Williamson S. Oldham and George W. White, comps. and eds., *A Digest of General Statutes and Laws of the State of Texas* (Austin: J. Marshall

and Co., 1854), Colonization Law of 24 March 1825, arts. 12–16, 22, 26, pp. 763–65; H. P. N. Gammel, comp., *The Laws of Texas, 1822–1897,* 10 vols. (Austin: Gammel Book Co., 1898), Act of 22 December 1836, sec. 24, 1:223; Act of 14 December 1837, secs. 23, 29, 30, 1:71–73; Act of 22 January 1845, 2:1075; Act of 7 February 1853, 3:1550–52; Act of 13 February 1854, 4:474; John Sayles and Henry Sayles, eds., *Early Laws of Texas* (Saint Louis: Gilbert Book Co., 1888), 18; Michael Q. Hooks and Jesús F. de la Tejá, "The Texas General Land Office: Preserving East Texas Land Records," *East Texas Historical Journal,* 27(1)(1989): 55–62.

8. Newton and Gambrell, *A Social and Political History,* 113; Jean L. Epperson, "Notes and Documents: 1834 Census—Anáhuac Precinct, Atascosito District," *Southwestern Historical Quarterly* 92(3)(January 1989): 437–47; Corrie Pattison Haskew, "1850 Census, Austin County, Texas," *Historical Records of Austin and Waller Counties* (Houston: Premier Printing and Letter Service, 1989), 75–84.

9. Frank Louis Halla, Jr., "El Paso, Texas, and Juárez, Mexico: A Study of a Bi-Ethnic Community, 1846–1881" (Ph.D. diss., University of Texas, Austin, December 1978), 64.

10. Oldham and White, *A Digest,* Colonization Law of 4 January 1823, art. 27, p. 761; Colonization Law of 24 March 1825, arts. 15, 31, p. 765.

11. De León, *They Called Them Greasers,* 5–6, 20, 36; Newton and Gambrell, *A Social and Political History,* 46.

12. Jordan et al., *Texas: A Geography,* 58; Mark E. Nackman, "Anglo-American Migrants to the West: Men of Broken Fortunes? The Case of Texas, 1821–46," *Western Historical Quarterly* 5 (October 1974): 446–48; Cashin, *A Family Venture,* 48; Henry F. Foster, "Indian and Common Law Marriages," in *Law, Society, and Domestic Relations,* ed. Kermit Hall (New York: Garland Publishing, 1987), 87.

13. General Mier y Terán to President Guadalupe Victoria, Nacogdoches, 30 June 1828, "Mexican Policy on Immigration to Texas," in *A Documentary History of the Mexican Americans,* ed. Wayne Moguin and Charles Van Doren (New York: Praeger, 1971), 142; Siegel, *A Political History of the Texas Republic,* 6; Edmund S. Morgan, *American Slavery, American Freedom: The Ordeal of Colonial Virginia* (New York: Norton, 1975), 316–38. See also Michael Ignatieff, *Journeys into the New Nationalism* (New York: Farrar, Strauss and Giroux, 1994).

14. Cashin, *A Family Venture,* 32, 99, 102–105; Dysart, "Mexican Women," 367. For particularly candid reports, see *The Diary of William Barrett Travis, August 30, 1833–June 26, 1834,* ed. Robert E. Davis (Waco: Texian Press, 1966).

15. Odie B. Faulk, "The Comanche Invasion of Texas, 1743–1836," *Great Plains Journal* 9(1)(fall 1969): 20; Diana Everett, *The Texas Cherokees: A People*

between Two Fires (Norman: University of Oklahoma Press, 1990), 19–22, 29, 52; Hogan, *The Texas Republic*, 14–15, 103; William W. Newcombe, Jr., *The Indians of Texas: From Prehistoric to Modern Times* (Austin: University of Texas Press, 1961), 340–43; F. Todd Smith, "Kadohadacho Indians and the Louisiana-Texas Frontier, 1803–1815," *Southwestern Historical Quarterly* 95(2)(1991): 176–204; Nancy Bonvillain, "Gender Relations in Native North America," *American Indian Culture and Research Journal* 13(2)(1989): 1–28.

16. Theda Perdue, "Columbus Meets Pocahontas in the American South," *Southern Culture* 3(1)(1977): 4–21.

17. Francis S. Latham, *Travels in the Republic of Texas, 1842*, ed. Gerald S. Pierce (Austin: Encino Press, 1971), 31–32. See also George W. Kendall, *Narrative of an Expedition across the Southwestern Prairies, from Texas to Santa Fe*, 2 vols. (London: D. Bogue, 1845), 2:428.

18. David D. Smits, "Abominable Mixture: Toward the Repudiation of Anglo-Indian Intermarriage in Seventeenth-Century Virginia," *Virginia Magazine of History and Biography* 95(2)(1987): 159–66, 170–71, 188; De León, *They Called Them Greasers*, 5, 36, 63.

19. Gary B. Nash, *Red, White, and Black: The Peoples of Early America*, 2d ed. (Englewood Cliffs, N.J.: Prentice Hall, 1982), 65, 86, 105–106, 150–51, 162–63, 193, 241, 277; Gilberto M. Hinojosa, "The Religious-Indian Communities: The Goals of the Friars," in *Tejano Origins in Eighteenth-Century San Antonio*, ed. Gerald E. Poyo and Gilberto M. Hinojosa (Austin: University of Texas, 1991), 61; Gilberto M. Hinojosa and Anne A. Fox, "Indians and Their Culture in San Fernando de Béxar," in *Tejano Origins*, 107–108; De León, *They Called Them Greasers*, 6–9, 15, 19–20, 36, 63; Elizabeth A. John, "Independent Indians and the San Antonio Community," in *Tejano Origins*, 123–24; Gordon Bronitsky, "Indian Assimilation in the El Paso Area," *New Mexico Historical Review* 62(2)(1987): 151–68.

20. Williams and Barker, *The Writings of Sam Houston*, 7:340; Chabot, *With the Makers of San Antonio*, 314–18; Jack Gregory and Rennard Strickland, *Sam Houston with the Cherokees, 1829–1833* (Austin: University of Texas Press, 1967), 42; Alicia V. Tjarks, "Comparative Demographic Analysis of Texas, 1777–1793," *Southwestern Historical Quarterly* 77 (January 1974): 291–388; Andrew Anthony Tijerina, "Tejanos and Texas: The Native Mexicans of Texas, 1820–1850" (Ph.D. diss., University of Texas, Austin, 1977), 10–14, 37–39, 44–45; De León, *They Called Them Greasers*, 6, 19; Elizabeth A. H. John, "Portrait of a Wichita Village, 1808," *Chronicles of Oklahoma* 60(4)(1982–83): 412–15; Alfred M. Williams, "Life among the Cherokees," *Lippincott's Magazine*, 27 (February 1881): 200.

21. "Treaty of Bird's Fort, September 29, 1843," in *Texas Indian Papers*, ed.

Dorman H. Winfrey and James M. Day (Austin: Pemberton Press, 1966), 1: 24–26; Everett, *The Texas Cherokees*, 99, 105–18. See generally Kelly Frank Himmel, "Anglo-Texans, Karankawas, and Tonkawas, 1821–1859: A Sociological Analysis of Conquest" (Ph.D. diss., University of Texas, Austin, 1995).

22. Richard Irving Dodge, *Our Wild Indians: Thirty-three Years' Personal Experience among the Red Men of the Great West* (New York: Archer House, 1959), 198, 205, 211, 217–18; Jean Louis Berlandier, *The Indians of Texas in 1830*, ed. John C. Ewers, trans. Patricia Reading Leclercq (Washington, D.C.: Smithsonian Institution Press, 1969), 35, 37; Noah Smithwick, *The Evolution of a State; or, Recollections of Old Texas Days* (Austin: Gammel Book Co., 1900; reprint, Austin: W. Thomas Naylor, 1995), 131; John, "Portrait of a Wichita Village," 416–37; Newcombe, *The Indians of Texas*, 301; Thomas Schilz and Jayde Lynn Dickson, "Amazons, Witches, and 'Country Wives': Plains Indian Women in Historical Perspective," *Annals of Wyoming* 59(1)(1987): 48–56.

23. David G. Burnet, "The Comanches and Other Tribes of Texas and the Policy to Be Pursued Respecting Them," in *Ethnology of the Texas Indians*, ed. Thomas R. Hester (New York: Garland Publishing, 1991), 264; Albert S. Gilles, Jr., "Polygamy in Comanche Country," *Southwest Review* 51 (summer 1966): 294; Sylvia Vankirk, "The Role of Native Women in the Fur Trade Society of Western Canada," *Frontiers* 7(3)(1984): 10.

24. Burnet, "The Comanches and Other Tribes," 235; Malone, *Women on the Texas Frontier*, 6; Newcombe, *The Indians of Texas*, 72, 180–85, 200–208, 269; Dan McPike, "Native American Women of the West," *Gilcrease Magazine of American History and Art* 13(3)(1991): 28–30.

25. Dysart, "Mexican Women," 368–69; Woodrow Borah and Sherburne F. Cook, "Marriage and Legitimacy in Mexican Culture: Mexico and California," *California Law Review* 54 (May 1966): 960–61.

26. De León, *They Called Them Greasers*, 6; Jesús F. de la Tejá, "Forgotten Founders: The Military Settlers of Eighteenth-Century San Antonio de Béxar," in *Tejano Origins*, 33; Jesús F. de la Tejá and John Wheat, "Béxar: Profile of a Tejano Community, 1820–1832," in *Tejano Origins*, 2–5; Gerald E. Poyo, "Immigrants and Integration in Late Eighteenth-Century Béxar," in *Tejano Origins*, 96–97; Jesús F. de la Tejá, *San Antonio de Béxar: A Community on New Spain's Northern Frontier* (Albuquerque: University of New Mexico Press, 1995), 100–23; Gerald E. Poyo, "The Canary Islands Immigrants of San Antonio: From Ethnic Exclusivity to Community in Eighteenth-Century Béxar," in *Tejano Origins*, 46.

27. Dysart, "Mexican Women," 367–68; de la Tejá and Wheat, "Béxar: Profile of a Tejano Community," 2–5; De León, *They Called Them Greasers*, 6; Tijerina, "Tejanos and Texas," 10–14, 37–39, 44–45; Tjarks, "Comparative

Demographic Analysis," 310; David T. Courtwright, *Violent Land: Single Men and Social Disorder from the Frontier to the Inner City* (Cambridge, Mass.: Harvard University Press, 1996), 65.

28. Dysart, "Mexican Women," 364-68.

29. Kendall, *Narrative of an Expedition,* 1:46-48; Ferdinand Roemer, *Texas with Particular Reference to German Immigration and the Physical Appearance of the Country,* trans. Oswald Mueller (San Antonio: Standard Printing Co., 1935), 121-25; W. Eugene Holland and Ruth Lapham Butler, eds., *William Bollaert's Texas* (Norman: University of Oklahoma Press, 1956), 217-19; Aaron M. Boom, ed., "Texas in the 1850s, as Viewed by a Recent Arrival," *Southwestern Historical Quarterly* 70 (October 1966): 283-84; Dysart, "Mexican Women," 367-68.

30. Frederick Law Olmstead, *A Journey through Texas; or, A Saddle-Trip on the Southwestern Frontier* (New York: Mason Brothers, 1860; reprint, Austin: University of Texas Press, 1978), 151-52; Crisp, "Anglo-Texan Attitudes," 152; De León, *They Called Them Greasers,* 10, 36-39, 43.

31. Latham, *Travels in the Republic of Texas,* 37-38.

32. Quoted in De León, *They Called Them Greasers,* 37.

33. Dysart, "Mexican Women," 365-75; Frank D. Bean and Benjamin S. Bradshaw, "Intermarriage between Persons of Spanish and Non-Spanish Surname: Changes from the Mid-Twentieth Century," *Social Science Quarterly* 51 (September 1970): 389-94; *idem,* "An Exploratory Study of Intermarriage between Mexican Americans and Anglo Americans, 1850-1960," *Southwestern Sociological Association Proceedings* (1970): 120-25; De León, *They Called Them Greasers,* 44; Jovita Gonzales, "Social Life in Cameron, Starr, and Zapata Counties" (M.A. thesis, University of Texas, Austin, 1930), 26-27, 102-106.

34. Gammel, *Laws,* Act of 21 December 1836, sec. 23, 1:1250; Texas, *Penal Code* (1857), art. 392; Gammel, *Laws,* Act of 12 February 1858, 4:1037; Borah and Cook, "Marriage and Legitimacy," 960-63; Dysart, "Mexican Women," 369.

35. David C. Humphrey, "Prostitution in Texas: From the 1830s to the 1960s," *East Texas Historical Journal* 33 (1995): 27-43; James F. Elliott, "The Great Western: Sarah Bowman, Mother and Mistress to the U. S. Army," *Journal of Arizona History* 30(1)(spring 1989): 1-26; Anne M. Butler, *Daughters of Joy, Sisters of Misery: Prostitutes in the American West, 1865-1890* (Urbana: University of Illinois Press, 1985), 4. See generally Jan Hutson, *The Chicken Ranch: The True Story of the Best Little Whorehouse in Texas* (New York, 1980), and H. Gordon Frost, *The Gentlemen's Club: The Story of Prostitution in El Paso* (El Paso: Mangan Books, 1983).

36. Quoted in De León, *They Called Them Greasers,* 43.

37. Kendall, *Narrative of an Expedition,* 2:422.

38. Olmstead, *A Journey through Texas,* 161.

39. William Physick Zuber, *My Eighty Years in Texas*, ed. Janis Boyle Mayfield (Austin: University of Texas Press, 1971), 23.

40. De León, *They Called Them Greasers*, 36–48.

41. De la Tejá, *San Antonio de Béxar*, 27–29; Poyo, "Immigrants and Integration," 86–87; *idem*, "The Canary Islands Immigrants," 47; Borah and Cook, "Marriage and Legitimacy," 960–61.

42. Halla, "El Paso, Texas," 105–107, 130; Dysart, "Mexican Women," 366–67; Robert C. Hunt, "Components of Relationships in the Family: A Mexican Village," in *Kinship and Culture*, ed. Francis Hsu (Chicago: Aldine, 1971), 114–17, 126, 134–37; Santiago Ramirez and Ramón Farres, "Some Dynamic Patterns in the Organization of the Mexican Family," *International Journal of Social Psychiatry* 3 (summer 1957): 18–21.

43. Latham, *Travels in the Republic of Texas*, 37.

44. Crisp, "Anglo-Texan Attitudes," 152.

45. *Ibid.*, 155–57; Dysart, "Mexican Women," 366.

46. Frederick C. Chabot, ed., *The Perote Prisoners: Being the Diary of James L. Trueheart....* (San Antonio: Naylor Co., 1934), 8; *idem, With the Makers of San Antonio*, 243–55; Smithwick, *The Evolution of a State*, 97; Williams and Barker, *The Writings of Sam Houston*, 1:306, 323–25, 339–47, 363–64; Bean and Bradshaw, "Intermarriage," 390–95; Carland Elaine Crook, "San Antonio, Texas, 1846–1861" (M.A. thesis, Rice University, Houston, 1964), ch. 2; Dysart, "Mexican Women," 369–70; Crisp, "Anglo-Texan Attitudes," 155–57.

47. Boom, "Texas in the 1850s," 283; Dysart, "Mexican Women," 370–71.

48. Chabot, *The Perote Prisoners*, 8; *idem, With the Makers of San Antonio*, 202–206, 274–76; *Corpus Christi Caller*, 28 April 1893, 5 May 1893; Williams and Barker, *The Writings of Sam Houston*, 3:278; Crisp, "Anglo-Texan Attitudes," 155; Crystal Sasse Ragsdale, *The Women and Children of the Alamo* (Austin: State House Press, 1994), 27–41.

49. Chabot, *The Perote Prisoners*, 2–3; Dysart, "Mexican Women," 370.

CHAPTER 2

1. Williams and Barker, *The Writings of Sam Houston*, 1:30; John Hoyt Williams, *Sam Houston: A Biography of the Father of Texas* (New York: Simon and Schuster, 1993), 64; Martha Anne Turner, *Sam Houston and His Twelve Women: The Ladies Who Influenced the Life of Texas' Greatest Statesman* (Austin: Pemberton Press, 1966), 14–19; Gregory and Strickland, *Sam Houston with the Cherokees*, 33, 44, 134–35, 157–64.

2. Gregory and Strickland, *Sam Houston with the Cherokees*, 84, 96–116, 126–31, 134–35, 157–64; Turner, *Sam Houston and His Twelve Women*, 16–18, 21; Marquis James, *The Raven: A Biography of Sam Houston* (Indianapolis: Bobbs-Merrill, 1929), 157, 183; Alfred M. Williams, "Houston's Life among the

Indians," *Magazine of American History* 10 (November 1883): 406–408; James F. Corn, "Sam Houston, the Raven," *Journal of Cherokee Studies* 6(1)(1981): 34–39.

3. Williams and Barker, *The Writings of Sam Houston,* 1:277–79; Gregory and Strickland, *Sam Houston with the Cherokees,* 48–50, 84–85, 157–64; Turner, *Sam Houston and His Twelve Women,* 16–17, 29–30, 35, 40–43, 61–64; James, *The Raven,* 199, 277, 299–300, 314; Williams, *Sam Houston: A Biography,* 10; Paulsen, "Remember the Alamo(ny)!" 9–12; Dorman Winfrey, "Chief Bowles of the Texas Cherokees," *Chronicles of Oklahoma* 8 (spring 1954): 35.

4. Gregory and Strickland, *Sam Houston with the Cherokees,* 32.

5. *Ibid.,* 42–43, 86–87; Alfred M. Williams, *Sam Houston and the War of Independence of Texas* (Boston: Houghton, Mifflin, 1893), 51.

6. Berlandier, *The Indians of Texas in 1830,* 35; Foster, "Indian and Common Law Marriages," 89–96; Newcombe, *The Indians of Texas,* 201; Andre F. Sjoberg, "Lipan Apache Culture in Historical Perspective," *Southwestern Journal of Anthropology* 9 (1953): 91–92.

7. Dodge, *Our Wild Indians,* 197; Newcombe, *The Indians of Texas,* 141–42, 170, 262, 267, 299; Susan M. Hartmann, "Women's Work among Plains Indians," *Gateway Heritage* 3(4)(1983): 2–9; Sjoberg, "Lipan Apache Culture," 91; Morris E. Opler, "The Lipan Apaches' Death Complex and Its Extensions," *Southwestern Journal of Anthropology* 1 (spring 1945): 122–41.

8. Berlandier, *The Indians of Texas in 1830,* 35; Malone, *Women on the Texas Frontier,* 6; Everett, *The Texas Cherokees,* 111; Sjoberg, "Lipan Apache Culture," 92; *idem,* "The Culture of the Tonkawa: A Texas Indian Tribe," *Texas Journal of Science* 5(3)(1953): 290; Newcombe, *The Indians of Texas,* 121, 141–43, 170, 201–202, 267, 301; Gilles, "Polygamy in Comanche Country," 291.

9. Berlandier, *The Indians of Texas in 1830,* 36; William W. Newcombe, Jr., "Karankawa," in *Handbook of North American Indians,* vol. 10, ed. Alfonso Ortiz (Washington, D.C.: Smithsonian Institution, 1978), 359–67; Malone, *Women on the Texas Frontier,* 6; Newcombe, *The Indians of Texas,* 170.

10. Dodge, *Our Wild Indians,* 206–207, 213; Burnet, "The Comanches and Other Tribes," 265; Newcombe, *The Indians of Texas,* 301; Foster, "Indian and Common Law Marriages," 89–96.

11. Dodge, *Our Wild Indians,* 206–10; Newcombe, *The Indians of Texas,* 201–203.

12. Dodge, *Our Wild Indians,* 194, 198, 205; Burnet, "The Comanches and Other Tribes," 264; Joel Prentiss Bishop, *Commentaries on the Law of Marriage and Divorce,* 2 vols. (Boston: Little, Brown, 1881), 1:184–91; Berlandier, *The Indians of Texas in 1830,* 36, 61; Foster, "Indian and Common Law Marriages," 88–89; De León, *They Called Them Greasers,* 2–5; Gilles, "Polygamy in Comanche Country," 286–97.

13. Bishop, *Commentaries* (1881), 1:21–47; Foster, "Indian and Common Law Marriages," 88–89; Grossberg, *Governing the Hearth,* 18–19, 34–38.

14. Dodge, *Our Wild Indians,* 208–209.

15. Smithwick, *The Evolution of a State,* 130; Dodge, *Our Wild Indians,* 207–10, 213, 219; Newcombe, *The Indians of Texas,* 44, 70, 123, 141–42, 172, 201–203, 263, 301; Sjoberg, "The Culture of the Tonkawa," 286–90; Foster, "Indian and Common Law Marriages," 89–90.

16. Dodge, *Our Wild Indians,* 219; Cashin, *A Family Venture,* 106; Gregory and Strickland, *Sam Houston with the Cherokees,* 33, 36, 48, 84–85; Albert V. Goodpasture, "The Paternity of Sequoyah," *Chronicles of Oklahoma* 1 (October 1921): 129; A. M. Murchison, "Intermarried Whites in the Cherokee Nation, 1865–1887," *Chronicles of Oklahoma* 6 (September 1928): 299.

17. Mason, *Patterns of Dominance,* 81–83; Fredrickson, *White Supremacy,* 94–135.

18. *Morgan v. McGhee,* 5 Humph. 13 (Tenn. 1844); *Johnson v. Johnson's Administrator,* 30 Mo. 72 (1860); *Boyer v. Dively,* 58 Mo. 510 (1875); *Kelly v. County of Kitsap,* 5 Wash. 521 (1893); *Follansbee v. Wilbur,* 14 Wash. 242, 44 Pac. 262 (1896); *La Riviere v. La Riviere,* 97 Mo. 80, 10 S.W. 840 (1896); *Kobagum v. Jackson Iron Co.,* 76 Mich. 498, 43 N.W. 602 (1889); *Earl v. Godley,* 42 Minn. 361, 44 N.W. 254 (1890); *Roche v. Washington,* 19 Ind. 53 (1862); *State v. Ta-cha-na-tah,* 64 N.C. 614 (1870); Bishop, *Commentaries* (1881), 1:184–87; Foster, "Indian and Common Law Marriages," 83–102.

19. *Jones v. Laney et al.,* 2 Tex. 348 (1847); *Tarpley v. Poage's Administrator,* 2 Tex. 136 (1847).

20. Gammel, *Laws,* Act of 20 January 1840, 2:177–78; *Grigsby v. Reib,* 105 Tex. 597 (1913); Ford W. Hall, "An Account of the Adoption of the Common Law by Texas," *Texas Law Review* 28 (1950): 808–18.

21. *G. M. Patterson v. W. T. Patterson* (Travis County District Court, Cause No. 10,393); *Estate of Wm. T. Patterson* (Travis County District Court, Cause No. 11,078).

22. *First National Bank of Austin v. Sharpe,* 12 Tex. Civ. App. [3d Dist.] 225, 335 S.W. 676 (1896).

23. Most jurisdictions of the United States had adopted the procedure by the Civil War. Grossberg, *Governing the Hearth,* 215–18. When the United States Supreme Court compelled Texas to do so in 1973, it was the last state in the Union not to have an affiliation procedure through which an unwed mother might establish the paternity of her child. See *Gomez v. Perez,* 409 U.S. 535 (1973); Comment, "The Rights of an Illegitimate Child," *Saint Mary's Law Journal* 12 (1980): 199.

24. Texas (Republic) *Constitution,* General Provisions, § 10; Gammel,

Laws, Act of 14 January 1840, sec. 2, 2:197; Texas, *Constitution* (1845), Art. III, §§ 1 and 2; Gammel, *Laws*, Joint Resolution of 29 April 1846, sec. 15, 2:155; Crisp, "Anglo-Texan Attitudes," 140–48, 209–15, 337; Anna Muckleroy, "The Indian Policy of the Republic of Texas," *Southwestern Historical Quarterly* 25(4)(April 1922): 230–60; Siegel, *A Political History of the Texas Republic*, 39, 107–109, 166; Everett, *The Texas Cherokees*, 99, 108–10; Jere Franco, "The Alabama-Coushatta and Their Texas Friends," *East Texas Historical Journal* 27(1)(1989): 31–43.

25. Sidney Kaplan, "Historical Efforts to Encourage White-Indian Inter-marriage in the United States and Canada," *International Social Science Review* 65(3)(1990): 126–28; Bernard W. Sheehan, *Seeds of Extinction: Jeffersonian Philanthropy and the American Indian* (Chapel Hill: University of North Carolina Press, 1973), 183–275; Robert E. Beider, "Scientific Attitudes toward Indian Mixed-Bloods in Early Nineteenth Century America," *Journal of Ethnic Studies* 8(2)(1980): 18.

26. Quoted in Fawn Brodie, *Thomas Jefferson: An Intimate History* (New York: Norton, 1974), 434.

27. William Stanton, *The Leopard's Spots: Scientific Attitudes toward Race in America, 1815–59* (Chicago: University of Chicago Press, 1960), 3–14; Beider, "Scientific Attitudes," 1–23; see generally Samuel G. Morton, *Crania Americana; or, A Comparative View of the Skulls of Various Aboriginal Nations of North and South America: To Which is Prefixed an Essay on the Varieties of the Human Species* (Philadelphia: J. Dobson, 1839; London: Simpkin and Marshall, 1839); Josiah C. Nott and George Gliddon, *Indigenous Races of the Earth; or New Chapters of Ethnological Enquiry* (Philadelphia: J. B. Lippincott, 1857). See also Thomas E. Will, "The American School of Ethnology: Science and Scripture in the Proslavery Argument," *Southern Historian* 19 (1998): 14–34.

28. Texas, *Journals of the Sixth Congress of the Republic of Texas*, 3 vols., ed. Harriet Smither (Austin: Von Boeckmann-Jones Co., 1940–45), "Report of the Secretary of War [Branch T. Archer]," 30 September 1841, 3:358; Crisp, "Anglo-Texan Attitudes," 122.

29. Texas, *House Journal, Third Congress*, "Message of President [Mirabeau B.] Lamar to Congress," 20 December 1838, 173–74. See also Mirabeau B. Lamar, "Second Annual Message to Congress," 12 November 1839, in *The Papers of Mirabeau Buonaparte Lamar*, 6 vols., ed. Charles A. Gulick, Jr. et al. (Austin: A. C. Baldwin, Printers, 1920–27), 3:167.

30. *Texas Sentinel* (Austin), 22 January 1840, 1 May 1840.

31. *Morning Star* (Houston), 21 January 1843, 26 January 1843; Stanton, *The Leopard's Spots*, 3–14, 31–34.

32. Roy Harvey Pearce, *The Savages of America: A Study of the Indian and*

the Idea of Civilization (Baltimore: Johns Hopkins Press, 1965), 3–5; Robert F. Berkhofer, Jr., *The White Man's Indian* (New York: Knopf, 1978), 2, 23–28.

33. A. J. Sowell, *Rangers and Pioneers of Texas* (1884) (New York: Argosy-Antiquarian, 1964), 7–9.

34. *Ibid.*, 10.

35. Gammel, *Laws*, Act of 5 June 1837, sec. 9, 1:233; Texas, *Penal Code* (1857), art. 386, p. 72; Gammel, *Laws*, Act of 12 February 1858, 4:164–65.

36. Gammel, *Laws*, Act of 21 December 1836, sec. 23, 1:1250; Texas, *Penal Code* (1857), Art. 392; Gammel, *Laws*, Act of 12 February 1858, 4:1037.

37. *Jones v. Laney*, 2 Tex. at 348.

38. *Medway v. Natick*, 7 Mass. 88 (1810); *Medway v. Needham*, 16 Mass. 157 (1819); *State v. Fore*, 1 Ired. 378 (N.C. 1841); *State v. Hooper*, 5 Ired. 201 (N.C. 1844); *State v. Brady*, 9 Humph. 74 (Tenn. 1848); *Bailey v. Fiske*, 34 Maine 77 (1852); Bishop, *Commentaries* (1881), 1:268; Robert Beverly, *History and Present State of Virginia*, ed. Louis B. Wright (Chapel Hill: University of North Carolina Press, 1969), 38–39; Nash, *Red, White, and Black*, 277–78; Morgan, *American Slavery, American Freedom*, 335.

39. "Treaty of Bird's Fort, September 29, 1843," in *Texas Indian Papers*, 1:24–46; Everett, *The Texas Cherokees*, 99, 105–18.

40. Williams and Barker, *The Writings of Sam Houston*, 7:340; Chabot, *With the Makers of San Antonio*, 314–18; H. Allen Anderson, "The Delaware and Shawnee Indians and the Republic of Texas, 1820–1845," *Southwestern Historical Quarterly* 94(2)(1990): 231–60; David R. Jennys, "Holland Coffee: Fur Trader on the Red River," *Museum of the Fur Trade Quarterly* 29(3)(1993): 1–9. See also Jane Lynn Scarborough, "George Washington Paschal: Texas Unionist and Scalawag Jurisprudent" (Ph.D. diss., Rice University, Houston, 1972).

41. Judith N. McArthur, "Myth, Reality, and Anomaly: The Complete World of Rebecca Hagerty," *East Texas Historical Journal* 24(2)(1986): 18–32.

42. Gammel, *Laws*, Act of 28 January 1840, 1:132; Act of 18 March 1848, 2:129; Act of 16 January 1850, 3:474; Joseph W. McKnight, "Legitimation and Adoption on the Anglo-Hispanic Frontier of the United States," *Tijdschrift voor Rechtsgeschiedenis* (Netherlands) 53(1)(1985): 135–50; Grossberg, *Governing the Hearth*, 200–205; Dysart, "Mexican Women," 368–69.

43. Olmstead, *A Journey through Texas*, 336.

44. Dysart, "Mexican Women," 369.

45. Republic of Mexico, *Constitution* (1824), Art. IV; *Jones v. Laney*, 2 Tex. at 348; Hans W. Baade, "The Form of Marriage in Spanish North America," *Cornell Law Review* 61(1)(November 1975): 7, 84–85; Comment, "The Rights of an Illegitimate Child," 199.

46. Courtwright, *Violent Land*, 65.

47. Dysart, "Mexican Women," 365, 372; Crisp, "Anglo-Texan Attitudes," 156; Mason, *Patterns of Dominance*, 87–103; Courtwright, *Violent Land*, 65.

48. Dysart, "Mexican Women," 372; Gonzales, "Social Life," 26–27, 69–70.

49. Caroline Remy, "Hispanic-Mexican San Antonio: 1836–1861," *Southwestern Historical Quarterly* 71 (April 1968): 569; Sidney W. Mintz and Eric R. Wolf, "An Analysis of Ritual Co-parenthood (*Compadrazgo*)," in *Marriage, Family, and Residence*, ed. Paul Bohannan and John Middleton (Garden City, N.Y.: Natural History Press, 1968), 327–54; Dysart, "Mexican Women," 372–73.

50. Crook, "San Antonio, Texas," 14; Dysart, "Mexican Women," 372; Francis Jerome Woods, *Mexican Ethnic Leadership in San Antonio, Texas* (Washington, D.C.: Catholic University of America Press, 1949), 96.

51. Félix D. Almáraz, Jr., "The Historical Heritage of the Mexican American in 19th-Century Texas, An Interpretation" (paper presented at "The Role of the Mexican American in the History of the Southwest," a conference sponsored by the Inter-American Institute, Pan-American College, Edinburg, Texas, 17–18 November 1969); Dysart, "Mexican Women," 375; Crook, "San Antonio, Texas," 14–15.

52. Crisp, "Anglo-Texan Attitudes," 43, 53, 57–58; De León, *They Called Them Greasers*, 4, 13, 17, 19, 22, 40.

53. Gilberto M. Hinojosa, "The Texas Mexico Border: A Turbulent History," *Texas Humanist* 6 (March–April 1984): 18–20; De León, *They Called Them Greasers*, 49–86. See generally David Montejano, *Anglos and Mexicans in the Making of Texas* (Austin: University of Texas Press, 1987); Abel Rubio, *Stolen Heritage: A Mexican American's Rediscovery of His Family's Lost Land Grant* (Austin: Eakin Press, 1986).

54. De León, *They Called Them Greasers*, 49–62.

55. Bardaglio, *Reconstructing the Household*, 177.

56. Crisp, "Anglo-Texan Attitudes," 148, 181. For a discussion of the concept of racial degradation and its historical relationship with totalitarianism, see Hannah Arendt, *The Origins of Totalitarianism* (New York: Harcourt, Brace, 1951), 171.

57. Texas (Republic), *Constitution*, General Provisions, §§ 8 and 10.

58. Juan A. Ortega Y Medina, "Race and Democracy," in *Texas Myths*, ed. Robert F. O'Connor (College Station, 1986), 60–69; Crisp, "Anglo-Texan Attitudes," 12; Lorenzo Meyer, "Las Dos Constituciones," *Excelsio*, 27 December 1984.

59. Crisp, "Anglo-Texan Attitudes," 331–36, 364.

60. *Journals of the Texas Convention* (Austin: Miner and Cruger, 1845), 93,

341–46; William F. Weeks, comp., *Debates of the Texas Convention* (Houston: J. W. Cruger, 1846), 153–56.

61. Weeks, *Debates of the Texas Convention*, 235–36; Crisp, "Anglo-Texan Attitudes," 242–43, 426–30.

62. Weeks, *Debates of the Texas Convention*, 157.

63. *Ibid.*, 211–12; *Journals of the Texas Convention*, 97–98.

64. Crisp, "Anglo-Texan Attitudes," 331–36, 418.

65. Bishop, *Commentaries* (1881), 1:269–71; Halla, "El Paso, Texas," 64.

66. Helen Ellsworth Blair Chapman to Emily Welles Blair, Ft. Brown, 20 July 1849, in *The News from Brownsville: Helen Chapman's Letters from the Texas Military Frontier, 1848–52*, ed. Caleb Coker (Austin: Texas State Historical Association, 1992), 134.

67. *Memoirs of Mary A. Maverick*, ed. Rena Maverick Green (San Antonio: Alamo Printing Co., 1921; reprint, Lincoln: University of Nebraska Press, 1989), 12–14; Glenda Riley, "Frontierswomen's Changing Views of Indians in the Trans-Mississippi West," *Montana* 34(1)(1984): 20, 25–35.

68. Smithwick, *The Evolution of a State*, 124, 174; Maverick, *Memoirs*, 25, 38–40, 91; Jonnie Lockhart Wallis and Lawrence L. Hill, eds., *Sixty Years on the Brazos: The Life and Letters of Dr. John Washington Lockhart, 1824–1900* (Waco: Texian Press, 1967), 121–23; Rupert N. Richardson, "Cynthia Ann Parker," in *Women of Texas*, ed. James M. Day et al. (Waco, 1972), 73–86; James F. Brooks, "'This Evil Extends Especially . . . to the Feminine Sex': Negotiating Captivity in the New Mexico Borderlands," *Feminist Studies* 22(2)(1996): 279–309.

69. Maverick, *Memoirs*, 38–39.

70. Fredrickson, *White Supremacy*, 99; Mason, *Patterns of Dominance*, 80–92; Necah Furman, "Texas Women versus the Texas Myth," in *The Texas Heritage*, ed. Ben Proctor and Archie McDonald (Saint Louis: Forum Press, 1980), 167–84; Henrietta Andreadis, "True Womanhood Revisited: Women's Private Writings in Nineteenth-Century Texas," *Journal of the Southwest* 31 (summer 1989): 170–204; Sandra L. Myres, "Cowboys and Southern Belles," in *Texas Myths*, 122–38.

71. Dysart, "Mexican Women," 365, 370; Crisp, "Anglo-Texan Attitudes," 156; Bean and Bradshaw, "Intermarriage," 395; Crook, "San Antonio, Texas," ch. 2.

72. Dodge, *Our Wild Indians*, 215–20; Boom, "Texas in the 1850s," 283; Mason, *Patterns of Dominance*, 80–92; Dysart, "Mexican Women," 370–71.

CHAPTER 3

1. Malone, *Women on the Texas Frontier*, 44.

2. C. R. Patton, N. C. M. Dec'd [*non compos mentis*, decided] Probate

Record No. 450, 690, and Suits, 1857, Brazoria County Court Records; Malone, *Women on the Texas Frontier*, 43−44.

3. Testimonial of Anthony Christopher, a slave of Charles F. Patton, in *The American Slave: A Composite Autobiography: Supplement, Series 2*, 10 vols., ed. George P. Rawick (Westport, Conn.: Greenwood Press, 1979), vol. 3, pt. 2, pp. 718−24; Malone, *Women on the Texas Frontier*, 45; Folder No. 2, Estate of C. R. Patton, N. C. M. Dec'd, Probate Record No. 453, 690, Brazoria County Court Records; testimonial of Sarah Ford, a slave of Columbus R. Patton, in Rawick, *The American Slave: A Composite Autobiography: Supplement, Series 2* (1979), vol. 4, pt. 3, pp. 1358−69; testimonial of Sarah Ford in *The American Slave: A Composite Autobiography*, 19 vols., ed. George P. Rawick (Westport, Conn.: Greenwood Press, 1972), vol. 4, pt. 2, pp. 41−46.

4. Malone, *Women on the Texas Frontier*, 44−46.

5. *Ibid.*, 45; Will of Columbus R. Patton, 1 June 1853, Brazoria County Court Records; Statement of Charles F. Patton et al., challenging the legality of the Will of Columbus R. Patton, 31 March 1857, Brazoria County Court Records.

6. Sarah Ford, in Rawick, *The American Slave: A Composite Autobiography: Supplement, Series 2* (1979), vol. 4, pt. 3, pp. 1358−69; Sarah Ford, in Rawick, *The American Slave: A Composite Autobiography* (1972), vol. 4, pt. 2, pp. 41−46; statement accompanying Exhibit B of John Adriance, 1860, Folder No. 3, Estate of Columbus R. Patton, Brazoria County Court Records; Malone, *Women on the Texas Frontier*, 44−46.

7. Tjarks, "Comparative Demographic Analysis of Texas," 291−388; Jordan et al., *Texas: A Geography*, 77.

8. Jordan et al., *Texas: A Geography*, 77; Randolph B. Campbell, *An Empire for Slavery: The Peculiar Institution in Texas, 1821−1865* (Baton Rouge, 1989), 11.

9. Oldham and White, *A Digest*, Colonization Law of 1823, art. 3, p. 761; *Guess v. Lubbock*, 5 Tex. 547−51 (1851); Jordan et al., *Texas: A Geography*, 75−78; Rupert N. Richardson, Ernest Wallace, and Adrian Anderson, *Texas: The Lone Star State*, 14th ed. (Englewood Cliffs, N.J.: Prentice Hall, 1981), 76; Jean L. Epperson, "Notes and Documents," 443.

10. John B. Boles, *Black Southerners, 1619−1869* (Lexington: University Press of Kentucky, 1984), 76−79, 134; Winthrop D. Jordan, *White over Black: American Attitudes toward the Negro, 1550−1812* (New York: W. W. Norton, 1968), 346−48, 413−14; Genovese, *Roll, Jordan, Roll*, 400; Gerald Ashford, "Jacksonian Liberalism and Spanish Law in Early Texas," *Southwestern Historical Quarterly* 57 (July 1953): 2, 8, 10−11.

11. Cashin, *A Family Venture*, 26; Genovese, *Roll, Jordan, Roll*, 3−7;

George M. Fredrickson, *The Black Image in the White Mind: The Debate on Afro-American Character and Destiny, 1817–1914* (New York: Harper and Row, 1971), 55–68; Morgan, *American Slavery, American Freedom*, 335–36; Jordan, *White over Black*, 139. See generally Drew Gilpin Faust, ed., *Ideology of Slavery: Proslavery Thought in the Antebellum South, 1830–1860* (Baton Rouge: Louisiana State University Press, 1981); James Oakes, *The Ruling Race: A History of American Slave Holders* (New York: Alfred A. Knopf, 1982).

12. Schoen, "The Free Negro in the Republic of Texas," *Southwestern Historical Quarterly* 39(4)(April 1936): 292–302; Alwyn Barr, "African Americans in Texas: From Stereotype to Diverse Roles," in *Texas through Times: Evolving Interpretations*, ed. Walter L. Buenger and Robert A. Calvert (College Station: Texas A&M Press, 1991), 50–58; Jerry B. Caine, "The Thought and Action of Some Early Texas Baptists Concerning the Negro," *East Texas Historical Journal* 13 (spring 1975): 3–12.

13. Barr, "African Americans in Texas," 52; Cashin, *A Family Venture*, 27; De León, *They Called Them Greasers*, 36, 44; Wyatt-Brown, *Southern Honor*, 97, 300–308.

14. *Honey v. Clark*, 37 Tex. 699–707 (1872–73); *Siete Partidas*, II. 2.6, 2.11; *Guess*, 5 Tex. at 535, 549–50; *Gortario v. Cantu*, 7 Tex. 46 (1851); Ocie Speer, *A Treatise on the Law of Married Women in Texas* (Rochester, N.Y.: Lawyers Co-Operative Publishing Co., 1901), 4; Hall, "El Paso, Texas," 64.

15. *Guess*, 5 Tex. at 550; Lawrence D. Rice, *The Negro in Texas, 1874–1900* (Baton Rouge: Louisiana State University Press, 1971), 36–37; Barr, "African Americans in Texas," 50–58; *Honey*, 37 Tex. at 706; Malone, *Women on the Texas Frontier*, 28; Schoen, "The Free Negro in the Republic of Texas," *Southwestern Historical Quarterly* 39(4)(April 1936): 293–302; Genovese, *Roll, Jordan, Roll*, 402.

16. George R. Woolfolk, *The Free Negro in Texas, 1800–1860: A Study in Cultural Compromise* (Ann Arbor, University Microfilms for the *Journal of Mexican American History*, 1976), 81; *idem*, "Turner's Safety Valve and Free Negro Migration," *Journal of Negro History* 50 (July 1965): 185–97.

17. Barr, "African Americans in Texas," 50–58; Malone, *Women on the Texas Frontier*, 28, 42; Schoen, "The Free Negro in the Republic of Texas," *Southwestern Historical Quarterly* 39(4)(April 1936): 293–302; 41(1)(July 1937): 92; Woolfolk, *The Free Negro in Texas*, 81–85; Fredrickson, *White Supremacy*, 96–99.

18. Smithwick, *The Evolution of a State*, 166; Schoen, "The Free Negro in the Republic of Texas," *Southwestern Historical Quarterly* 39(4)(April 1936): 294–95.

19. Billy Don Ledbetter, "White over Black in Texas: Racial Attitudes

in the Antebellum Period," *Phylon* 34 (December 1973): 406–18; Boles, *Black Southerners*, 76–79; Barr, "African Americans in Texas," 52; Cashin, *A Family Venture*, 105, 113.

20. Campbell, *An Empire for Slavery*, 51–55; Jordan et al., *Texas: A Geography*, 72–78; Kerr, "Migration to Texas," 184–216; Jordan, "Population Origins," 83–103.

21. Richardson et al., *Texas*, 82, 182, 193; Campbell, *An Empire for Slavery*, 55–58; Jordan et al., *Texas: A Geography*, 77.

22. Amos Andrew Parker, *Trip to the West and Texas* (Concord, N.H.: White and Fisher, 1835), 186; Lewis Cecil Gray, *History of Agriculture in the Southern United States to 1860*, 2 vols. (Washington, D.C.: Carnegie Institution of Washington, 1933), 1:530; *The 1840 Census of the Republic of Texas*, ed. Gifford White (Austin: Pemberton Press, 1966); U.S. Census Office, *Agriculture of the United States in 1860* (Washington, D.C.: U.S. Government Printing Office, 1864), 240–42; Genovese, *Roll, Jordan, Roll*, 7; Peter Kolchin, "Reevaluating the Antebellum Slave Community: A Comparative Perspective," *Journal of American History* 70 (December 1983): 579–601; Campbell, *An Empire for Slavery*, 118, 128–29, 191–95.

23. Rawick, *The American Slave: A Composite Autobiography* (1972), vol. 4, pt. 2, p. 77; see also *ibid.*, pp. 88, 174.

24. *Ibid.*, vol. 4, pt. 1, p. 26; G. Featherstone, *Excursion through the Slave States . . .* (London: J. Murray, 1844; reprint, New York: Negro Universities Press, 1968), 125; Genovese, *Roll, Jordan, Roll*, 53.

25. Rawick, *The American Slave: A Composite Autobiography* (1972), vol. 5, pt. 3, p. 45. See also *ibid.*, vol. 5, pt. 3, pp. 133–35; and *ibid.*, vol. 4, pt. 2, pp. 77, 88, 174.

26. Rawick, *The American Slave: A Composite Autobiography* (1972), vol. 5, pt. 3, p. 46; vol. 4, pt. 2, p. 88; Malone, *Women on the Texas Frontier*, 42; Cashin, *A Family Venture*, 102–105. See generally Catherine Clinton, "'Southern Dishonor': Flesh, Blood, and Bondage," in *In Joy and in Sorrow: Women, Family, and Marriage in the Victorian South*, ed. Carol Bleser (New York: Oxford University Press, 1991), 52–68.

27. *Timmins v. Lacy*, 30 Tex. 135–36 (1867); *Blakely's Administrator v. Duncan*, 4 Tex. 184 (1849); Texas, *Penal Code* (1857), art. 523, p. 103; Gammel, *Laws*, Act of 13 May 1846, 2:383; Speer, *A Treatise*, 5; Campbell, *An Empire for Slavery*, 55, 154, 160, 201; Malone, *Women on the Texas Frontier*, 47–50; Barry A. Crouch, "'The Chords of Love': Legalizing Black Marital and Family Rights in Postwar Texas," *Journal of Negro History* 79(4)(1994): 334–51; Bardaglio, *Reconstructing the Household*, 66; Deborah Gray White, *Ar'n't I a Woman? Female Slaves in the Plantation South*, rev. ed. (New York: W. W. Norton, 1999), 142–160; Genovese, *Roll, Jordan, Roll*, 450–457, 482–534; John Blassingame, *The*

Slave Community: Plantation Life in the Antebellum South (New York: Oxford University Press, 1972), 77–102; Leslie Howard Owens, *This Species of Property: Slave Life and Culture in the Old South* (Oxford University Press, 1976), 182–213.

28. Malone, *Women on the Texas Frontier,* 42–43.

29. *Ibid.,* 28; Campbell, *An Empire for Slavery,* 195–97.

30. Edward S. Abdy, *Journal of a Residence and Tour in the United States,* 3 vols. (London: J. Murray, 1835), 2:291; James Sterling, *Letters from the Slave States* (London: J. W. Parker, 1857), 46; Fredrika Bremer, *The Homes of the New World: Impressions of America,* 2 vols. (New York: Harper and Brothers, 1853), 2:249, 527; Daniel R. Hundley, *Social Relations in Our Southern States* (New York: H. B. Price, 1860), 352–53.

31. Rawick, *The American Slave: A Composite Autobiography* (1972), vol. 4, pt. 2, p. 3. See also *ibid.,* vol. 5, pt. 3, pp. 53, 83–84.

32. *Ibid.,* vol. 4, pt. 2, pp. 6, 8, 56, 105, 145, 159; *ibid.,* vol. 5, pt. 4, p. 6; Frederick Law Olmstead, *A Journey in the Back Country, 1853–54* (New York: Mason Brothers, 1860; reprint, New York: B. Franklin, 1970), 64–65; James Dunwoody Brownson De Bow, ed., *Industrial Resources, Statistics, etc. of . . . the Southern and Western States,* 3 vols. (New Orleans: Office of De Bow's Review, 1852–53), 2:337; Joseph Halt Ingraham, *The South-West, by a Yankee,* 2 vols. (New York: Harper and Brothers: 1835; reprint, New York: Negro Universities Press, 1968), 2:26; Philip Graham, ed., "Texas Memoirs of Amelia E. Barr," *Southwestern Historical Quarterly* 69(4)(April 1966): 487; Genovese, *Roll, Jordan, Roll,* 7–8, 109.

33. Schoen, "The Free Negro in the Republic of Texas," *Southwestern Historical Quarterly* 39(4)(April 1936): 293–302; Malone, *Women on the Texas Frontier,* 42–43; Cashin, *A Family Venture,* 102–103; Genovese, *Roll, Jordan, Roll,* 414–15. See also White, *Ar'n't I a Woman,* 24–46; John Hope Franklin and Alfred A. Moss, Jr., *From Slavery to Freedom,* 6th ed. (New York: Alfred A. Knopf, 1988), 128; Boles, *Black Southerners,* 132.

34. Nance, *Attack and Counterattack,* 642; Campbell, *An Empire for Slavery,* 200–204; Rice, *The Negro in Texas,* 34–37; Malone, *Women on the Texas Frontier,* 40–44. The Texas WPA narratives provide many references to female slave concubinage. See generally Rawick, *The American Slave: A Composite Autobiography: Supplement, Series 2* (1979), vols. 4, 5.

35. *Oldham v. McIver,* 49 Tex. 556 (1878).

36. Williams and Barker, *The Writings of Sam Houston,* 2:500; *Honey,* 37 Tex. at 688–89.

37. *Honey,* 37 Tex. at 697.

38. *Hagerty v. Harwell,* 16 Tex. 663 (1856); *Guess,* 5 Tex. at 557–58; *Hilliard v. Frantz,* 21 Tex. 192 (1858); *Hunt v. White,* 24 Tex. 643 (1859); Campbell, *An*

Empire for Slavery, 154, 200–205; Rice, *The Negro in Texas,* 33–38; Malone, *Women on the Texas Frontier,* 43–46. For coverage of the petitions and memorials to the Texas Congress regarding slave mistresses and their mulatto children, see Harold Schoen, "The Free Negro in the Republic of Texas" (Ph.D. diss., University of Texas, Austin, 1938).

39. Smithwick, *The Evolution of a State,* 165–66; Schoen, "The Free Negro in the Republic of Texas," *Southwestern Historical Quarterly* 41(1)(July 1937): 94.

40. Texas (Republic), *Constitution,* General Provisions, § 10; Gammel, *Laws,* Act of 13 May 1846, 2:363; Schoen, "The Free Negro in the Republic of Texas," *Southwestern Historical Quarterly* 40(4)(April 1937): 267–89; 41(1)(July 1937): 86–89.

41. Gammel, *Laws,* Act of 14 December 1837, 1:43; Gammel, *Laws,* Joint Resolution of 5 June 1837, 1:232.

42. Texas (Republic), *Constitution,* General Provisions, § 9; Gammel, *Laws,* Act of 5 February 1840, 2:151; Schoen, "The Free Negro in the Republic of Texas," *Southwestern Historical Quarterly* 40(2)(October 1936): 85–113; 40(3)(January 1937): 169–99; Earl W. Farnell, "The Abduction of Free Negroes and Slaves in Texas," *Southwestern Historical Quarterly* 60(3)(January 1957): 377–79; Andrew Forest Muir, "The Free Negro in Harris County, Texas," *Southwestern Historical Quarterly* 46 (January 1943): 214–38; *idem,* "The Free Negro in Jefferson and Orange Counties, Texas," *Journal of Negro History* 35 (April 1950): 183–206; *idem,* "The Free Negro in Galveston County, Texas," *Negro History Bulletin* 22 (December 1958): 68–70.

43. Texas (Republic), *Constitution,* General Provisions, § 9; Paul D. Lack, "Slavery and the Texas Revolution," *Southwestern Historical Quarterly* 89(2)(1985): 181–202; Crisp, "Anglo-Texan Attitudes," 209–15, 454; Cashin, *A Family Venture,* 112. See generally Reginald Horsman, *Josiah Nott of Mobile: Southerner, Physician, and Racial Theorist* (Baton Rouge: Louisiana State University Press, 1987).

44. *Guess,* 5 Tex. at 535–46; Schoen, "The Free Negro in the Republic of Texas," *Southwestern Historical Quarterly* 40(2)(October 1936): 98–99; 40(4)(April 1937): 276, 281–83.

45. Muir, "The Free Negro in Harris County, Texas," 214–38; Schoen, "The Free Negro in the Republic of Texas," *Southwestern Historical Quarterly* 39(4)(April 1936): 302; 40(4)(April 1937): 276, 281–83; 41(1)(July 1937): 90–94.

46. Gammel, *Laws,* Act of 5 June 1837, sec. 9, 1:233; Woolfolk, *The Free Negro in Texas,* 91; Fredrickson, *White Supremacy,* 98–99. But see Texas (Republic), *Constitution,* General Provisions, § 10; Gammel, *Laws,* Joint Resolution of 5 June 1837, 1:232.

47. Gammel, *Laws,* Act of 20 January 1840, secs. 1 and 2, 2:177–78; *Brad-*

shaw v. Mayfield, 18 Tex. 21–29 (1856); *Barkley v. Dumke*, 87 S.W. 1147 (1905); *Honey*, 37 Tex. at 699, 707; Grossberg, *Governing the Hearth*, 126–29.

48. Schoen, "The Free Negro in the Republic of Texas," *Southwestern Historical Quarterly* 39(4)(April 1936): 293–302; Bardaglio, *Reconstructing the Household*, 55–56; Genovese, *Roll, Jordan, Roll*, 423.

49. *Honey*, 37 Tex. at 699; *Siete Partidas*, IV. 5.1, 2.7, 2.11; *Guess*, 5 Tex. at 535, 549–50.

50. Gammel, *Laws*, Ordinance and Decree of 16 January 1836, 1:1041; *ibid.*, Act of 5 June 1837, 1:1293–94; Act of 5 February 1841, 1:640; *Guess*, 5 Tex. at 547; *Honey*, 37 Tex. at 702.

51. Nash, *Red, White, and Black*, 282, 285; Eva Saks, "Representing Miscegenation Law," *Raritan* 8(2)(1988): 46–47; Bardaglio, *Reconstructing the Household*, 101; Grossberg, *Governing the Hearth*, 126, 128.

52. *Fitts v. Fitts*, 14 Tex. 443, 450 (1853); Joseph W. McKnight, "Family Law: Husband and Wife," *Southwest Law Journal* 35 (1981): 93, 136.

53. Woolfolk, *The Free Negro in Texas*, 90–92.

54. Gammel, *Laws*, Act of 6 January 1841, 1:483–84; Speer, *A Treatise*, 4–5, 388; Saks, "Representing Miscegenation Law," 46–47; Bishop, *Commentaries* (1881), 1:128, 269–70; Grossberg, *Governing the Hearth*, 102.

55. Gammel, *Laws*, Act of 5 June 1837, 1:234.

56. *Tarpley*, 2 Tex. at 136; *Yates v. Houston*, 3 Tex. 694 (1848); *Lockhart v. White*, 18 Tex. 104 (1856); *Babb v. Carroll*, 21 Tex. 765 (1858); *Honey*, 37 Tex. at 707.

57. Act of 12 February 1858, Gammel, *Laws*, 4:164–65, 174–77, 188–89; *Timmins*, 30 Tex. at 115; Speer, *A Treatise*, 5; David M. Potter, *The Impending Crisis, 1848–1861* (New York: Harper and Row, 1976), 386–87, 449, 455–56; Franklin and Moss, *From Freedom to Slavery*, 175–76; Jordan, *White over Black*, 470; Juan F. Perea, "The Black/White Binary Paradigm of Race: The 'Normal Science' of American Racial Thought," *California Law Review* 85(5)(October 1997): 1213–58.

58. Texas, *Senate Journal, Second Legislature*, Memorial No. 33, File 94, 11 November 1841; Memorial No. 139, File 74, n.d., 186.

59. Schoen, "The Free Negro in the Republic of Texas," *Southwestern Historical Quarterly* 39(4)(April 1936): 295; 41(1)(July 1937): 92; Douglas C. McMurtrie, "Pioneer Printing in Texas," *Southwestern Historical Quarterly* 35(3) (January 1932): 173–94.

60. Gammel, *Laws*, Act of 21 December 1836, sec. 23, 1:1250; Texas, *Penal Code* (1857), arts. 387–91, p. 72; Gammel, *Laws*, Act of 12 February 1858, 4:165; *Honey*, 37 Tex. at 686; *Oldham*, 49 Tex. at 556; *Clements v. Crawford*, 42 Tex. 601 (1875); *State v. Moore*, 7 Tex. App. 609 (1880).

61. Smithwick, *The Evolution of a State*, 109.

62. Paul D. Lack, "Slavery and Vigilantism in Austin, Texas, 1840–1860," *Southwestern Historical Quarterly* 85(1)(July 1981): 1–20.

CHAPTER 4

1. Williams and Barker, *The Writings of Sam Houston,* 1:322; Hogan, *The Texas Republic,* 268–69; Pat Ireland Nixon, *The Medical Story of Early Texas, 1528–1853* (Lancaster, Pa.: Lancaster Press, 1946), 324–27; James E. Winston, "Virginia and the Independence of Texas," *Southwestern Historical Quarterly* 16 (January 1913): 281; Cashin, *A Family Venture,* 106–107.

2. Hogan, *The Texas Republic,* 269.

3. Quoted in Cashin, *A Family Venture,* 106–107; W. Randolph, "Genealogy of Archer Family," 50, Virginia State Archives, Richmond; Branch T. Archer, 22 October 1854, 21 October 1853, Archer Papers, Eugene C. Barker Texas History Center, University of Texas, Austin; Nixon, *The Medical Story of Early Texas,* 326.

4. Cashin, *A Family Venture,* 107; Nixon, *The Medical Story of Early Texas,* 325.

5. Nettie Lee Benson, "Texas Viewed from Mexico, 1820–1834," *Southwestern Historical Quarterly* 90(3)(1987): 219–91.

6. Oldham and White, *A Digest,* Colonization Law of March 24, 1825, 763–64; [Imperial] Colonization Law of 1823, 760; Henderson Yoakum, *History of Texas,* 2 vols. (New York: J. S. Redfield, 1855), 1:193–208; Donald E. Chipman, *Spanish Texas, 1519–1821* (Austin: University of Texas, 1992), 212, 216, 222–23; Nettie L. Benson, "A Governor's Report on Texas in 1809," *Southwestern Historical Quarterly* 71 (April 1968): 603–66; Fane Downs, "Governor Martínez and the Defense of Texas from Foreign Invasion, 1817–1822," *Texas Military History* 7 (spring 1968): 30–31; Newton and Gambrell, *A Social and Political History of Texas,* 30–33; Félix D. Almáraz, Jr., *Tragic Cavalier: Governor Manuel Salcedo of Texas, 1808–1813* (Austin: University of Texas, 1971), 50–59.

7. Mary Austin Holley, *The Texas Diary, 1835–38,* ed. J. P. Bryan (Austin: University of Texas, 1965), 44; Richardson et al., *Texas,* 63–72; Newton and Gambrell, *A Social and Political History,* 30–33; Nackman, "Anglo-American Migrants," 446–48; Siegel, *A Political History of the Texas Republic,* 6–12; Elizabeth York Enstam, "The Family," in *Texas Myths,* 139–58.

8. Texas (Republic), *Constitution,* General Provisions, § 10; Gammel, *Laws,* Act of 22 December 1836, 1:1276–85; Act of 14 December 1837, 1:1405–1419; Act of 22 January 1845, 2:1073–75; Act of 7 February 1853, 3:1317; Act of 13 February 1854, 3:1550–52. For a good treatment of early land policy and discussion of the relatively few women who homesteaded independently, see Gould and Pando, *Claiming Their Land,* 1–28.

9. *Laws and Decrees of the State of Coahuila and Texas, in Spanish and English. To Which is Added the Constitution of Said State...*, trans. J. P. Kimball (Houston: Telegraph Power Press, 1839), Actas del Congreso, 12 January 1829, 937; 13 January 1829, 938. For a discussion of Mexican colonization Decree No. 70 and its repeal on 8 April 1831, see Joseph W. McKnight, "Protection of the Family Home from Seizure by Creditors: The Sources and Evolution of a Principle," *Southwestern Historical Quarterly* 86(3)(1983): 369–99.

10. Courtwright, *Violent Land*, 66.

11. Gammel, *Laws*, Act of 26 January 1839, 2:125–26; Act of 5 February 1840, 2:267–68; *Journals of the Fourth Congress of the Republic of Texas, 1839–1840, to Which Are Added the Relief Laws*, 3 vols., ed. Harriet Smither (Austin: Von Boeckmann-Jones Co., 1929), 1:253, 348; 2:191, 193–94, 262; Gammel, *Laws*, Act of 5 February 1840, 2:347; Act of 22 December 1840, 2:525–26; Texas, *Constitution* (1845), Art. IV, § 22; *Wood v. Wheeler*, 7 Tex. 13, 24 (1851); *Coleman v. Cobbs*, 14 Tex. 598 (1855); McKnight, "Protection of the Family Home," 391–96.

12. Joseph W. McKnight, "Texas Community Property Law—Its Course of Development and Reform," *California Western Law Review* 8 (fall 1971): 110–20; *idem*, "The Spanish Legacy to Texas Law," *American Journal of Legal History* 3 (July 1959): 220–23; William Defuniak and Michael J. Vaughn, *Principles of Community Property*, 2d ed. (Tucson: University of Arizona Press, 1971), 1–4, 44–48, 52–53, 58, 127–28, 160–61, 168–69; Kay Ellen Thurman, "Married Women's Property Acts" (L.L.M. thesis, University of Wisconsin, Madison, 1966), 40–44; Harriet Spiller Daggett, *Legal Essays on Family Law* (Baton Rouge: Louisiana State University Press, 1935), 100–106; Fred Walter Householder, "The Sources of the Texas Law of Married Women" (M.A. thesis, University of Texas, Austin, 1909), 48–59. The Spanish matrimonial law had been in effect in Louisiana since 1769. Its rules were codified in the *Louisiana Digest* of 1808 and then recodified in the *Louisiana Civil Code* and the *Louisiana Code of Practice*, both of which were published in 1825. The *Louisiana Civil Code* was very influential among the large number of Louisianians settling in Texas during the late 1820s and 1830s. McKnight, "Texas Community Property Law: Conservative Attitudes, Reluctant Change," 74. See generally José R. Remacha et al., *The Influence of Spain on the Texas Legal System* (Austin: State Bar of Texas, 1992).

13. Willis E. Myers, ed., *Syllabus of the Honorable Henry D. Harlan's Lectures on the Law of Domestic Relations* (Baltimore: King Brothers, 1898), 49–51; Bardaglio, *Reconstructing the Household*, 30–31.

14. *Yates*, 3 Tex. at 452–56; *Babb*, 21 Tex. at 767; *Moore v. Bullard*, 24 Tex. 150 (1859); *Wood v. Wheeler*, 7 Tex. 13 (1851); George E. Howard, *A History of Matrimonial Institutions*, 3 vols. (Chicago, 1904), 2:200–203; McKnight, "Texas

Community Property Law: Conservative Attitudes, Reluctant Change," 75; Vaughn, "The Policy of Community Property," 20, 32–33; Grossberg, *Governing the Hearth*, 7, 34–35.

15. Smithwick, *The Evolution of a State*, 169; Cashin, *A Family Venture*, 79; Newton and Gambrell, *A Social and Political History*, 103.

16. Address of John W. Lockhart to the Daughters of the Republic, from the *Galveston Daily News*, 10 December 1893, in Wallis, *Sixty Years on the Brazos*, 121.

17. *Ibid.*, 225; Williams and Barker, *The Writings of Sam Houston*, 2:393, 3:442.

18. Caroline von Hinueber, "Life of German Pioneers in Early Texas. Caroline von Hinueber (Born Ernst)," ed. Rudolph Kleberg, Jr., *Texas Historical Association Quarterly* 2(3)(1898): 229.

19. Parker, *A Trip to the West in Texas*, 164; Newton and Gambrell, *A Social and Political History*, 107–26.

20. Smithwick, *The Evolution of a State*, 173; Zuber, *My Eighty Years in Texas*, 29; Holley, *The Texas Diary*, 17, 23, 36; Maverick, *Memoirs*, 34, 90–100; Richardson et al., *Texas*, 129–39, 140–46, 174–81; de la Tejá and Wheat, "Béxar: Profile of a Tejano Community," 7–34.

21. Smithwick, *The Evolution of a State*, 14–15, 169, 173; Newton and Gambrell, *A Social and Political History*, 105, 114–27; Malone, *Women on the Texas Frontier*, 16–25.

22. Smithwick, *The Evolution of a State*, 173–76, 201, 235; Zuber, *My Eighty Years in Texas*, 25, 29, 120–27.

23. Wallis, *Sixty Years on the Brazos*, 14; Sandra L. Myres, *Westering Women and the Frontier Experience, 1800–1915* (Albuquerque: University of New Mexico Press, 1982), 172–73; Newton and Gambrell, *A Social and Political History*, 107; Malone, *Women on the Texas Frontier*, 13–26; Enstam, "The Family," 141, 152.

24. Smithwick, *The Evolution of a State*, 5.

25. Douglas, *Famous Texas Feuds*, 5–8; Wallis, *Sixty Years on the Brazos*, 14–15; Holley, *The Texas Diary*, 20–23.

26. Eugene C. Barker, ed., *The Austin Papers*, 3 vols. (Washington, D.C.: U.S. Government Printing Office, 1924–28), 1:705.

27. Nackman, "Anglo-American Migrants," 440–48; Newton and Gambrell, *A Social and Political History*, 110–12; Siegel, *A Political History of the Texas Republic*, 4–7.

28. Cashin, *A Family Venture*, 30–32, 99–106.

29. Quoted in Hogan, *The Texas Republic*, 268.

30. Courtwright, *Violent Land*, 66; Allen Walker Read, "'G.T.T.': Gone to Texas," *Southern Folklore Quarterly* 27(3)(1963): 223–28.

31. Quoted in Hogan, *The Texas Republic*, 269.

32. *Houston Morning Star*, 25 September 1841, 5 May 1842, 19 May 1842, 4 October 1842; *Houston Telegraph and Texas Register*, 24 June 1837, 18 November 1837, 20 January 1838, 31 March 1838, 24 June 1840, 8 July 1840, 14 June 1843, 5 February 1845; Frederick Law Olmstead, *The Cotton Kingdom: A Traveler's Observations on Cotton and Slavery in the American States*, ed. Arthur M. Schlesinger (New York: Knopf, 1953), 414; Francis Richard Lubbock, *Six Decades in Texas; or, Memoirs of Francis Richard Lubbock: A Personal Experience in Business, War, and Politics*, ed. C. W. Raines (Austin: Ben C. Jones and Co., 1900), 54–57; Smithwick, *The Evolution of a State*, 54; William Ransom Hogan, "Rampant Individualism in the Republic of Texas," *Southwestern Historical Quarterly* 44 (1941): 459–61; Newton and Gambrell, *A Social and Political History*, 109–15; Crisp, "Anglo-Texan Attitudes," 165; Dickson D. Bruce, Jr., *Violence and Culture in the Antebellum South* (Austin: University of Texas Press, 1979), 4, 21–22, 103–107. See generally *Humor of the Old Southwest*, ed. Hennig Cohen and William B. Dillingham, 2d ed. (Athens: University of Georgia Press, 1975).

33. Betsy Downey, "Battered Pioneers: Jules Sandoz and the Physical Abuse of Wives on the American Frontier," *Great Plains Quarterly* 12 (Winter 1992): 46–49.

34. Elizabeth Pleck, *Domestic Tyranny: The Making of Social Policy against Family Violence from Colonial Times to the Present* (New York: Oxford University Press, 1987), 3–121; idem, "Wife Beating in Nineteenth-Century America," *Victimology* 4(1)(1979): 60–74; idem, "Feminist Responses to 'Crimes against Women,'" *Signs* 8 (spring 1983): 451–70. See generally Linda Gordon, *Heroes of Their Own Lives: The Politics and History of Family Violence: Boston, 1880–1960* (New York: Viking Press, 1988); William A. Stacey and Anson Shupe, *The Family Secret: Domestic Violence in America* (Boston: Beacon Press, 1983).

35. Downey, "Battered Pioneers," 33–38, 46–49; Susan Armitage and Elizabeth James, eds., *The Women's West* (Norman: University of Oklahoma Press, 1987), 3–5; Glenda Riley, *The Female Frontier* (Lawrence: University Press of Kansas, 1988), 1–2, 96–97; idem, *Frontierswomen: The Iowa Experience* (Ames: Iowa State University Press, 1981), vii–xiii; Julie Roy Jeffrey, *Frontier Women: The Trans-Mississippi West, 1840–1880* (New York: Hill and Wang, 1979), 7, 30. See generally R. E. Mather and Louis Schmittroth, *Scandal of the West: Domestic Violence on the Frontier* (Oklahoma City: History West Publishing, 1998).

36. Jayme A. Sokolaw and Mary Ann Lamanna, "Women and Utopia: The Woman's Commonwealth of Belton, Texas," *Southwestern Historical Quarterly* 87 (April 1984): 378–79.

37. Barbara L. Wold, "Courageous Messenger," *E. C. Barksdale Student*

Lectures II (1989–90): 79–103; Ragsdale, *Women and Children of the Alamo*, 53–69; C. Richard King, *Susanna Dickinson: Messenger of the Alamo* (Austin: Shoal Creek Publishers, 1976), 99–122.

38. *Wright v. Wright*, 6 Tex. 17–18 (1851); *Nogees v. Nogees*, 7 Tex. 546 (1852).

39. Weeks, *Debates of the Texas Convention*, 1053–55; Kathleen Elizabeth Lazarou, "Concealed under Petticoats: Married Women's Property and the Law of Texas, 1840–1913" (Ph.D. diss., Rice University, Houston, 1980), 100–101; Sokolaw and Lamanna, "Women and Utopia," 375–80.

40. Olmstead, *A Journey through Texas*, 125–26; *Tuberville v. Tuberville*, 4 Tex. 129 (1849). Regarding the "frolics" of married men in southern Texas during the Mexican War, see Coker, *The News from Brownsville*, 65–71. See also Malone, *Women on the Texas Frontier*, 2–13, 26–52; Dysart, "Mexican Women," 365–75; Sokolaw and Lamanna, "Women and Utopia," 378–81. Cashin, *A Family Venture*, 33, 99, 106–107.

41. Ellen Garwood, "Early Texas Inns: A Study in Social Relationships," *Southwestern Historical Quarterly* 55(2)(October 1956): 219–45; William Ransom Hogan, "Pamelia Mann: Texas Frontierswoman," *Southwestern Review* 20 (summer 1935): 364; Martha Anne Turner, "Jane Wilkinson Long," in *Women of Texas*, ed. James M. Day et al. (Waco, 1972), 24; Elliott, "The Great Western," 1–26; Butler, *Daughters of Joy*, 5–13.

42. Texas, *Penal Code* (1857), arts. 339–41; Gammel, *Laws*, Act of 12 February 1858, 4:1037; Act of 6 January 1841, sec. 12, 2:485–86.

43. *Cartwright v. Cartwright*, 18 Tex. 626 (1857); *Hagerty v. Harwell*, 16 Tex. 663 (1856); *Hilliard*, 21 Tex. at 192; *Hunt*, 24 Tex. at 643; Malone, *Women on the Texas Frontier*, 26–52; Campbell, *An Empire for Slavery*, 195–97; Cashin, *A Family Venture*, 24, 78–79, 102–105.

44. Helen E. Fisher, *Anatomy of Love: The Natural History of Monogamy, Adultery, and Divorce* (New York: W. W. Norton, 1992), 91–96; Jordan et al., *Texas: A Geography*, 1–2.

45. Dysart, "Mexican Women," 376.

46. Olmstead, *A Journey through Texas*, 125–26.

47. *Simons v. Simons*, 13 Tex. 470 (1857); *Sheffield v. Sheffield*, 3 Tex. 84 (1848); *Cartwright*, 18 Tex. at 624; *Pinkard v. Pinkard*, 14 Tex. 356 (1855); *Wright*, 6 Tex. 18; *Camp v. Camp*, 18 Tex. 534 (1857); *Sharman v. Sharman*, 18 Tex. 522 (1857); Enstam, "The Family," 140–53.

48. *Lewis*, 44 Tex. 323; *Wheat v. Owens*, 15 Tex. 241 (1851); Henry Smith, "Reminiscences of Henry Smith," *Texas Historical Association Quarterly* 14(1) (July 1910): 24–31.

49. Holley, *The Texas Diary*, 13–14.

50. Weeks, *Debates of the Texas Convention*, 597; *Besch v. Besch*, 27 Tex. 390–92 (1864); Linda Peavy and Ursula Smith, *Women in Waiting in the West-*

ward Movement (Norman: University of Oklahoma Press, 1994), 8–9, 17–18, 23, 34–35, 38.

51. Oldham and White, *A Digest*, Colonization Law of 1825, art. 20, p. 764; Act of 4 September 1827, art. 6, p. 768; Colonization Law of 1832, art. 28, p. 772; Newton and Gambrell, *A Social and Political History*, 103.

52. *Lewis*, 44 Tex. 338–39; Peavy and Smith, *Women in Waiting*, 8–9, 18–23, 34–38; Baade, "The Form of Marriage," 86; Grossberg, *Governing the Hearth*, 121–26.

53. Gammel, *Laws*, "Decree of the Emperor, February 18, 1821, Fifth Recital," 1:31; Republic of Mexico, *Constitution* (1824), Art. IV; *Sharman*, 23 Tex. at 522–24; Speer, *A Treatise*, 385; Bennett Smith, *Marriage by Bond in Colonial Texas* (Fort Worth: Branch-Smith, Inc., 1972), 6; Newton and Gambrell, *A Social and Political History*, 117–19; Richardson et al., *Texas*, 74–75.

54. Mary Austin Holley, *Texas* (Lexington, Ky.: J. Clarke, 1836; reprint, Austin: Texas State Historical Association, 1990), 181; Wallis, *Sixty Years on the Brazos*, 15; William B. De Wees, *Letters from an Early Settler of Texas* (Louisville: Morton and Griswold, 1852), 137; John J. Linn, *Reminiscences of Fifty Years in Texas* (New York, 1883), 283; William S. Red, *The Texas Colonists and Religion* (Austin: E. L. Shettles, 1924; reprint, Temecula, 1993), 5; Baade, "The Form of Marriage," 7; Newton and Gambrell, *A Social and Political History*, 118–20; Smith, *Marriage by Bond*, 37–62.

55. *Lewis*, 44 Tex. at 338–39; *Routh v. Routh*, 57 Tex. 592–93 (1882); *Middlebrook v. Wideman*, 203 S.W.2d 686 (Tex. Civ. App.–Texarkana 1947, no writ); Richardson et al., *Texas*, 129–45, 174–75; Enstam, "The Family," 140–52; Malone, *Women on the Texas Frontier*, 15–25.

56. Baade, "The Form of Marriage," 86; Smith, "Reminiscences," 24, 31.

57. Nick Malavis, "Equality under the Lord's Law: The Disciplinary Process in Texas Baptist Churches, 1833–1870," *East Texas Historical Journal* 31(1)(1993): 3–23; "The Records of an Early Texas Baptist Church," *Quarterly of the Texas State Historical Association* 11(2)(October 1907): 142–43; 12(1)(July 1908): 11; Angela Boswell, "The Meaning of Participation: White Protestant Women in Antebellum Houston Churches," *Southwestern Historical Quarterly* 99(1)(1995): 26–47.

58. *Simon v. State*, 31 Tex. Crim. Rep. 199 (1892); *Foote v. State*, 65 Tex. Crim. Rep. 368 (1912); Bishop, *Commentaries* (1881), 1:368–69; James Kent, *Commentaries on American Law*, 4 vols. (New York: O. Halsted, 1826–30), 2:211–12; Bardaglio, *Reconstructing the Household*, 5; Grossberg, *Governing the Hearth*, 202.

59. Fredrickson, *White Supremacy*, 104–105; Malone, *Women on the Texas Frontier*, 42; Dysart, "Mexican Women," 367; Sandra L. Myres, "Cowboys and Southern Belles," 122–38.

60. *Pridgen v. Pridgen*, Harrison County District Court Civil Papers, Case No. 1697; *Hagerty*, 16 Tex. at 663; *Cartwright*, 18 Tex. at 626; Campbell, *An Empire for Slavery*, 201; Cashin, *A Family Venture*, 108–109.

61. *Lewis*, 44 Tex. at 338–39.

62. *Routh*, 57 Tex. at 592–93.

63. Hogan, "Pamelia Mann," 364; Andrew Forest Muir, "In Defense of Mrs. Mann," in *Mexican Border Ballads and Other Lore*, ed. Mody Boatright (Austin: Texas Folk-Lore Society, 1946); King, *Susanna Dickinson*, 95–121; Wold, "Courageous Messenger," 79–103; Ragsdale, *Women and Children of the Alamo*, 53–69.

64. Furman, "Texas Women versus the Texas Myth," 168; Myres, "Cowboys and Southern Belles," 130; Dysart, "Mexican Women," 367–68; Bardaglio, *Reconstructing the Household*, 30–31.

65. Enstam, "The Family," 150–51; Malone, *Women on the Texas Frontier*, 18–20; Myres, "Cowboys and Southern Belles," 168. See generally Henson, *Anglo-American Women in Texas, 1820–1850* (Boston: American Press, 1982).

66. Enstam, "The Family," 139, 150–51; Cashin, *A Family Venture*, 24, 78–79.

67. Gammel, *Laws*, Act of 20 January 1840, secs. 3 and 4, 2:177–78; Texas Constitution (1845), Art. VII, § 20; Gammel, *Laws*, Act of 13 March 1848, 3:78; Act of 26 August 1856, 4:469; Speer, *A Treatise*, 385; McKnight, "Texas Community Property Law: Conservative Attitudes, Reluctant Change," 72–98; Lazarou, "Concealed under Petticoats," 86, 133–44; Defuniak and Vaughn, *Principles*, 36, 83, 234, 297; Leo Kanowitz, *Women and the Law: The Unfinished Revolution* (Albuquerque: University of New Mexico Press, 1969), 64; Daggett, *Legal Essay*, 106–107; George McKay, *A Treatise on the Law of Community Property*, 2d ed. (Indianapolis: Bobbs-Merrill, 1925), 739–40; idem, *A Commentary on the Law of Community Property* (Denver: W. H. Courtwright, 1910), 17–19, 40–42, 46–47, 724, 760–63; Householder, "The Sources," 41–42; Mattie Lloyd Wooten, "The Status of Women in Texas" (Ph.D. diss., University of Texas, Austin, 1941), 304.

68. Gammel, *Laws*, Act of 20 January 1840, secs. 4, 9–10, 2:178–79; *Black v. Bryan*, 18 Tex. 453 (1857); *Fullerton v. Doyle*, 18 Tex. 2 (1856); *Harvey v. Hill*, 7 Tex. 591 (1852); *Wright v. Hayes*, 10 Tex. 130 (1853); *Thomas v. Chance*, 11 Tex. 634 (1854); *Cheeks v. Bellows*, 17 Tex. 613 (1856); Gammel, *Laws*, Act of 13 March 1848, secs. 3–5, 3:78; Act of 26 August 1856, 4:469; Speer, *A Treatise*, 48–49, 55, 60–61; McKnight, "Texas Community Property Law: Conservative Attitudes, Reluctant Change," 72–98; Lazarou, "Concealed under Petticoats," 68–69; Defuniak and Vaughn, *Principles*, 234–97; Kanowitz, *Women*

and the Law, 60–66; Daggett, *Legal Essays,* 100–110; McKay, *A Treatise,* 235–41, 738–42; Householder, "The Sources," 50.

69. De la Tejá, *San Antonio de Béxar,* 75, 137, 97–121; de la Tejá and Wheat, "Béxar: Profile of a Tejano Community," in *Tejano Origins,* 17–18; Arnoldo De León, *The Tejano Community, 1836–1900* (Albuquerque: University of New Mexico Press, 1982), 34–35; *idem,* "*Rancheros, Comerciantes,* and *Trabajadores* in South Texas, 1848–1900," in *Reflections of the Mexican Experience in Texas,* ed. Margarita B. Melville and Hilda Castille Phariss (Houston: Mexican American Studies, University of Houston, 1979), 78; Dysart, "Mexican Women," 364–66; Robert Staples, "The Mexican-American Family: Its Modification over Time and Space," *Phylon* 32 (summer 1971): 179–92. See generally Michael Thurgood Haynes, "Crowning Achievement: Reproducing Elite Class and Gender Roles in San Antonio" (Ph.D. diss., University of Texas, Austin, 1994).

70. De León, *They Called Them Greasers,* 13; Enstam, "The Family," 143–44; Dysart, "Mexican Women," 366; De León, *The Tejano Community,* 130; Ann M. Pescatello, *Power and Pawn: The Female in Iberian Families, Societies, and Culture* (Westport, Conn.: Greenwood Press, 1976), 176.

71. Olmstead, *A Journey through Texas,* 161.

72. Robert C. Hunt, "Components of Relationships," 114–15, 117, 126, 134–37; Halla, "El Paso, Texas," 100–103, 105–108, 116, 120–24.

73. Richard R. B. Powell, "Community Property: A Critique of Its Regulation of Intra-Family Relations," *Washington Law Review* 12 (1936): 38–40; McKay, *A Treatise,* 65; Halla, "El Paso, Texas," 131–32; Dysart, "Mexican Women," 375; Richard Griswold del Castillo, "'Only for My Family': Historical Dimensions of Chicano Family Solidarity—The Case of San Antonio in 1860," *Aztlán* 16(1–2)(1985): 145–76.

74. Enstam, "The Family," 141–52; Malone, *Women on the Texas Frontier,* 18–25; Myres, "Cowboys and Southern Belles," 130–34; Jolene Maddox Snider, "Sarah Devereux: A Study of Southern Femininity," *Southwestern Historical Quarterly* 97(3)(1994): 479–508.

75. Furman, "Texas Women versus the Texas Myth," 160–67. See generally Paula Mitchell Marks, *Turn Your Eyes toward Texas: Pioneers Sam and Mary Maverick* (College Station: Texas A&M University Press, 1989); Henson, *The Cartwrights of San Augustine.* But see Henrietta Andreadis, "True Womanhood Revisited," 179–204.

76. Elizabeth York Enstam, "Women on the Urban Frontier," in *The Texas Experience,* ed. Archie P. McDonald (College Station: Texas A&M University Press, 1986), 96–98; *idem,* "The Family," 142–49; *idem, Women and the Creation of Urban Life: Dallas, Texas, 1843–1920* (College Station: Texas A&M University Press, 1998), chs. 1 and 2; Furman, "Texas Women versus the Texas

Myth," 168; Richardson et al., *Texas*, 194; David G. McComb, *Texas: A Modern History* (Austin: University of Texas Press, 1989), 67.

77. Holley, *Texas*, 145; Wallis, *Sixty Years on the Brazos*, 226; Furman, "Texas Women versus the Texas Myth," 159–68; Myres, "Cowboys and Southern Belles," 163–69; Malone, *Women on the Texas Frontier*, 17–25; Enstam, "The Family," 150–51. See generally Mattie Lloyd Wooten, "The Roles of Pioneer Women in the Texas Frontier Community" (M.A. thesis, University of Texas, Austin, 1929); Rubye Du Terrail, "The Role of Women in Nineteenth-Century San Antonio" (M.A. thesis, Saint Mary's University, San Antonio, 1949).

78. McKnight, "Texas Community Property Law: Conservative Attitudes, Reluctant Change," 72–98.

79. Weeks, *Debates of the Texas Convention*, 595; *Wright*, 10 Tex. at 130; *Harvey*, 7 Tex. at 591; *Thomas*, 11 Tex. at 634; *Cheeks*, 17 Tex. at 613; *Wood*, 7 Tex. at 13; *Yates*, 3 Tex. at 452–56; *Babb*, 21 Tex. at 767; *Burris v. Wideman*, 6 Tex. 232 (1851); *Carroll v. Carroll*, 20 Tex. 742 (1858); Speer, *A Treatise*, 205, 233; McKnight, "Texas Community Property Law: Conservative Attitudes, Reluctant Change," 72, 75; Vaughn, "The Policy of Community Property," 20, 32–33; Ford W. Hall, "An Account of the Adoption of the Common Law," 801–36.

80. Gammel, *Laws*, Act of 20 January 1840, secs. 2–12, 2:178–80; Texas, *Constitution* (1845), Art. 7, § 20; Gammel, *Laws*, Act of 13 March 1848, 3:78; Act of 26 August 1856, 4:469; *Burris*, 6 Tex. at 232; Speer, *A Treatise*, 60–61, 205; Defuniak and Vaughn, *Principles*, 234–93; Richardson et al., *Texas*, 163, 174–75, 181–82; Campbell, *An Empire for Slavery*, 51–55; Jordan et al., *Texas: A Geography*, 48–49.

81. *Yates*, 3 Tex. at 433; Siegel, *A Political History*, 39, 107–109, 166; De León, *They Called Them Greasers*, 49–86; Hinojosa, "The Texas Mexico Border," 10–20; Ellen Schneider and Paul H. Carlson, "Gunnysackers, *Carreteros*, and Teamsters: The South Texas Cart War of 1857," *Journal of South Texas* 1 (spring 1988): 1–9. See generally Rubio, *Stolen Heritage*.

82. Campbell, *An Empire for Slavery*, 192; Malone, *Women on the Texas Frontier*, 18–20.

83. Enstam, "The Family," 145–51; Furman, "Texas Women," 168; Myres, "Cowboys and Southern Belles," 125–30.

CHAPTER 5

1. *Nichols v. Stewart*, 15 Tex. 226–32 (1855); Yoakum, *History of Texas*, 1:301–304.

2. Edward A. Lukes, *De Witt Colony of Texas* (Austin: Jenkins Publishing, 1976), 142–44, 183; *Nichols*, 15 Tex. at 227–35.

3. *Nichols*, 15 Tex. at 230–32.

4. *Ibid.*

5. Deed of Rachel [Sowell] Nichols and George W. Nichols to A. W. G. Davis, authenticated by J. M. Baker, Chief Justice, 27 October 1845, Gonzales County Court Deed Records.

6. *Nichols*, 15 Tex. at 231–35.

7. Gammel, *Laws*, Ordinance and Decree of 16 January 1836, 1:1041; *ibid.*, Act of 5 June 1837, 1:1293–94; *Nichols*, 15 Tex. at 227–35.

8. *Nichols*, 15 Tex. at 232.

9. James M. Day, comp., *The Texas Almanac, 1857–1873* (Waco: Texian Press, 1967), 109; Joseph W. McKnight, "Stephen Austin's Legalistic Concerns," *Southwestern Historical Quarterly* 89(3)(January 1986): 251–54. While Austin modeled his criminal and civil laws on the codes of various jurisdictions in the United States, the local ordinances were subject to the provisions of *Novísima Recopilación* and *Las Siete Partidas*. For the version of the *Partidas* familiar to early Texas jurists, see Moreau Lislet and Henry Carleton, *The Laws of "Las Siete Partidas" Which Are Still in Force in the State of Louisiana*, 2 vols. (New Orleans: James M'Karaher, 1820). McKnight, "The Spanish Legacy," 220–24; Daffan Gilmer, "Early Courts and Lawyers of Texas," *Texas Law Review*, 12(4)(June 1934): 439–40; Louis J. Wortham, *A History of Texas* (Fort Worth: Molyneaux Co., 1924), 388.

10. Baade, "The Form of Marriage," 8–11, 84; Smith, *Marriage by Bond*, 5–7, 86; Smithwick, *The Evolution of a State*, 25; Howard Miller, "Stephen F. Austin and the Anglo-Texan Response to the Religious Establishment in Mexico, 1821–1836," *Southwestern Historical Quarterly* 91(3)(1988): 283–316.

11. Smith, *Marriage by Bond*, 26–27.

12. Holley, *Texas*, 177–81.

13. *Ibid.*, 178–79.

14. Douglas, *Famous Texas Feuds*, 5; Smithwick, *The Evolution of a State*, 238.

15. *Ibid.*, 46.

16. Smith, "Reminiscences," 34.

17. *Ibid.*

18. Smithwick, *The Evolution of a State*, 46.

19. Holley, *Texas*, 178.

20. Smith, "Reminiscences," 34–35.

21. Holley, *Texas*, 178.

22. Smith, "Reminiscences," 34–35.

23. *Ibid.*, 37.

24. Howard, *Matrimonial Institutions*, 2:200–203; Grossberg, *Governing the Hearth*, 34–35.

25. Smith, *Marriage by Bond*, 6–86.

26. Smithwick, *The Evolution of a State*, 46.

27. Smith, *Marriage by Bond*, 28; Grossberg, *Governing the Hearth*, 6–9, 12–13, 17–19, 25–27.

28. Henry Smith to Vice-President Mirabeau B. Lamar, 18 November 1836, quoted in Smith, *Marriage by Bond*, 37; Smith, "Reminiscences," 24, 31.

29. *Lewis*, 44 Tex. at 340–41; Gammel, *Laws*, Act of 5 February 1841, 2:640; Smith, *Marriage by Bond*, 5.

30. *Lewis*, 44 Tex. at 339–41; Baade, "The Form of Marriage," 86.

31. Gammel, *Laws*, Ordinance and Decree of 16 January 1836, 1:1041; *ibid.*, Act of 5 June 1837, 1:1293–94; Act of 5 February 1841, 2:640; *Nichols*, 15 Tex. at 226, 232; *Sapp v. Newsome*, 27 Tex. 537 (1864); Smith, *Marriage by Bond*, 4–10; Richardson et al., *Texas*, 74–75; Baade, "The Form of Marriage," 10.

32. Bardaglio, *Reconstructing the Household*, 14, 23–24, 84, 106; Cashin, *A Family Venture*, 24, 78–79; Enstam, "The Family," 139, 151.

33. Gammel, *Laws*, Ordinance and Decree of 22 January 1836, 1:1041.

34. Gammel, *Laws*, Act of 5 June 1837, 1:1293–94; Texas (Republic), *Constitution*, Declaration of Rights, Sec. 3; Texas, *Constitution* (1845), Art. I, §§ 3 and 4.

35. *Tarpley*, 2 Tex. at 149. The Texas Supreme Court relied on the seminal 1809 New York decision of *Fenton v. Reed*, which was based on a majority opinion that Chancellor James Kent wrote. 4 Johns. 52–54 (N.Y. 1809); Bishop, *Commentaries* (1881): 1:203, 223; Grossberg, *Governing the Hearth*, 70–78; Otto E. Koegel, *Common Law Marriage and Its Development in the United States* (Washington, D.C.: J. Byrne, 1922), 11–13.

36. *Nichols*, 15 Tex. at 232.

37. *Middlebrook*, 203 S.W. 2d at 686–87; *McChesney v. Johnson*, 79 S.W. 2d 658–69 (Tex. Civ. App.– 1934, no writ) (dictum); Newton and Gambrell, *A Social and Political History*, 115–23; W. M. Bonesio, "Marriage and Divorce under the Texas Family Code," *Houston Law Review* 8 (1970–71): 109–12.

38. Gammel, *Laws*, Act of 21 December 1836, 1:1250; Texas, *Penal Code* (1857), art. 392; Gammel, *Laws*, Act of 12 February 1858, 4:1037; Adele B. Looscan, "Harris County, 1822–1845," *Southwestern Historical Quarterly* 18 (October 1914): 195–207; 19 (July 1915): 37–64.

39. Gammel, *Laws*, Act of 18 December 1837, sec. 2, 1:95; *Sharman v. Sharman*, 18 Tex. 524–25 (1857).

40. Gammel, *Laws*, Act of 6 January 1841, 2:483–86.

41. *Lewis*, 44 Tex. at 338–39.

42. Gammel, *Laws*, Ordinance and Decree of 16 January 1836, 1:1041; *ibid.*, Act of 5 June 1837, 1:1293–94; Baade, "The Form of Marriage," 9–11.

43. Gammel, *Laws*, Act of 5 February 1841, 2:640.

44. Gammel, *Laws,* Act of 28 January 1840, 2:132; Act of 18 March 1848, 3:129; see also *ibid.,* Act of 29 November 1841, 2:6; *Hartwell v. Jackson,* 7 Tex. 577—78 (1852); Grossberg, *Governing the Hearth,* 200—204; Daniel Scott Smith, "The Long Cycle in American Illegitimacy and Premarital Pregnancy," in *Bastardy and Its Comparative History,* ed. Peter Laslett (Cambridge, Mass.: Harvard University Press, 1980), 372; James Dundas White, "Legitimation by Subsequent Marriage," *Law Quarterly Review* 36 (1920): 256; Dennis Fitzpatrick, "Legitimation by Subsequent Marriage," *Journal of Comparative Law,* N.S. (1905): 43.

45. Gammel, *Laws,* Act of 20 January 1840, 2:177—80; Tapping Reeve, *Law of Baron and Femme* (New Haven, Conn.: Oliver Steele, 1816), 277; Kent, *Commentaries,* 2:216—17; Deborah J. Venezia, "The Rights of an Illegitimate Child Post—*Gomez v. Perez:* A Legitimate Situation?" *St Mary's Law Journal* 12 (1980): 199—201; John J. Sampson, "Chapter 13. Determination of Paternity" (commentary in "The Texas Family Code Symposium," [special issue]), *Texas Tech Law Review* 13(3)(1982): 897—900; Grossberg, *Governing the Hearth,* 215—18; William Nelson, *The Americanization of the Common Law: The Impact of Legal Change on Massachusetts Society, 1760—1830* (Cambridge: Harvard University Press, 1975), 25—26, 76.

46. *Tarpley,* 2 Tex. at 136, 149; *Yates,* 3 Tex. at 447—49; *Lockhart,* 18 Tex. at 104; *Babb,* 21 Tex. at 765; *Honey,* 36 Tex. at 68; Clarence M. Davis, "Common Law Marriage in Texas," *Southwestern Law Journal* 21(3)(1967): 643—47; Comment, "Recent Cases," *Texas Law Review* 9(4)(June 1931): 613—14; M. L. C., "Persons—Common Law Marriage—Validity After Removal of Impediment," *Texas Law Review* 8(3)(April 1930): 439; H. E. S., "Judicial Presumptions Respecting Irregular Marriages," *University of Pennsylvania Law Review* (March 1934): 508. For a discussion of the Scottish origins of "habit and repute," see *Dalrymple v. Dalrymple,* 161 E.R. 665 (1811); *Cunningham v. Cunningham,* 2 Dow. 483 (Eng. 1814).

47. *Morgan,* 5 Humph. at 13; *Johnson,* 30 Mo. at 72; William Blackstone, *Commentaries on the Laws of England,* 4 vols. (Oxford: Clarendon Press, 1765—69), 1:436, 4:163—64; Zephaniah Swift, *A System of Laws for the State of Connecticut,* 2 vols. (Windham, Conn.: John Byrne, 1795—96), 1:186—87; William Paley, *The Principles of Political and Moral Philosophy,* 5th ed., 2 vols. (Philadelphia: Thomas Dobson, 1788), 1:352, 2:293—95; Kent, *Commentaries,* 2:177; Francis Lieber, *Manual of Political Ethics,* 2 vols. (Boston: C. C. Little and J. Brown, 1838—39), 2:291; Grossberg, *Governing the Hearth,* 120—26; Foster, "Indian and Common Law Marriages," 83—102; Bishop, *Commentaries* (1881), 1:184—87.

48. Gammel, *Laws,* Ordinance and Decree of 16 January 1836, 1:135; *ibid.,* Act of 21 December 1836, sec. 22, 1:190; Act of 18 December 1837, secs. 1, 2,

and 8, 1:94; Act of 5 February 1841, sec. 1, 2:176; Act of February 9, 1854, 4:1509–10; Texas, *Penal Code* (1857), arts. 384–85, pp. 71–72; *Smith,* 1 Tex. 621; *Yates,* 3 Tex. 433; *Lee,* 18 Tex. 145; *Lockhart,* 18 Tex. 103, *Carroll,* 20 Tex. 741, *Babb,* 21 Tex. 765, *Hartwell,* 7 Tex. 576; *Moore,* 24 Tex. 149 (1859); *Gorman v. State,* 23 Tex. 646 (1859); *Lewis,* 44 Tex. 339–41; *Routh,* 57 Tex. 590–91; *Morgan v. Morgan,* 1 Tex. Civ. App. 315 (2d Dist. 1892); Joel Prentiss Bishop, *Commentaries on the Law of Marriage and Divorce,* 5th ed., 2 vols. (Boston: Little and Brown, 1873), 1:259–65; *Century Edition of the American Digest: A Complete Digest of All Reported American Cases from the Earliest Times to 1896,* 50 vols. (Saint Paul, Minn.: West, 1897–1904), 34:254–58; Grossberg, *Governing the Hearth,* 103–105.

49. *Smith,* 1 Tex. 625–35; *Siete Partidas* IV. 13.1.

50. *Carroll,* 20 Tex. at 732–36. The rule set forth in *Carroll* was similar to that utilized in the 1854 Mississippi decision *Hull v. Rawls,* 27 Miss. 471. See also *Sellers v. Davis,* 12 Tenn. 503 (1833); *Gathing v. Williams,* 5 Ired. 487 (N.C. 1848); *Mount Holly v. Andover,* 11 Vt. 226 (1839); *Rawdon v. Rawdon,* 28 Ala. 565 (1856); *Middleborough v. Rochester,* 12 Mass. 363 (1815); *Higgins v. Breen,* 9 Mo. 493 (1845); *Heffner v. Heffner,* 11 Harris 104 (Pa. 1854); Bishop, *Commentaries* (1881), 1:101, 257; Grossberg, *Governing the Hearth,* 121.

51. *Yates,* 3 Tex. at 447; *Lockhart,* 18 Tex. at 104. The rule drew on holdings in the English settlement and removal decisions of *Rex v. The Inhabitants of Twyning,* 2 B. & Ald. 387 (1819) and *Rex v. The Inhabitants of Harborne,* 2 A.D. & E. 540 (1835). *Yates* was unusual, if not unique, in its reasoning and result. The decision handed down ten years later in the Mississippi decision *Spears v. Burton,* however, was quite similar. 31 Miss. 547 (1856).

52. *Hiram v. Pierce,* 45 Maine 367 (1858); *Valleau v. Valleau,* 6 Paige 207 (N.Y. 1836); *Commonwealth v. Mash,* 7 Met. 474 (Mass. 1844); *Jackson v. Claw,* 18 Johns. 346 (N.Y. 1820); *Rhea v. Rhenner,* 26 U.S. (1 Pet.) 105, 76 L. Ed. 72 (U.S. 1828); *Wood v. Wood's Adm'r,* 2 Bay 476 (S.C. 1802); *Loring v. Steineman,* 1 Met. 204 (Mass. 1840); *Northfield v. Plymouth,* 20 Vt. 582 (1848); *Canady v. George,* 6 Rich Eq. 103 (S.C. 1853); Joel Prentiss Bishop, *Commentaries on the Law of Marriage and Divorce,* 2d ed. (Boston: Little and Brown, 1856), 171; *idem, Commentaries* (1881), 1:257–61; Grossberg, *Governing the Hearth,* 121; Homer Clark, *The Law of Domestic Relations in the United States,* 2d ed. (Saint Paul: West, 1988), 67; Samuel Adams, "Two Score and Three of Enoch Ardens," *Journal of Family Law* 5 (1965): 159–69; Charles Feit, "The Enoch Arden: A Problem of Family Life," *Brooklyn Law Review* 6 (1937): 434.

53. Lester G. Bugbee, "The Old Three Hundred: A List of Settlers in Austin's First Colony," *Quarterly of the Texas State Historical Association* 1 (October 1897): 108–17.

54. *Yates*, 3 Tex. at 452–65.

55. Joseph W. Hawes, "The Reform Impulse," in *The Social Fabric: American Life from 1607 to 1877*, 2 vols., 4th ed., ed. John H. Carey and Julius Weinberg (Boston: Little, Brown, 1984), 193–94; Grossberg, *Governing the Hearth*, 8, 234–43.

56. *Yates*, 3 Tex. at 451.

57. Hogan, *The Texas Republic*, 268.

58. *Babb*, 21 Tex. at 767–68. See also *Moore*, 24 Tex. at 150.

59. *Carroll*, 20 Tex. at 742–43.

60. *Harrington v. Harrington*, 742 S.W. 2d 722–24 (Tex. Civ. App.–Houston 1987, no writ). See also *Small v. Harper*, 638 S.W. 2d 24 (Tex. Civ. App.–Houston [1st Dist.] 1982, no writ); *Negrini v. Plus Two Advertising, Inc.*, 695 S.W. 2d 624 (Tex. Civ. App.–Houston [1st Dist.] 1985, no writ); Carol S. Bruch, "Property Rights of De Facto Spouses Including Thoughts on the Value of Homemakers' Services," *Family Law Quarterly* 10(2)(1976): 101; Herma Hill Kay and Carol Amyx, "*Marvin v. Marvin*: Preserving the Options," *California Law Review* 65(5)(1977): 937; William A. Reppy, Jr., "Property and Support Rights for Unmarried Couples: A Proposal for Creating a New Legal Status," *Louisiana Law Review* 44(6)(1984): 1677.

61. *Earle and McNier v. Daws*, 3 Md. Chan. 230 (1849); *Kelly's Heirs v. McGuire and Wife*, 15 Ark. 555 (1855); *Flintham v. Holder*, 1 Dew Eq. 349 (N.C. 1829); *Little v. Lake*, 8 Ohio 289 (1838); *Miller v. Stewart*, 8 Gill. 128 (Md. 1849); *Bacon v. McBride*, 32 Vt. 585 (1860); *Black v. Cartmell*, 10 B. Mon. 188 (Ky. 1849); *Woodstock v. Hooker*, 6 Conn. 36 (1825); *Burlington v. Fosby*, 6 Vt. 83 (1834); *Kent v. Backer*, 2 Gray 535 (Mass. 1854); Tapping Reeve, *A Treatise on the Law of Descent* (New York, 1825), 26; Kent, *Commentaries*, 2: 212–13; *Lange v. Richous*, 6 La. 560 (1834); Grossberg, *Governing the Hearth*, 196–228; Stanley Katz, "Republicanism and the Law of Inheritance," *Michigan Law Review* 76 (1976) 1–29.

62. *Wilkie v. Collins*, 48 Miss. 496 (1873); *Michaels v. Michaels*, 91 N.J. Eq. 408, 110 Atl. 573 (1920); *Johnson v. Johnson*, 114 Ill. 611, 3 N.E. 232, 55 Am. St. Rep. 884 (1885); *Wagoner v. Wagoner*, 128 Mich. 635, 87 N.W. 898 (1901); *Keller v. Linsenmyer*, 101 N.J. Eq. 664, 139 Atl. 33 (1927); *Harris v. Harris*, 8 Ill. App. 57 (1880); *Brown v. Parks*, 173 Ga. 228, 150 S.E. 238 (1931); *Smith v. Fuller*, 108 N.W. 765 (Iowa 1906); H. E. S., "Judicial Presumptions," 508–15; Clark, *The Law of Domestic Relations*, 70–75.

63. *Boulden v. McIntire*, 119 Ind. 574, 21 N.E. 445, 12 Am. St. Rep. 453 (1889); *Coal Run Coal Co. v. Jones*, 127 Ill. 379, 8 N.E. 865 (1886); *Maier v. Brock*, 222 Mo. 74, 120 S.W. 1167, 133 Am. St. Rep. 513 (1909); *Scott v. Scott*, 25 Ky. Law 1356, 77 S.W. 1122 (1904); *Chancy v. Whinney*, 47 Okla. 272, 147 Pac. 1036

(1915); *Hamlin v. Grogan,* 257 F. 59 (C.C.A. 8th Cir. 1919); *Wilson v. Allen,* 108 Ga. 275, 33 S.W. 975 (1899); *Industrial Comm. v. Dell,* 104 Ohio St. 389, 135 N.E. 669 (1922); In re *Hamilton,* 76 Hun. 200, 27 N.Y. Supp. 107 (1915); *Nelson v. Jones,* 245 Mo. 579, 151 S.W. 80 (1912); Annot., 34 A.L.R. 474 (1925); Annot., 77 A.L.R. 735 (1932).

64. Robert A. Allen, "Presumption of the Validity of a Second Marriage," *Baylor Law Review* 20(2)(spring 1968): 209–14; Clark, *The Law of Domestic Relations,* 71–73; Joseph W. McKnight, "Chapter 2. Validity of Marriage. Subchapter A. General Provisions. Sec. 201. State Policy" (commentary in "The Texas Family Code Symposium" [special issue]), *Texas Tech Law Review* 13(3)(1982): 655–56; H. E. S., "Judicial Presumptions," 507–14; Francis H. Bohlen, "The Effect of Rebuttable Presumptions of Law upon the Burden of Proof," *University of Pennsylvania Law Review* 68(4)(1920): 307, 318; Edmund M. Morgan, "Some Observations Concerning Presumptions," *Harvard Law Review* 44 (March 1931): 906; Grossberg, *Governing the Hearth,* 19–20; Morton J. Horwitz, *The Transformation of American Law, 1780–1860* (Cambridge, Mass.: Harvard University Press, 1977), 73, 160, 253.

65. Rosalee Morris Curtis, *John Hemphill: First Chief Justice of the State of Texas* (Austin: Pemberton Press, 1971), 37, 76, 83; J. E. Ericson and Mary P. Winston, "Civil Law and Common Law in Early Texas," *East Texas Historical Journal* 2 (February 1964): 26; Dumas Malone, *Dictionary of American Biography* (New York: Charles Scribner and Sons, 1932), 52; Reuben Reid Gaines, "John Hemphill, 1803–1862," in *Great American Lawyers,* ed. William Draper Lewis (Philadelphia: John C. Winston Co., 1908), 5; C. W. Raines, "Enduring Laws of the Republic of Texas," *Southwestern Historical Quarterly* 1 (1897): 96; James D. Lynch, *Bench and Bar of Texas* (Saint Louis: Nixon-Jones Printing Co., 1885), 72.

66. James W. Ely, Jr., and David J. Bodenhamer, "Regionalism and American Legal History: The Southern Experience," *Vanderbilt Law Review* 39 (April 1986): 539–567; Michael Stephen Hindus, *Prison and Plantation: Crime, Justice, and Authority in Massachusetts and South Carolina, 1767–1878* (Chapel Hill: University of North Carolina Press, 1980), 15, 20–21; Bardaglio, *Reconstructing the Household,* 2122.

67. Gammel, *Laws,* Act of 20 January 1840, secs. 5–12, 2:178–80; *Black,* 18 Tex. at 464; *Hollis v. Francois,* 5 Tex. 195 (1849); McKnight, "Texas Community Property Law: Conservative Attitudes, Reluctant Change," 70–74; Kanowitz, *Women and the Law,* 63–66; Defuniak and Vaughn, *Principles,* 233–97; Wooten, "The Status of Women in Texas," 303–305; Householder, "The Sources," 39–50; McKay, *A Treatise,* 738–41; Daggett, *Legal Essays,* 105–108; Speer, *A Treatise,* 54–58.

68. Gammel, *Laws,* Act of 3 February 1841, 2:608–609; Act of 30 April

1846, 2:1462; Act of 18 December 1849, 3:449; *Coleman,* 14 Tex. at 594; Gammel, *Laws,* Act of 26 January 1839, 2:125–26; Richardson et al., *Texas,* 136, 143; Texas, *Constitution* (1845), Art. VII, §§ 9, 19, and 22; Weeks, *Debates of the Texas Convention,* 423, 596–97, 1054–55; Gammel, *Laws,* Act of 29 April 1846, 2:1459; Act of 13 March 1848, 3:469; *Love v. Robertson,* 7 Tex. 6 (1851); *DeBlanc v. Lynch,* 23 Tex. 25 (1859); Speer, *A Treatise,* 116; McKnight, "Texas Community Property Law: Conservative Attitudes, Reluctant Change," 72–77; *idem,* "Texas Community Property Law—Its Course of Development and Reform," 117–45; *idem,* "The Spanish Legacy to Texas Law," 222–41; Lawrence M. Friedman, *History of American Law* (New York: Simon and Schuster, 1973), 148; Thurman, "Married Women's Property Acts," 40–42; William Huie, "The Constitutional Definition of the Wife's Separate Property," *Texas Law Review* 35 (October 1957): 1054–55; *idem,* "Some Principles of Texas Community Property Law," in *Comparative Studies in Community Property Law,* ed. Jan P. Charmatz and Harriet S. Daggett (Baton Rouge: Louisiana State University Press, 1955), 117–18.

69. Weeks, *Debates of the Texas Convention,* 423, 596–601, 1054–55; Hall, "An Account of the Adoption of the Common Law," 801–36; Lazarou, "Concealed under Petticoats," 100–101, 120–21; Bardaglio, *Reconstructing the Household,* 30–32; Gerald R. Leslie, *The Family in Social Context,* 2d ed. (New York: Oxford University Press, 1973), 189–91.

CHAPTER 6

1. Yoakum, *History of Texas,* 1:329–54; *Wheat,* 15 Tex. at 241–42.

2. *Ibid.*

3. Yoakum, *History of Texas,* 2:140–42, 361–63; *Wheat,* 15 Tex. at 241–43; Gammel, *Laws,* Act of 22 December 1836, sec. 15, 1:1279–80; Act of 14 December 1837, sec. 29, 1:1414.

4. *Wheat,* 15 Tex. at 242–44.

5. For authority that a wife's abandonment justified a forfeiture of her community estate under the traditional Hispanic law, the court referred to Joaquín Escriche, *Diccionario Razonado de Legislación y Jurisprudencia* (1851), "Mujer Casada." To hold that simple female adultery also warranted such a forfeiture, at least before 1840, it cited Escriche, *Diccionario,* "Bienes Gananciales," which referred to *Siete Partidas* VII. 17.15; *Febrero Novísimo,* 1:111; and *Novísima Recopilación* X. 4.11. Regarding the exceptions to the adultery forfeiture rule, the court cited Escriche, *Diccionario,* "Adulterio," which referred to *Siete Partidas* VII. 17.4, 17.8; *Fuero Real* IV. 7; and *Novísima Recopilación* XII. 28.4. On this point, it also relied on *Armstrong v. Stelber,* 3 La. Ann. 713 (1848). *Wheat,* 15 Tex. at 245–47.

6. For this holding, the court cited Escriche, *Diccionario*, "Bienes Gananciales," which referred to *Febrero Novísimo*, 1:114. *Wheat*, 15 Tex. at 244.

7. *Wheat*, 15 Tex. at 247.

8. Gammel, *Laws*, Act of 6 January 1841, sec. 3, 2:484. In *Sheffield* (3 Tex. at 79), the court relied on *Tourne v. Tourne*, 9 La. 450 (1836); Leonard Shelford, *Practical Treatise on the Law of Marriage and Divorce* (Philadelphia: J. S. Littel, 1841), 240; Kent, *Commentaries*, 2:155; and *Evans v. Evans*, 4 Eng. Eccl. 310 (1790). In *Wright* (6 Tex. at 3), it cited *Popkin v. Popkin*, 3 Eng. Eccl. 325 (1794); *Westmeath v. Westmeath*, 4 Eng. Eccl. 263 (1826); *Harris v. Harris*, 1 Eng. Eccl. 205 (1813); *Waring v. Waring*, 1 Eng. Eccl. 211 (1813); *Bray v. Bray*, 3 Eng. Eccl. 76, (1828); and *Durant v. Durant*, 3 Eng. Eccl. 327 (1825). See also discussions in *Nogees*, 7 Tex. at 537; *Pinkard*, 14 Tex. at 356; *Camp*, 18 Tex. at 528; *Taylor v. Taylor*, 18 Tex. 574 (1857).

9. *Tourne*, 9 La. at 452; *Ghoulston v. Ghoulston*, 31 Ga. 625 (1860); *Waskam v. Waskam*, 31 Miss. 154 (1856); *Rose v. Rose*, 9 Ark. 507 (1849); Bishop, *Commentaries* (1881), 1:528-36, 552; Howard, *Matrimonial Institutions*, 3:52-54, 93-97; Censer, "'Smiling through Her Tears,'" 27-34; Roderick Phillips, *Putting Asunder: A History of Divorce in Western Society* (Cambridge: Cambridge University Press, 1988), 446-51; Catherine Clinton, *The Plantation Mistress*, 80-85; Joseph S. Ferrell, "Early Statutory and Common Law Divorce in North Carolina," *North Carolina Law Review* 41 (1963): 608-20.

10. Curtis, *John Hemphill*, 37, 76, 83. For an opinion in which Chief Justice Hemphill expressed the strong solicitude of the court for homesteading women, see *Wood*, 7 Tex. at 22.

11. Gammel, *Laws*, Act of 6 January 1841, sec. 2, 2:484; *Hare v. Hare*, 10 Tex. 359 (1853); *Pinkard*, 14 Tex. at 356; *Besch*, 27 Tex. at 390-92 (1864); Bishop, *Commentaries* (1881), 1:590-622; Weeks, *Debates of the Texas Convention*, 595-98; Peavy and Smith, *Women in Waiting*, 8-9, 17-18, 23, 34-35, 38.

12. *Morris v. Morris*, 20 Ala. 168 (1852); *Kinsey v. Kinsey*, 37 Ala. 393 (1861); *Harding v. Harding*, 22 Md. 337 (1864); Bishop, *Commentaries* (1881), 1:597; Note, "Constructive Desertion—A Broader Basis for Breaking the Bond," *Iowa Law Review* 51 (1965): 108-28; Annot., 19 A.L.R. 2d 1428-65.

13. *Camp*, 18 Tex. at 535. Compare *Morris*, 20 Ala. at 168; *Holston v. Holston*, 23 Ala. 777 (1853); *Wood v. Wood*, 27 N.C. 674 (1845); *Levering v. Levering*, 16 Md. 213 (1860); *Gillinwaters v. Gillinwaters*, 28 Miss. 60 (1859). See Bishop, *Commentaries* (1881), 1:595-603, 610-12.

14. *Wheat*, 15 Tex. at 244.

15. *Lovett v. Lovett*, 11 Ala. 763 (1847); *Richardson v. Wilson*, 8 Yerg. 67 (Tenn. 1835); Joel Prentiss Bishop, *New Commentaries on Marriage, Divorce, and Separation*, 2 vols. (Chicago: T. H. Flood, 1891), 2:436-45; Bardaglio,

Reconstructing the Household, 31; Censer, "'Smiling through Her Tears,'" 41–47.

16. Gammel, *Laws,* Act of 6 January 1841, secs. 4, 6, 8–10, 2:484–85; Speer, *A Treatise,* 416–17.

17. Section 4 of the 1841 divorce act provided trial judges with broad discretion in property division. Neither the act nor any affirmative holding of the Texas Supreme Court guaranteed a community share for a wife found at fault. The court, however, repeatedly maintained that culpability in divorce litigation did not impair a woman's community and separate property rights. In the 1848 decision of *Byrne v. Byrne,* for example, a man secured a divorce on the ground of cruelty by proving his wife tried to poison him. The court, nonetheless, held that "the wife, although degraded, was entitled to her share of the [community] property and to her own separate property. . . ." 3 Tex. at 336, 341. Jurists agreed, furthermore, the adultery forfeiture rule relied on in *Wheat v. Owens* was not decisive in Texas after 1840, when the Texas Congress adopted simultaneously the common law and Hispanic marital rights systems. *Routh,* 57 Tex. 596–97 (1882); Gammel, *Laws,* Act of 20 January 1840, 2:178–80. Indicative of the obsolescence of the adultery penalty is that the high court upheld an equal division of community property for Elizabeth Simons in 1859 even though her husband Paul had divorced her for infidelity. *Simons,* 13 Tex. at 469–71; *Simons v. Simons,* 23 Tex. 344 (1859). The court routinely relied on the civilian jurisprudence of the Louisiana Supreme Court, which provided an equal division of community property as a matter of law. *Routh,* 57 Tex. at 596. See, for example, *Taylor v. Felps,* 10 La. 114 (1836); *Headen v. Headen,* 15 La. 61 (1840); *Rawley v. Rawley,* 19 La. 557 (1841); *Ledoux v. Boyd,* 10 La. Ann. 66 (1855).

18. *Trimble v. Trimble,* 15 Tex. 18–20 (1855); *Fitts,* 14 Tex. at 451; *Rice v. Rice,* 21 Tex. 58, 68–69 (1858); *Wright v. Wright,* 3 Tex. 179 (1848); *Wright,* 6 Tex. at 2; Paulsen, "Remember the Alamo(ny)," 15–16; Joseph W. McKnight, "Family Law," 93, 136. But see Lazarou, "Concealed under Petticoats," 55, 99, 101.

19. *Fitts,* 14 Tex. at 443, 450; *Wright,* 6 Tex. at 33; *Wright,* 3 Tex. at 178. Compare *McGee v. McGee,* 10 Ga. 477 (1852); *Roseberry v. Roseberry,* 17 Ga. 29 (1855); *Lovett,* 11 Ala. at 763; *Wilson v. Wilson,* 19 N.C. 377 (1857); N.C., *Code* (1855), ch. 39, sec. 15; *Lawson v. Shotwell,* 27 Miss. 63 (1854); and *Sheafe v. Laighton,* 36 N.H. 240 (1858). See Bishop, *Commentaries* (1881), 1:336–39, 348–50, 402, 418; McKnight, "Family Law," 93, 136; Paulsen, "Remember the Alamo(ny)," 8–69; Censer, "'Smiling through Her Tears,'" 36, 41; Marylynn Salmon, *Women and the Law of Property in Early America* (Chapel Hill: University of North Carolina Press, 1986), 66–67.

20. Gammel, *Laws,* Act of 6 January 1841, sec. 13, 2:484; *Trimble,* 15 Tex. at 18–20; *Fitts,* 14 Tex. at 445; *Rice,* 21 Tex. at 58; *Byrne v. Love,* 14 Tex. 81

(1855); *Faulk v. Faulk*, 23 Tex. 653 (1859). Compare *Cornelius v. Cornelius*, 31 Ala. 479 (1858); Ala., *Code* (Ormand, Bagby, and Goldthwaite 1852), secs. 1977, 1980, pp. 379–80; *Foster v. Alston*, 7 Miss. 406 (1842); *Armstrong v. Stone*, 50 Va. 102 (1852); Va., *Digest of the Laws*, 2d ed. (Tate 1841), p. 288; *State v. Paine*, 23 Tenn. 523 (1843); *Hutson v. Townsend*, 6 Rich. Eq. 249 (S.C. 1854); *Thomas v. Tailleau*, 13 La. Ann. 127 (1858); Ga., *Digest of the Statute Laws* (Cobb 1851), ch. 149, p. 335; Miss., *Revised Code* (Sharkey, Harris, and Ellet 1857), ch. 40, art. 17, pp. 334–35; Tenn., *Code* (1858), sec. 2490, p. 489; Va., *Code* (Patton and Robinson 1849), ch. 109, secs. 10, 12, p. 473; *Dedham v. Natick*, 16 Mass. 135 (1819); *Ahrenfeldt v. Ahrenfeldt*, 1 Hoffm. Chan. 497 (N.Y. 1840); *Wand v. Wand*, 14 Cal. 12 (1860); *Miner v. Miner*, 11 Ill. 43 (1849). See Blackstone, *Commentaries*, 1:442, 3:427; Bishop, *New Commentaries* (1891), 2:449–58, 464–65; James Schouler, *A Treatise on the Law of Domestic Relations*, (Boston: Little and Brown, 1870), 2:234–35; Censer, "'Smiling through Her Tears,'" 43, 45–46; Bardaglio, *Reconstructing the Household*, 79–80, 82–88, 92–94; Wyatt-Brown, *Southern Honor*, 234–44; Clinton, *The Plantation Mistress*, 84–85; Grossberg, *Governing the Hearth*, 155–56, 234–46, 250–55; Jay Fliegelman, *Prodigals and Pilgrims: The American Revolution against Patriarchal Authority, 1750–1800* (New York: Cambridge University Press, 1982), 95; Howard Neil Cozen, "English Background: Origins of *Parens Patriae*," *South Carolina Law Review* 22 (1976): 147–51; Matilda Fenberg, "Blame Coke and Blackstone," *Women Lawyers Journal* 34(2)(spring 1948): 7–10.

21. Ten of the fifteen Texas appeals were granted to women, one was granted to a man, and four were remanded. The proportion of appeals women instituted was comparable to that in at least seven other antebellum states: Alabama, 75 percent; Arkansas, 100 percent; Georgia, 42 percent; Louisiana, 73 percent; Mississippi, 60 percent; North Carolina, 60 percent; Tennessee, 86 percent. Censer, "'Smiling through Her Tears,'" 46–47.

22. In 1845, the Eleventh District Court issued two final divorce decrees: Cause No. 1316, *Sarah Renshaw v. James Renshaw;* Cause No. 1380, *Esther O. Fall v. James S. Fall.* Three divorce cases were continued: Cause No. 725, *W. K. Wilson v. Robert Wilson;* Cause No. 1407, *Anne Earl v. Charles Earl, Sr.;* Cause No. 1405, *Jsp. Whiting v. Whiting.* One suit was discontinued: Cause No. 1465, *Emily Robinson v. Thomas Robinson.* Eleventh Judicial District Court, Minutes District Court E, Harris County, 14 April 1845 to 8 December 1848. Minutes and trial documents are available at Harris County Records Library, 102 San Jacinto, Houston, Texas. Court minutes are also on microfilm and available through the Texas State Library, State Archives Division, Austin, Texas.

23. In 1860, women instituted ten of the divorce suits, in contrast to five that men began. Harris County Records Library, Eleventh District Court Minutes, Vol. J, Harris County, 12 December 1859 to 26 September 1865.

24. Cause No. 4591, *Eliza Stephanes v. Charles Stephanes;* Cause No. 4953, *August Hentze v. Augustee Hentze;* Cause No. 5038, *Felitia Ingraham v. R. C. Ingraham;* Cause No. 4968, *Mary Reeves v. E. B. Reeves;* Cause No. 5095, *John J. Cain v. Alitha Cain;* Harris County Records Library, Eleventh District Court Minutes, Vol. J, Harris County, 12 December 1859 to 26 September 1865.

25. *Sheffield,* 3 Tex. at 86.

26. *Ibid.*

27. Gammel, *Laws,* Act of 6 January 1841, secs. 4 and 12, 2:484–86.

28. *Moore v. Moore,* 22 Tex. 239–41 (1858).

29. *Nogees,* 7 Tex. at 546.

30. See Censer, "'Smiling through Her Tears,'" 37; Bardaglio, *Reconstructing the Household,* 34–36; Bishop, *Commentaries* (1881), 1:554–55. See *David,* 27 Ala. at 222; *Rose,* 9 Ark. at 507; *Robinson v. Robinson,* 26 Tenn. 440 (1846). But see *Harrison v. Harrison,* 29 N.C. 484 (1847); *Rutledge v. Rutledge,* 37 Tenn. 554 (1858); *Tourne,* 9 La. at 452.

31. *Nogees,* 7 Tex. at 540, 546; *Sheffield,* 3 Tex. at 79; Texas, *Penal Code* (1857), arts. 475, 483; *Owen v. State,* 7 Tex. App. 329 (1875); *Gorman v. State,* 42 Tex. 221 (1879). Compare *Bradley v. State,* 1 Miss. 156 (1824); *Bread's Case,* 2 Bland 562 (Md. 1830); *Joyner v. Joyner,* 6 Jones Eq. 322 (N.C. 1862); *State v. Rhodes,* 61 N.C. 453 (1868); *Fulgham v. State,* 46 Ala. 143 (1871); *Lawson v. State,* 115 Ga. 578, 41 S.E. 993 (1902); *Carpenter v. Commonwealth,* 92 Ky. 452, 18 S.W. 9 (1892); *Harris v. State,* 71 Miss. 462, 14 So. 266 (1893); *State v. Oliver,* 70 N.C. 60 (1874). See Blackstone, *Commentaries,* 1:445; Kent, *Commentaries,* 2:181; Bynum, *Unruly Women,* 61; Beirne Stedman, "Right of Husband to Chastise Wife," *Virginia Law Register* (N.S.) 3(4)(August 1917): 241–43.

32. *Rice,* 21 Tex. at 59–60.

33. *Ibid.* at 60. See also *Byrne,* 3 Tex. at 336–41.

34. *Nogees,* 7 Tex. at 546, *aff'd Taylor,* 18 Tex. at 574; Speer, *A Treatise,* 31, 191.

35. Gammel, *Laws,* Act of 6 January 1841, sec. 12, 2:486; *Wright,* 6 Tex. at 20–25, *aff'd Nogees,* 7 Tex. at 539–40. The *Wright* court cited *Ferrers v. Ferrers,* 3 Eng. Eccl. 334 (1792); *Weastmeath,* 4 Eng. Eccl. at 238; and Shelford, *Practical Treatise,* 436, 447.

36. See Censer, "'Smiling through Her Tears,'" 35–39.

37. *Wright,* 6 Tex. at 22–23.

38. Myres, *Westering Women,* 174.

39. *Durant,* 3 Eng. Eccl. at 327; *Bramwell v. Bramwell,* 162 E.R. 1285 (1831); *Ferrers,* 3 Eng. Eccl. at 354; *D'Aguilar v. D'Aguilar,* 3 Eng. Eccl. 329 (1794); *Dance v. Dance,* 3 Eng. Eccl. 341 (1799); *Turton v. Turton,* 5 Eng. Eccl. 130 (1830); *Hughes v. Hughes,* 19 Ala. 307 (1851); *Reese v. Reese,* 21 Ala. 785 (1853); *Bowic v. Bowic,* 3 Md. Ch. 51 (1850); *Armstrong v. Armstrong,* 32 Miss. 279, 298

(1856); *Gardner v. Gardner*, 2 Gray 434 (Mass. 1854); *Wood v. Wood*, 2 Paige 108 (N.Y. 1830); *Hollister v. Hollister*, 6 Pa. 449 (1849). See Bishop, *New Commentaries* (1891), 2:124, 139, 157–63; Annot., 16 A.L.R. 2d 590; J. E. Thompson, "Divorce—Condonation—Effect of a Marital Offense Insufficient for Divorce," *Texas Law Review* 24 (1945–46): 386–87.

40. Gammel, *Laws*, Act of 6 January 1841, sec. 2, 2:483. Compare *Mehle v. Lapeyrollerie*, 16 La. Ann. 4 (1861); *Tewksbury v. Tewksbury*, 4 How. 109 (Miss. 1839). See Bishop, *Commentaries* (1881), 1:510–13, 518–19. But see N.C., *Revised Statutes* (1837), ch. 39, sec. 2; *Whittington v. Whittington*, 2 Dev. & Bat. 64 (N.C. 1836); *Moss v. Moss*, 2 Ired. 55 (N.C. 1841); *Wood*, 27 N.C. at 674. For a discussion of traditional Hispanic law making simple adultery a ground for separation, see *Sharman*, 18 Tex. at 524.

41. Speer, *A Treatise*, 398.

42. Gammel, *Laws*, Act of 21 December 1836, sec. 23, 1:1250; Texas, *Penal Code* (1857), arts. 392–95, p. 73; Bishop, *Commentaries* (1881), 1:637; idem, *Commentaries on the Law of Statutory Crimes* (Boston: Little, Brown, 1873), 426. For discussions of statutes in other states penalizing only "living in adultery," see *Cameron and Cooper v. State*, 14 Ala. 546 (1848); *McLeland v. State*, 25 Ga. 477 (1858); *Wright v. State*, 8 Blackf. 385 (Ind. 1847); *Searls v. People*, 13 Ill. 597 (1852); *Crouse v. State*, 16 Ark. 566 (1855).

43. *Wheat*, 15 Tex. at 246.

44. Bishop, *Commentaries* (1881), 1:518; Shelford, *Practical Treatise*, 395; Phillips, *Putting Asunder*, 136–37; Carol Lynn Halem, *Divorce Reform: Changing Legal and Social Perspectives* (New York: Free Press, 1980; London: Collier Macmillan, 1980), 17.

45. *Wright*, 6 Tex. at 17; *Sharman*, 18 Tex. at 526. Both decisions referred to *Popkin*, 3 Eng. Eccl. at 225; *Durant*, 3 Eng. Eccl. at 327; and *Bray*, 3 Eng. Eccl. at 76.

46. *Cartwright*, 18 Tex. at 644.

47. *Ibid.* at 642–43; Texas, *Penal Code* (1857), art. 394, p. 73.

48. Hemphill's opinion in this regard involved a complex analysis of various Spanish commentators, the 1808 and 1825 Louisiana civil codes, Louisiana judicial decisions, and traditional Hispanic law, including *Siete Partidas* IV. 11.20; *Novísima Recopilación* X. 4.1, 4.3; *Fuero Real* III. 3.1, 3.3, 7.2; *Childers v. Johnson*, 6 La. Ann. 634 (1851); *Ducrest's Heirs v. Bijeau's Estate*, 8 Martin N.S. 198 (La. 1829); *Deshautels v. Fontenot*, 6 La. Ann. 689 (1851); *Frederic v. Frederic*, 10 Martin N.S. 189 (La. 1821); and *Goner v. Goner*, 11 Rob. 526 (La. 1845). See *Cartwright*, 18 Tex. at 629–41.

49. *Hagerty*, 16 Tex. at 663; McArthur, "Myth, Reality, and Anomaly," 18–32.

50. Curtis, *John Hemphill*, 38, 60, 76, 83.

51. Gammel, *Laws*, Act of 12 February 1858, 4:1037.

52. Texas, *Penal Code* (1857), art. 562, p. 110. The law of the Visigoths empowered a man who discovered his wife in the act of adultery to kill both her and her lover. The old Hispanic rule, deriving therefrom, only permitted a husband to kill the paramour. S. P. Scott, trans. and ed., *The Visigothic Code: Forum Judicum* (Boston: Boston Book Co., 1910), III. 4.4, p. 96; *Siete Partidas* VII. 12.8. Regarding the traditional Hispanic criminal penalties for female adultery, including death, public whipping, and the disposition and permissible vengeance of a husband, see *Fuero Real* IV. 7.1; *Novísima Recopilación* XII. 28.1, 28.4, 28.5. See also Blackstone, *Commentaries*, 4:191; George Wilfred Stumberg, "Defense of Person and Property under Texas Criminal Law," *Texas Law Review* 21(1)(November 1942): 17–18; C. S. Potts, "Is the Husband's Act in Killing Wife Taken in Act of Adultery Justifiable Homicide in Texas?" *Texas Law Review* 2(1)(1923): 111; William M. Ravkind, "Justifiable Homicide in Texas," *Southwestern Law Journal* 13(2)(1959): 509–11.

53. Texas, *Penal Code* (1857), art. 563, p. 110.

54. *Wright*, 6 Tex. at 18; *Pinkard*, 14 Tex. at 356; *Camp*, 18 Tex. at 535; *Cartwright*, 18 Tex. at 644. Beginning with *Wright*, these decisions referred to *Durant*, 3 Eng. Eccl. at 327, and *Bray*, 3 Eng. Eccl. at 76. Among southern states, only the supreme courts of Texas, Tennessee, and North Carolina held repeated false accusations of female adultery constituted actionable cruelty. See *Everton v. Everton*, 50 N.C. 202 (1857); *Sharp v. Sharp*, 34 Tenn. 496 (1855); Bishop, *Commentaries* (1881), 1:535–36.

55. Gammel, *Laws*, Act of 6 January 1841, sec. 12, 2:486. The Texas statutory defenses of recrimination, condonation, and connivance appear strikingly similar to those set forth in a Pennsylvania statute, Act of 13 March 1815, Pub. L. No. 150, sec. 7. See Annot. 16 A.L.R. 2d 592. For a discussion of the origins and development of recrimination doctrine, see *Beeby v. Beeby*, 3 Eng. Eccl. 338 (1799); *Brisco v. Brisco*, 2 Eng. Eccl. 294 (1824); M. M. Moore, "Critique of the Recrimination Doctrine," *Dickenson Law Review* 68 (1963–64): 157; and Bishop, *New Commentaries* (1891), 2:167–77, 184–85. For the development of adultery condonation principles, see *Parnell v. Parnell*, 1 Eng. Eccl. 220 (1814); *Westmeath*, 4 Eng. Eccl. at 238; *Durant*, 3 Eng. Eccl. at 310, 323; *Burr v. Burr*, 10 Paige 20 (N.Y. 1842); *Masten v. Masten*, 15 N.H. 159 (1844); *Jeans v. Jeans*, 2 Harr. 38 (Del. 1835); *Threewits v. Threewits*, 4 Des. 560 (S.C. 1815); *Earp v. Earp*, 1 Jones Eq. 239 (N.C. 1854); *J.F.C. v. M.E.*, 6 Rob. 135 (La. 1843); *Bienvenue v. Her Husband*, 14 La. Ann. 386 (1859); Annot. 16 A.L.R. 2d 587; Bishop, *New Commentaries* (1891), 2:147–63. The connivance principle traditionally applied with more force against husbands than wives because English law and custom supported the obligation of a man to be vigilant in the protection of his wife's chastity. That section 12 denied the defense to men quite likely

stemmed, to a large degree, from the difficulty a woman would have had conniving at her husband's abandonment and adulterous cohabitation. Regarding the development of the defense, see *Forster v. Forster,* 4 Eng. Eccl. 358 (1790); *Dillon v. Dillon,* 7 Eng. Eccl. 377 (1842); *Hamerton v. Hamerton,* 4 Eng. Eccl. 13–15 (1828); Bishop, *New Commentaries* (1891), 2:112–20.

56. *Simons,* 13 Tex. at 469–71.

57. The court cited Simon Greenleaf, *A Treatise on the Law of Evidence,* 6th ed., 2 vols. (Boston: Little and Brown, 1852–54), 2: §46. See also *Crowley v. State,* 13 Ala. 172 (1848); *Thompson v. Thompson,* 10 Rich. Eq. 416, 424 (S.C. 1859); Bishop, *New Commentaries* (1891), 2:509–12, 518–24.

58. *Simons,* 13 Tex. at 474–75.

59. *Sheffield,* 3 Tex. at 83.

60. *Ibid.* Regarding presumptions of guilt, the court cited *Burgess v. Burgess* 2 Hagg. Con. 229 (1817). Gammel, *Laws,* Act of 6 January 1841, sec. 4, 2:484.

61. Bishop, *Commentaries* (1873), 451.

62. Texas, *Penal Code* (1857), arts. 392–93, p. 73.

63. *Cartwright,* 18 Tex. at 644.

64. Bertram Wyatt-Brown, *Honor and Violence in the Old South* (New York: Oxford University Press, 1986), 105; Bardaglio, *Reconstructing the Household,* 5–6; Stumberg, "Defense of Person and Property," 18–19; Ravkind, "Justifiable Homicide," 510.

65. *Sheffield,* 3 Tex. at 84; *Simons,* 13 Tex. at 474; *Cartwright,* 18 Tex. at 624; *Pinkard,* 14 Tex. at 356; *Wright,* 6 Tex. at 18; *Sharman,* 18 Tex. at 522; and *Camp,* 18 Tex. at 534.

66. As had been the case under Mexican colonization law and headright rules in the Republic of Texas, various preemption acts after 1845 required grantees of land to reside upon and cultivate their tracts for at least three years to obtain a clear title. Gammel, *Laws,* Act of 22 January 1845, 2:1073–75; Act of 7 February 1853, 3:1317; Act of 13 February 1854, 3:1550–52; Gould and Pando, *Claiming Their Land,* 7–10.

67. Holley, *Texas,* 148; Dysart, "Mexican Women," 367.

68. Bishop, *New Commentaries* (1891), 2:165–69, 177. See also *Beeby,* 3 Eng. Eccl. at 338; *Bush v. Brainard,* 1 Cow. 78 (N.Y. 1823); *Mattox v. Mattox,* 2 Ohio 233 (1826); Moore, "Critique of the Recrimination Doctrine," 156–58.

69. Texas, *Penal Code* (1857), art. 563, p. 110.

70. The connivance defense stemmed from the fundamental rule that a person could not be heard to complain of an act tainted by his or her own wrong. In Anglo-American divorce law, the principle encompassed a "married party's corrupt consenting to evil conduct in the other whereof afterward he complains." Courts generally invoked the precept when a suspicious husband,

NOTES TO PAGES 157–163

eager to obtain a divorce, had surreptitiously watched his wife after setting up a situation that might lure her into adultery. Bishop, *New Commentaries* (1891), 2:110–11, 123. See also *Timmings v. Timmings*, 5 Eng. Eccl. 22 (1792); *Dillon*, 7 Eng. Eccl. at 377; *Harris v. Harris*, 4 Eng. Eccl. 160, 178 (1829); *Bray v. Bray*, 2 Halst. Ch. 628 (N.J. 1849).

71. Censer, "'Smiling through Her Tears,'" 35–39.

72. Jurists in the United States through the antebellum period agreed that the renewed adultery of a forgiven wife could provide the basis for a divorce suit regardless of statutory bars against a suit based on condoned female infidelity. This consensus included the justices of the Delaware Supreme Court, who in 1835 construed a statutory condonation rule virtually identical to the Texas provision, and the few supreme courts in the antebellum South dealing with the issue. Bishop, *New Commentaries* (1891), 2:148–51, 162; Annot. 16 A.L.R. 2d 591–93; *Jeans*, 2 Harr. at 38; *Collier v. Collier*, 16 N.C. 356 (1829); *Earp*, 1 Jones Eq. at 239; *J.F.C.*, 6 Rob. at 135; *Bienvenue*, 14 La. Ann. at 386. The decisions of the Texas Supreme Court were entirely consistent with the standard interpretation. *Wright*, 6 Tex. at 22; *Nogees*, 7 Tex. at 543; *Hare*, 10 Tex. at 355.

73. Annot. 16 A.L.R. 2d 588–89; Bishop, *New Commentaries* (1891), 2:148.

74. Bishop, *Commentaries* (1881), 1:368–69; Kent, *Commentaries*, 2:211–12; *Simon*, 31 Tex. Crim. Rep. at 199.

CONCLUSION

1. Frederick Jackson Turner, *The Frontier in American History* (New York: H. Holt, 1920; reprint, Tucson: University of Arizona Press, 1986), 320, 343–44. The first chapter of *The Frontier in American History* constitutes Turner's celebrated paper "The Significance of the Frontier in American History," which he presented to the American Historical Association in Chicago on 12 July 1893. Subsequent chapters flesh out Turner's basic theory. Conclusions regarding the southern frontier are found in Chapter 12, "Social Forces in American History," and Chapter 13, "Middlewestern Pioneer Democracy." For a commentary on the implications of the Turner thesis for the study of the antebellum southern frontier, see John D. Guice, "Turner's Forgotten Frontier: The Old Southwest," *Historian* 52(4)(1990): 602–12.

2. See generally Gordon Morris Bakken, *The Development of Law on the Rocky Mountain Frontier: Civil Law and Society, 1850–1912* (Westport, 1983) and *Practicing Law in Frontier California* (Lincoln: University of Nebraska Press, 1991).

Bibliographical Commentary

The following essay identifies the scholarship and source materials most useful in the writing of this book. See the introduction for a discussion of works that were particularly important in influencing its conceptualization. The discussion that follows is not comprehensive, in that it covers neither all of the literature this book builds upon nor all of that bearing on particular subjects discussed. Included are references to important source materials, but the list is not exhaustive.

ANGLO-TEXAN PIONEER LIFE

While the number of firsthand accounts of pioneer life in Texas often seems unlimited, a handful of published journals, diaries, and travel narratives provide unusually discerning descriptions of its early social development. Many of the cogent and often amusing observations of Texas patriot and leader Henry Smith on social conditions in Mexican Texas and the early Republic of Texas can be found in "Reminiscences of Henry Smith," *Texas Historical Association Quarterly* 14(1)(1910). Noah Smithwick's *The Evolution of a State; or, Recollections of Old Texas Days* (1900; reprint Austin, 1990) is an indispensable work. Smithwick possessed not only a flair for grasping the essence of social situations, but also the entertaining wit of a Southwest humorist. For vivid descriptions of various growing towns, such as Houston, in the early republic and of the day-to-day life of a well-educated visitor with a refined sensibility, see Mary Austin Holley, *The Texas Diary, 1835–38*, ed. J. P. Bryan (Austin, 1965). Regarding the living conditions of common settlers and the contacts of Anglo-Texan frontiersmen and soldiers with various Native American peoples and Tejanos in the turbulent early 1840s, see Francis M. Latham, *Travels in the Republic of Texas, 1842*, ed. Gerald S. Pierce (Austin, 1971) and George M.

Kendall, *Narrative of an Expedition across the South-Western Prairies, from Texas to Santa Fe*, 2 vols. (London, 1845). For the trenchant observations of a reform-minded northerner, and thus a critical perspective on Texas society late in the antebellum period, see Frederick Law Olmstead, *A Journey through Texas; or, A Saddle-Trip on the Southwestern Frontier* (1857; reprint Austin, 1978). Most of the foregoing works also include useful commentary on the gender roles and relationships of women and men among various peoples and cultures.

LAND POLICY

Numerous historians have emphasized that abundant and inexpensive land was the primary shaping agent of social structure in frontier Texas and of the polity's law and politics. Thomas Miller's *The Public Lands of Texas, 1519–1979* (Norman, 1971) assessed land policy, showing how various constitutional and legislative measures promoted Anglo-American settlement and provided for "defense" against conquered and dispossessed indigenous groups. A work that includes a concise description of the impact of the land and environment on early social development is David G. McComb's *Texas: A Modern History* (Austin, 1989). For a detailed account of how land policy preoccupied lawmakers through the colonial, national, and antebellum statehood periods, see volume one of Henderson Yoakum, *History of Texas*, 2 vols. (New York, 1855).

GEOGRAPHY AND IMMIGRATION

Geographers have used statistical approaches for the study of Texas history for decades, particularly tying the early social development of the state to land policy and immigration. For an innovative use of manuscript census records and a useful account of the geographic origins of early settlers, see Barnes F. Lathrop and William W. White, *Migration into East Texas, 1835–1860: A Study from the United States Census* (Austin, 1949). Lathrop and White showed a certain restlessness of background in the prevailing pattern of geographical mobility, noting a widespread movement of immigrants from one part of the southern back country to another. This book also includes a cogent discussion of the "cultural baggage" lower southern immigrants brought with them to Texas. In "Heads of Families in Antebellum Texas: A Profile," *Red River Valley Historical Review* 5 (1980), Richard G. Lowe and Randolph B. Campbell further documented the large inflow of lower southerners after about 1840. A good treatment of the settlement patterns and cultures of immigrants from the upper and lower South is included in Terry G. Jordan, "A Century and a Half of Ethnic Change in Texas, 1836–1986," *Southwestern Historical Quarterly* 89(4)(1986) and *Immigration to Texas* (Boston, 1980). For a work that explores the plurality of early Texas society, the confluence of cultures within it, and descriptions of the influence of environment on the development of various societies, see Terry G. Jordan, John L. Bean, and William H. Holmes, *Texas: A Geography* (Boulder, 1984).

ANGLO-TEXAN FAMILY LIFE

Depictions of Anglo-Texan frontier families exist within a wide range of historical scholarship both old and new. Lewis W. Newton and Herbert P. Gambrell's *A Social and Political History of Texas* (Dallas, 1935) explained quite well how primitive conditions adversely affected pioneer households and made life particularly hard for women. An insightful account of social life among the Anglos at the end of the antebellum period is Llerena B. Friend's "The Texan of 1860," *Southwestern Historical Quarterly* 62 (July 1958). Friend examined immigration patterns, the shortage of marriageable women, and the high mortality affecting social relationships. For a community study relying on quantitative methods, see James Michael McReynolds, "Family Life in a Borderland Community: Nacogdoches, Texas, 1779–1861" (Ph.D. diss., Texas Tech University, Lubbock, 1978). McReynolds argued that the nuclear family was the central institution guaranteeing the economic well-being of Anglo-Texans regardless of its instability. Based on Mexican census data, Joella Dorothea Kite's "A Social History of the Anglo-American Colonies in Mexican Texas, 1821–1835" (Ph.D. diss., Texas Tech University, Lubbock, 1990) described the motivations of early settlers, marital and family relations, and how an ineffectual judicial system combined with the southern background of many immigrants to increase "community responses," rather than formal ones, to criminal behavior and violence.

ANGLO-TEXAN MEN

The "manly independence" of Anglo-Texan frontiersmen has received much consideration over the years. While investigating the unusual political factionalism centered on personalities that emerged in the Republic of Texas, Stanley Siegel's *A Political History of the Texas Republic, 1836–1845* (Austin, 1956) included one of the earliest discussions of the unsavory personal histories and characteristics of many men starting over in Texas. Mark E. Nackman's *A Nation within A Nation: The Rise of Texas Nationalism* (Port Washington, 1975) explored the linkage between political and social development from 1836 to 1846. He explained the legendary independent-mindedness of immigrants and concluded that a large number of settling men were often fleeing the law, creditors, and family relationships. A class of adventurers who gave Texas a deserved reputation for social instability thus built the new republic. See also Mark E. Nackman, "Anglo-American Migrants to the West: Men of Broken Fortunes? The Case of Texas, 1821–46," *Western Historical Quarterly* 5(4)(1974). William Ransom Hogan's *The Texas Republic: A Social and Economic History*

(Norman, 1976) also provides extremely useful insight into social conditions, particularly describing the "rampant individualism" of Anglo men. According to Hogan, the exaggerated independence of Texas frontiersmen manifested itself in a pattern of vigilantism, personalism, violence, and word-mongering. For a collection of letters often articulating quite well the response of a religious woman to the self-indulgent behavior of Anglo-American men in southern Texas before, during, and after the Mexican War, see *The News from Brownsville: Helen Chapman's Letters from the Texas Military Frontier, 1842–1852*, ed. Caleb Coker (Austin, 1992).

Other studies, however, have shown that some leaders made determined efforts to impose order on the chaotic social situation. Joseph W. McKnight, for example, argued that Stephen F. Austin based his "Civil Regulations" on Spanish procedures to provide a mechanism for settling disputes and punishing disorderly residents. See "Stephen Austin's Legalistic Concerns," *Southwestern Historical Quarterly* 89(3)(1986). A useful document source in this regard is *The Austin Papers*, 3 vols., ed. Eugene C. Barker (Washington, D.C., 1934). For an innovative study of how some church authorities attempted to rein in the disruptive behavior of unruly settlers, see Nick Malavis, "Equality under the Lord's Law: The Disciplinary Process in Texas Baptist Churches, 1833–1870," *East Texas Historical Journal* 31(1)(1993). Documentation of church disciplinary cases can be found in "The Records of an Early Texas Baptist Church," *Texas State Historical Association Quarterly* 11(2)(1907); 12(1)(1908).

ANGLO-TEXAN WOMEN

Several scholars in the last ten years have explored the highly individualistic and opportunistic behavior of Texas women in the sex business. In "Prostitution in Texas: From the 1830s to the 1960s," *East Texas Historical Journal* 33 (1995), David C. Humphrey examined the origins of prostitution in Texas and the motivations of both immigrant Anglo women and Tejano women who pursued this line of work. James F. Elliott's "The Great Western: Sarah Bowman, Mother and Mistress of the U.S. Army," *Journal of Arizona History* 30(1)(1989) traced the adventures of one of the more intrepid sex workers in southern Texas during and after the Mexican War. See also Gordon H. Frost, *The Gentlemen's Club: The Story of Prostitutes in El Paso* (El Paso, 1983). For a brief treatment of the bawdy house industry in antebellum Texas that places it in a larger pattern of frontier development, see Anne M. Butler, *Daughters of Joy, Sisters of Misery: Prostitutes in the American West, 1865–1890* (Urbana and Chicago, 1985).

For the most part, however, characterizations of Anglo-Texan women have focused on the great majority who homesteaded as family members. These descriptions have drawn on a number of competing conceptualizations of the frontier West, slave South, and urbanizing Northeast. According to Necah S. Furman, Texas women's history was skewed, before 1980 at least, because of its subjugation to nineteenth-century prescriptive and literary interpretations. In "Texas Women versus the Texas Myths," in *The Texas Heritage*, ed. Ben Proctor and Archie McDonald (St. Louis, 1980), Furman argued that Texas men attributed to frontier women the traits embodied in the northeastern "true womanhood" ideal. This idealization unrealistically placed them on a pedestal, made them the objects of protection, and painted a false collective picture of them as unduly submissive, domestic, and pious. For a more recent study showing how early churches in Houston attempted to reinforce this role, see Angela Boswell, "The Meaning of Participation: White Protestant Women in Antebellum Houston Churches," *Southwestern Historical Quarterly* 99(1)(1995). To a large degree, the "true womanhood" characterization meshes with that of late-nineteenth-century and early-twentieth-century folklorists, novelists, and historians, who often described Texas women as displaced southern belles. Men writing about antebellum Texas, both during that period and later, thus often idealized women as tragic, helpless heroines or refined paragons of virtue. According to Sandra Myres, however, the male-generated fiction, myth, and folklore of the late nineteenth century also typified the frontier woman as one who was "expected to be strong and capable . . . stand and fight when the menfolk are not around . . . and refrain from unseemly displays of emotion." See "Cowboys and Southern Belles," in *Texas Myths*, ed. Robert F. O'Connor (College Station, 1986). Resolving these apparently inconsistent characterizations has absorbed considerable scholarly attention.

Several historians writing in the 1980s described Texas frontier women as victims of adult male abuse. In "True Womanhood Revisited: Women's Private Writing in Nineteenth-Century Texas," *Journal of the Southwest* 31 (1989), Henrietta Andreadis characterized settling women as exploited drudges. Based on her analysis of forty manuscript diaries, Andreadis argued that many homesteading women felt isolated and lived monotonous and unsatisfactory lives with inattentive husbands. In "Women and Utopia: The Woman's Commonwealth of Belton, Texas," *Southwestern Historical Quarterly* 87 (1984), Jayme A. Sokolaw and Mary Ann Lamanna described the harsh and sometimes brutal treatment that Texas women endured at the hands of their spouses.

Other historians have rejected both the female victimization paradigm and the "true womanhood" model, arguing that Texas women were, in fact, quite assertive, capable, and thus worthy of admiration. Ann Patton Malone's *Women on the Texas Frontier: A Cross-Cultural Perspective* (El Paso, 1983) maintained that frontier life in Texas was very difficult for the first generation of women, and that the prescription of true womanhood under these circumstances fit very poorly. On the other hand, she emphasized the adaptability of homesteading women. In her view, harsh living conditions caused pioneer women to develop radically divergent attitudes toward the nature of community, home life, and family. Elizabeth York Enstam emphasized the autonomous role that women assumed in helping to manage family businesses, farms, and ranches. See "The Family," in *Texas Myths,* and "Women on the Urban Frontier," in *The Texas Experience,* ed. Archie P. McDonald and Ben Proctor (College Station, 1986). In *Anglo-American Women in Texas, 1820–1850* (Boston, 1982), Margaret Henson similarly argued that immigrant women frequently adapted with competence and vigor to the harsh frontier environment, regardless of the difficulties that many first-generation arrivals endured. A description of frontier women as hard-working individualists dealing successfully with difficult circumstances also can be found in Fane Downs, "'Tryels and Trubbles': Women in Early Nineteenth-Century Texas," *Texas Historical Quarterly* 90(1)(1986). For a study showing how one woman enlarged on gender ideals prevalent in the more settled South to run one of the largest plantations in East Texas for more than a decade, see Jolene Maddox Snider, "Sarah Devereux: A Study of Southern Femininity," *Southwestern Historical Quarterly* 97(3)(1994). In *Claiming Their Land: Women Homesteaders in Texas* (El Paso, 1991), Florence G. Gould and Patricia Pando focused on the 1,141 single women who homesteaded from 1845 to 1898. While portraying these women as spunky, adventurous, and hard-working, Gould and Pando emphasized how they stepped outside traditional southern female roles and "proved up" their land to make homes rather than to engage in speculation.

Well-known source materials certainly support the characterization of settling women as capable and resilient individualists. See, for example, *Memoirs of Mary A. Maverick,* ed. Rena Maverick Green (Lincoln and London, 1989). This candid and well-written account reveals how both Anglo-Texan women and men dealt effectively with deadly epidemics, hostile Comanches, and the rigors of daily life on the Anglo-Hispanic frontier beginning in the early 1840s. While combining romantic literary style with an effort to promote expansion in Texas, Mary Austin Holley's *Texas* (1836; reprint Austin, 1990) reveals how immigrant women and men vigorously pursued entrepreneurial opportunities after independence from Mexico.

Historians have increasingly described the relationships of unusually proficient Anglo-Texan women with their husbands and families. An eminently readable dual biography providing useful insights into frontier marriage and family life is Paula Mitchell Marks, *Turn Your Eyes toward Texas: Pioneers Sam and Mary Maverick* (College Station, 1989). This book blended the public life of Sam and the private life of Mary, while exploring the latter's trials and tribulations in dealing with an often neglectful and abusive spouse. In *The*

Cartwrights of San Augustine: Three Generations of Agrarian Entrepreneurs in Nineteenth-Century Texas (Austin, 1993), Margaret Swett Henson and Deolece Parmelee described the experiences of one Anglo family in the redlands of East Texas from 1835 through the nineteenth century, highlighting that the family was first and foremost a business enterprise. This chronicle also revealed the thorough involvement of women in family ventures and their not untypical business acumen. While certainly reflecting a distinct Texas nationalism, the writings of pioneer John Lockhart about early settlement clearly convey the independence and substantial capabilities of women, the strong commitments they had to their husbands and children, and their vital role in homesteading ventures. See *Sixty Years on the Brazos: The Life and Letters of Dr. John Washington Lockhart 1824–1900,* ed. Jonnie Lockhart Wallis and Lawrence L. Hill (Waco, 1967).

The turn toward a more ethnically inclusive approach to the history of Texas women began to bear fruit as early as 1983. In that year, Ann Patton Malone's *Women on the Texas Frontier: A Cross-Cultural Perspective* explored the similarities and differences in the antebellum experiences of Indian, black, and Anglo-American women. In "Myth, Reality, and Anomaly: The Complete World of Rebecca Hagerty," *East Texas Historical Journal* 24(2)(1986), Judith N. McArthur described the strong ties of slave-owner Rebecca Hagerty with her Creek heritage, while also showing how she shrewdly increased her landholdings and net worth through the years. For a study of gender roles of well-to-do women in San Antonio after independence from Mexico, see Michael Thurgood Haynes, "Crowning Achievement: Reproducing Elite Class and Gender Roles in San Antonio" (Ph.D. diss., University of Texas, Austin, 1994).

TEJANO FAMILY LIFE

A considerable body of traditional and contemporary scholarship has dealt directly with Tejano family life. Rubye Du Terrail's "The Role of Women in Nineteenth-Century San Antonio" (M.A. thesis, Saint Mary's University, San Antonio, 1949) presented useful information regarding the roles of Tejanas and their families. Detailed descriptions of the social experiences of Tejanos and their household relations after the firm establishment of Anglo-American rule can be found in Carland Elaine Crook, "San Antonio, Texas, 1846–1861" (M.A. thesis, Rice University, Houston, 1964) and Caroline Remy, "Hispanic-Mexican San Antonio: 1836–1861," *Southwestern Historical Quarterly* 71 (1968). In "The History of Mexicans in Texas, 1820–1845" (Ph.D. diss., Texas Tech University, Lubbock, 1970), Fane Downs described the everyday life of Tejanos from colonial times through the Republic of Texas, exploring the mores of the *ricos* and the *pobres* in San Antonio de Béxar, Goliad, Victoria, and Nacogdoches and on the *ranchos* in the San Antonio River Valley. For a comparative history of Anglo-Texan and Tejano settlement, which includes an examination of patriarchy, machismo, and their effects on family relations among Tejano villagers, see Frank Louis Halla, Jr., "El Paso, Texas, and Juárez, Mexico: A Study of a Bi-Ethnic Community, 1846–1881" (Ph.D. diss., University of Texas, Austin, 1978). In "Indians, Soldiers, and Canary Islanders: The Making of a Texas Frontier Community," (unpublished paper presented at the 1987 meeting of the Texas State Historical Association), Jesús F. de la Tejá argued that San Antonio society responded to the shared dangers, isolation, and limited economic opportunity on the frontier by forging strong kinship ties and producing a dynamic community. A similar discussion can be found in Armando C. Alonzo, *Tejano Legacy: Rancheros and Settlers in South Texas, 1734–1900* (Albuquerque, 1998). For a study showing the tendency among Tejanos to form extended families that featured more cohesiveness than was common in Anglo society, see Richard Griswold del Castillo, "'Only for My Family': Historical Dimensions of Chicano Family Solidarity—The Case of San Antonio in 1860," *Aztlán* 16(1–2)(1985).

INDIGENOUS TEXANS

Outdated by thirty-five years of specialized research, William W. Newcombe, Jr.'s *The Texas Indians: From Prehistoric to Modern Times* (Austin, 1961) remains the best single work describing the indigenous peoples of Texas and their family mores. Utilizing an ethnohistorical framework, Lawrence E. Aten's *Indians of the Upper Texas Coast* (New York, 1983) explored the connection of environment to the material cultures and social norms of the Caddo, Karankawa, Tlascalan, and Tonkawa. Based on Spanish documents and travel accounts, Andre F. Sjoberg's "Lipan Apache Culture in Historical Perspective," *Southwestern Historical Quarterly* 9 (1953) includes a thorough depiction of the life cycle, marriage customs, and childbearing patterns of the Lipan Apache. An interesting piece that dispels the conception of nineteenth-century Anglo-Americans that polygyny among the Comanche was an exploitative arrangement is Albert S. Gilles's "Polygamy in Comanche Country," *Southwest Review* 51(3)(1966). For a presentation of family customs among a number of indigenous Texan groups, including a discussion of Native American women, see Betsy Warren, *Indians of Texas* (Dallas, 1981).

Though consistently marked by a male perspective and pronounced Anglo-centrism, numerous firsthand accounts describe the sexual and family mores of various tribes residing in antebellum Texas. Vivid, albeit brief, descriptions of the courtship, marriage, and childbearing practices of almost all the immigrant and indigenous tribes toward the end of the Mexican period are contained in the journal of French naturalist Jean Louis Berlandier, *The Indians of Texas in 1830*, ed. John C. Ewers, trans. Patricia Reading Leclercq (Washington, D.C., 1969). A more extensive account of the sexual, marital, and family mores of the Lipan Apache and Comanche in the late antebellum years can be found in Richard Irving Dodge, *Our Wild Indians: Thirty-Three Years' Personal Experience among the Red Men of the Great West* (New York, 1959). David G. Burnet provided useful observations regarding the roles of Comanche women and men in his politically motivated essay "The Comanches and Other Tribes of Texas and the Policy to Be Pursued Respecting Them," in *Ethnology of the Texas Indians*, ed. Thomas R. Hester (New York, 1991).

AFRICAN-TEXANS

Studies focusing on the family life of slaves include Ruthe Winegarten's "Texas Slave Families," *Texas Humanist* 7 (1985) and Randolph B. Campbell's "The Slave Family in Antebellum Texas," *Victoria College Science Symposium* (1988). For a community study relying on demographic data that explored African-American kinship patterns, see Randolph B. Campbell, *A Southern Community in Crisis: Harrison County, Texas, 1850–1880* (Austin, 1984). Further insight into the African-Texan family before the Civil War can be gleaned from a number of works that examine the social and political transformations occurring during Reconstruction. In "Emancipation and the Black Family: A Case Study in Texas," *Social Science Quarterly* 57 (1977), James W. Smallwood, Barry A. Crouch, and Larry Madaras concluded that Texas blacks showed intense concern for reuniting and maintaining their families after emancipation. Crouch and Madaras bolstered this finding in "Reconstructing Black Families: Perspectives from the Texas Freedmen's Bureau Records," *Prologue* 18 (1986). See also Barry A. Crouch, "'The Chords of Love': Legalizing Black Marital Family Rights in Postwar Texas," *Journal of Negro History* 79(4)(1994). An indispensable source for understanding the society and family life of black Texans is, of course, the interviews of former slaves gathered in the 1930s under the direction of the WPA. See volumes 4 and 5 in *The American Slave: A Composite Autobiography*, 19 vols., ed. George P. Rawick (Westport, Conn., 1972), and volumes 2 through 10 in *The American Slave: A Composite Autobiography: Supplement, Series 2*, 10 vols., ed. George P. Rawick (Westport, Conn., 1979). See also *The Slave Narratives of Texas*, ed. Lawrence R. Murphy (Austin, 1974).

Scholarship describing the development of racial-caste organization certainly has investigated the situation of blacks in colonial Texas and the deterioration of their position after independence from Mexico. Alwyn Barr's *Black Texans: A History of Negroes in Texas, 1528–1971* (Austin, 1973) surveyed the experiences of blacks, both free and bonded, before and after the Anglo take-over. George R. Woolfolk demonstrated that free blacks in the Republic of Texas faced increasing discrimination, while friends of black veterans of the revolution, white relatives of free blacks, and former owners who had freed slaves fought efforts to oust those already present. See *The Free Negro in Texas, 1800–1860: A Study in Cultural Compromise* (Ann Arbor, 1976) and "Turner's Safety Valve and Free Negro Westward Migration," *Journal of Negro History* 50 (1965). Andrew Forest Muir examined how the status of free blacks deterio-rated with particular rapidity in the 1850s amid new legal restrictions and threats of violence. See "The Free Negro in Harris County, Texas," *Southwest-ern Historical Quarterly* 46 (1943); "The Free Negro in Fort Bend County, Texas," *Journal of Negro History* 33 (1948); "The Free Black in Jefferson and Orange Counties, Texas," *Journal of Negro History* 35 (1950); and "The Free Negro in Galveston County, Texas," *Negro History Bulletin* 22 (1958). In "Prot-estant Churches and Slavery in Matagorda County," *East Texas Historical Jour-nal* 14 (1976), Reba W. Palma described how whites arranged separate black congregations in the 1840s and 1850s, indicating the growing separation of the two groups. In "The Thought and Action of Some Early Texas Baptists Con-cerning the Negro," *East Texas Historical Journal* 13 (1975), however, Jerry B. Caine maintained that the stresses and dangers of the frontier pressured white and black churchgoers into relatively cooperative relationships.

Scholarship in the last twenty years has examined the extent to which slav-ery in Texas resembled that of the more settled southern states. A detailed description of Texas slavery, including statistical analyses of wealth distribu-tion, slave ownership, and agricultural property, can be found in Randolph B. Campbell and Richard G. Lowe, *Wealth and Power in Antebellum Texas* (Col-lege Station, 1977). In *An Empire for Slavery: The Peculiar Institution in Texas, 1821–1865* (Baton Rouge, 1989), Campbell relied on demographic data to con-clude that Texas slavery was essentially undifferentiated from the peculiar institution further east. Billy Don Ledbetter's "White over Black in Texas: Racial Attitudes in the Antebellum Period," *Phylon* 34 (1973) argued similarly.

Several articles have investigated Texas slavery as a legal institution and the implications of this for black-white relations. A. E. Keir Nash's "The Texas Supreme Court and Trial Rights of Blacks, 1845–1860," *Journal of American History* 58 (1971) examined the extent to which the rulings of the high court protected slaves from the worst kinds of mistreatment. Nash further developed the argument that the court sometimes extended rights to slaves in his article "Texas Justice in the Age of Slavery: Appeals Concerning Blacks and the Antebellum State Supreme Court," *Houston Law Review* 8 (1971). Bruce A. Glasrud's "Jim Crow's Emergence in Texas," *American Studies* 15(1)(1974) traced the legal and social history of segregation from the Texas War of Independence through the nineteenth and early twentieth centuries, including useful discussion of early antimiscegenation laws.

RACISM

The extent to which racism adversely shaped the relationship of Anglos and Tejanos has received extensive treatment. Early investigations along these lines can be found in *Foreigners in Their Native Land: Historical Roots of the Mexican Americans,* ed. David J. Weber (Albuquerque, 1973). In "Anglo-Texan Attitudes toward the Mexican, 1821–1845" (Ph.D. diss., Yale University, New Haven, 1976), James Ernest Crisp described how extremely negative attitudes toward Tejanos developed slowly as amicable social and political relations gave way to hostilities on the eve of the Mexican War. In *They Called Them Greasers: Anglo Attitudes toward Mexicans in Texas, 1821–1900* (Austin, 1983), Arnoldo De León revealed how the ethnocentrism of Anglo-Americans generated animosity toward Tejanos and persecution of them from the beginning of white settlement. De León's *The Tejano Community, 1836–1900* (Albuquerque, 1982) emphasized the increasing minority status of Texas Mexicans after the Anglo invasion and how Tejanos suffered racial discrimination and attacks against their property. One of the most comprehensive studies of racial prejudice and its relationship to the rise and fall of distinct social classes, however, is David Montejano's *Anglos and Mexicans in the Making of Texas, 1836–1986* (Austin, 1987). Montejano considered how class and landed property figured heavily in the Anglo subjugation of Mexicans. His book particularly explored the legalistic maneuvers Anglo-Texans used to accomplish this. Studies describing how Anglos dispossessed Tejanos of their land also include Abel Rubio, *Stolen Heritage: A Mexican American's Rediscovery of His Family's Lost Land Grant* (Austin, 1986) and Gilberto M. Hinojosa, "The Texas Mexico Border: A Turbulent History," *Texas Humanist* 6 (1984).

Several scholars in the last ten years have examined the pattern of both cooperation and conflict between Anglo-Texans and Native Americans during the antebellum period. Diana Everett's *The Texas Cherokees: A People between Two Fires* (Norman, 1990) investigated how immigrant Indians traded and interacted with increasingly hostile Anglos in East Texas through the early 1840s. Kelly Frank Himmel described the complicated forms of social interplay and conflict involving homesteaders and several indigenous groups in "Anglo-Texans, Karankawas, and Tonkawas, 1821–1859: A Sociological Analysis of Conquest" (Ph.D. diss., University of Texas, Austin, 1995). For firsthand accounts of these developments, see *The Papers of Mirabeau Buonaparte Lamar,* ed. Charles A. Gulick et al. (Austin, 1920–27), and *The Writings of Sam Houston, 1813–1863,* 8 vols., ed. Amelia W. Williams and Eugene C. Barker (Austin, 1943). Various documents related to the Indian trade, Indian removal, and the dispossession of indigenous East Texans can be found in *Texas Indian Papers,* ed. Dorman H. Winfrey and James M. Day (Austin, 1966).

INTERRACIAL RELATIONSHIPS

Scholarship exploring the connection between interracial sexual relations and emergent white supremacy has most thoroughly examined the situation of African-Texans. In her demographic analysis of the late Spanish period, "Comparative Demographic Analysis of Texas, 1777–1793," *Southwestern Historical Quarterly* 77 (1974), Alicia V. Tjarks provided valuable insights into the cross-racial marriages, sexual relationships, and families of whites, blacks, mestizos, and Native Americans. In "Mestizaje in Nineteenth-Century Texas," *Journal of Mexican American History* 2(2)(1972), Larry E. Dickens described the considerable intermixing of blacks and Tejanos through the Spanish and Mexican periods. Harold Schoen's seminal study of free blacks during the Republic of Texas entailed a thorough examination of mixed marriages, noting the unusually large incidence of this practice before about 1840. His work also explored the way Anglo-Texan racial dominance after independence from Mexico generated a legal regime increasingly oppressive to free blacks, one that notably included new antimiscegenation laws. See "The Free Negro in the Republic of Texas," *Southwestern Historical Quarterly* 39(4)–41(1) (1936–37). While scrutinizing the changing roles of free black women and female slaves during the antebellum period, Ann Patton Malone's *Women on the Texas Frontier* especially explored their complex intimate relationships with white men.

The Hispanic custom of *mestizaje* and the sexual relations of Tejanos with various indigenous groups have been studied extensively. While integrating Hispanic peoples into the history of the Southwest, John F. Bannon's *The Spanish Borderlands Frontier, 1813–1821* (New York, 1970) examined the sexual involvement of Spaniards with Native Americans in the early development of the Tejano population. In *San Antonio de Béxar: A Community on New Spain's Northern Frontier* (Albuquerque, 1995), Jesús F. de la Tejá described the subjugation of various tribes within the missions of early San Antonio and the cohabitative relationships of male settlers with Indian women. Various selections in *Tejano Origins in Eighteenth-Century San Antonio,* ed. Gerald E. Poyo and Gilberto Hinojosa (Austin, 1995), also dealt with these developments, examining particularly the interaction of Coahuiltecs and various independent tribes with the mestizo inhabitants of San Antonio de Béxar. For a description of the incorporation of various Indian peoples into the surrounding Hispanic communities of El Paso, see Gordon Bronitsky, "Indian Assimilation in the El Paso Area," *New Mexico Historical Review* 62(2)(1987). Jack Jackson's *Los Mesteños: Spanish Ranching in Texas, 1721–1821* (College Station, 1986) showed that the majority of the Texas population was mestizo by the late Spanish period. According to Jackson, regardless of the absence of class rivalry, racial-caste distinctions had developed in what would soon become Mexican Texas.

The sexual relationships of Tejanos with immigrating Anglos have also received considerable attention. Jane Dysart's "Mexican Women in San Antonio: The Assimilation Process, 1830–1860," *Western Historical Quarterly* 7 (1976) explored how Hispanic mores and racial-caste conceptions among both Tejanos and Anglos generated sexual involvements and marriages between Anglo men and Mexican women. In "Intermarriage between Persons of Spanish and Non-Spanish Surname: Changes from the Mid-Nineteenth Century," *Social Science Quarterly* 51 (1979), sociologists Frank D. Bean and Benjamin S. Bradshaw studied matrimony between Anglo-Americans and Tejanos from the late antebellum period to the mid-twentieth century, arguing that the incidence of Anglo-Hispanic marriage was a function of cultural norms, demographic factors such as population and sex ratios, the proximity of groups, and their respective age compositions. For an investigation of the rapid economic development of El Paso and the frequency with which rich Mexican women married wealthy Anglo tradesmen, especially before 1840, see W. H. Timmons's "The El Paso Area in the Mexican Period, 1821–1848," *Southwestern Historical Quarterly* 84(1)(1980). An examination of early Mexican-Texan efforts to assimilate into mainstream Anglo-Texan society for the purpose of group security can be found in a chapter of Jose A. Hernandez's *Mutual Aid for Survival: The Case of the Mexican American* (Malabar, Fla., 1983).

Only a handful of scholars have examined the sexual involvement in Texas of Native Americans with invading whites during the period under study. In "Portrait of a Wichita Village, 1808," *Chronicles of Oklahoma* 60(4)(1982–83), Elizabeth A. H. John described the Indian trade along the Red River and related tribal customs that permitted and encouraged white men to marry Wichita women. See also *Journal of an Indian Trader: Anthony Glass and the Texas Trading Frontier, 1790–1810*, ed. Dan L. Fores (College Station, 1987). Providing insight into the relationships of Anglo men and Indian women in East Texas through most of the Mexican period is Jack Gregory and Renard Strickland's *Sam Houston with the Cherokees, 1829–1833* (Austin, 1967). A study of the relationships of Plains Indians with invading whites and blacks can be found in Barbara A. Neal Ledbetter's *Belknap Frontier Saga: Indians, Negroes, and Anglo-Americans on the Texas Frontier* (Burnet, 1980). In "Indian and Common Law Marriage," in *Law, Society, and Domestic Relations*, ed. Kermit Hall (New York, 1987), Henry F. Foster described the informal marriage customs of several tribes that immigrated to Texas, including the Creek and Cherokee, "mixed" marriages involving Indian women and white men, and adjudication of these relationships in Anglo-American courts.

LEGAL HISTORY

A wide range of scholarship has described the law relevant to Anglo-Texan families. While numerous historical studies have appeared over the years, a large segment of the literature is located in law journals and legal treatises. A considerable amount of it was authored for the professional use of lawyers and judges dealing with the pressing issues of their times. Traditional legal writing on domestic relations focused primarily on the development of rules, while more recent works usually give more attention to the social and cultural contexts of legal developments. For references to both published and unpublished documents and important works on Texas legal history, see *A Reference Guide to Texas Law and Legal History: Sources and Documentation,* 2d ed., ed. Karl T. Gruben and James E. Hambleton (Austin, 1987), and *A Reference Guide to Texas Law and Legal History: Sources and Documentation,* ed. Marion Boner (Austin, 1976).

MARRIAGE

A number of scholars have explored bond marriage in Mexican Texas. Legal historian Hans W. Baade conducted the most thorough investigation of the influence of Spanish law on the development of matrimonial rules in the northern provinces of New Spain and Mexico. In particular, his article "The Form of Marriage in Spanish North America," *Cornell Law Review* 61(1)(1975) described how social disorganization, the ceremonial marriage requirements of the Roman Catholic Church, the shortage of priests, and the prohibition of absolute divorce generated an unusually large amount of bigamy in colonial Texas and thus problems for settling women and men who wanted to marry legally. In "Marriage Contracts in French and Spanish Louisiana: A Study in 'Notarial' Jurisprudence," *Tulane Law Review* 53 (1979), he investigated bond marriage prototypes used in early Louisiana and their origins in the civilian law. Bennett Smith's *Marriage by Bond in Colonial Texas* (Fort Worth, 1972) is the most focused discussion of the device in Texas. Smith demonstrated how primitive conditions, poorly organized provincial government, and a restrictive Mexican religious policy induced adoption of the instrument. While exploring yet another aspect of the intrepid life of Harriet Ames, James R. Norvell's "The Ames Case Revisited," *Southwestern Historical Quarterly* 63 (1959) described an important 1875 Texas Supreme Court ruling on the legality of colonial bond marriages and the validity of related community property claims.

Common law marriage has received a fair amount of scrutiny. A brief discussion of the historical development of informal marriage in Texas can be found in Clarence M. Davis, "Common Law Marriage in Texas," *Southwestern Law Journal* 21(3)(1967). W. M. Bonesio gave it a more detailed treatment in

"Marriage and Divorce under the Texas Family Code," *Houston Law Review* 8 (1970–71). A more sophisticated study is Kathryn S. Vaughn's "The Recent Changes to the Texas Informal Marriage Statute: Limitation or Abolition of Common-Law Marriage?" *Houston Law Review* 28(5)(1991). Vaughn discussed the roots of informal marriage in medieval England, its rejuvenation in the United States shortly after the American Revolution, and the social context of its 1847 establishment in Texas.

BIGAMY AND ILLEGITIMACY

Scholarship investigating how early Anglo-Texan jurists used Hispanic law to deal with bigamy is limited. Cecil Pruett's "The Requirements of a Marriage Ceremony for a Putative Relationship," *Baylor Law Review* 4 (1952) recounted how putative marriage survived in Texas after the adoption of the common law. In "The Rights of Parties to a Putative Marriage in Property Acquired by Their Joint Efforts," *Texas Law Review* 1(4)(1923), W. A. Rhea traced the adoption of putative marriage and its doctrinal alterations, while describing the rights of a putative wife to property acquired by the joint efforts of spouses. George B. Davis's "Family Law and Community Property—Putative Marriage—Division of Property," *Southwestern Law Journal* 11(2)(1957) also examined the early judicial development of rules protecting the community property of putative wives. For a more recent study comparing the development of putative marriage in Texas with that in California and Louisiana, see Christopher L. Blakesley, "The Putative Marriage Doctrine," *Tulane Law Review* 60(1)(1985).

The extensive reliance of early Texas lawmakers on Spanish civilian principles to deal with illegitimacy has received considerable coverage. Most noteworthy is the work of Joseph W. McKnight, the preeminent scholar and historian of the Hispanic legal tradition in Texas and of the state's family law. For decades, McKnight has studied the persistent aspects of Spanish law in both nineteenth-century and twentieth-century Texas. For an examination of how legitimation and adoption laws on the Texas frontier intermingled Castilian, English, and Roman legal traditions to create singular rules, see his article "Legitimation and Adoption on the Anglo-Hispanic Frontier of the United States," *Tijdschrift voor Rechtsgeschiedenis* (Netherlands) 53(1)(1985). In "Spanish Legitimacy in the United States—Its Survival and Decline," *American Journal of Comparative Law* 44 (1996), McKnight described the influence of early civilian legitimation procedures in nineteenth-century Texas and other jurisdictions during that period. Deborah J. Venezia's "The Rights of an Illegitimate Child Post–*Gomez v. Perez:* A Legitimate Situation?" *St. Mary's Law Journal* 12 (1980) argued that the 1840 statutory adoption of Hispanic civil law, by which an out-of-wedlock child could inherit from his or her mother and maternal relations diminished the harsh results of illegitimacy in frontier Texas. She also maintained that this development encouraged leaders to refrain from adopting an affiliation procedure through the nineteenth century and most of the twentieth century. For a shorter piece exploring this topic and related ones, see "The Rights of an Illegitimate Child" (comment), *St. Mary's Law Journal* 12 (1980).

The various ways that Texas leaders approached the interwoven problems of bigamy and bastardy with their own Anglo-American legal tradition has received some cursory attention over the years. A treatment of the development of the presumption of the validity of a second marriage can be found in W. E. D., "Husband and Wife—Presumption of Dissolution of Marriage," *Texas Law Review* 9(4)(1931). See also H. E. S., "Judicial Presumptions Respecting Irregular Marriages," *University of Pennsylvania Law Review* (1934), and Robert A. Allen, "Presumption of the Validity of a Second Marriage," *Baylor Law Review* 20(2)(1968). For a discussion of the early judicial adoption of the rule by which courts were authorized to uphold a common law marriage despite the existence of an undissolved union, see M. L. C., "Persons—Common Law Marriage—Validity after Removal of Impediment," *Texas Law Review* 8(3)(1930), and Robert A. Allen, "Presumption of the Validity of a Second Marriage," *Baylor Law Review* 20(2)(1968). A description of this innovation in other jurisdictions later is included in Homer H. Clark, Jr., *The Law of Domestic Relations in the United States*, 2d ed. (St. Paul, 1988). Richard B. Dewey's "Illegitimacy in Texas," *Texas Law Review* 37(4)(1959) traced the early development of common law marriage and ameliorative bigamy law in Texas, explaining how the shortage of clergymen, frontier social disorganization, and institutional disarray induced these innovations for the protection of "baseborn" children. Paul E. Martin's "Legitimation of Bastards," *Baylor Law Review* 8 (1956) constitutes a good survey of both the statutory and judicial development of the early Texas law of illegitimacy.

MATRIMONIAL PROPERTY LAW

Most of the scholarship on marriage and the family in Texas has focused on Hispanic matrimonial property law. For a detailed discussion of how Texas legislators spliced the Spanish community property system with the common law in 1840, see Ford W. Hall's "An Account of the Adoption of the Common Law by Texas," *Texas Law Review* 28 (1950). Hall argued that Texas lawmakers fashioned the Anglo-Hispanic amalgam to establish a legal regime that was suitable to the social, geographic, and climatic conditions of the state. In "The Reception of the Common Law of England in Texas and the Judicial Attitude toward that Reception, 1840–1859," *Texas Law Review* 29 (1951), Edward Lee

Markham, Jr., discussed the policy choice of the Texas Supreme Court to retain the civil law prescribing the rights of women. For a discussion of Spanish community property principles applicable in Texas before independence from Mexico and of the post-1840 establishment of premarital agreements, see William O. Huie, "Some Principles of Texas Community Property Law," in *Comparative Studies in Community Property*, ed. Jan P. Charmatz and Harriet S. Daggett (Baton Rouge, 1955). Several casebooks and textbooks describe the early Hispanic community property law in Texas, while comparing this regime with similar ones adopted in other United States jurisdictions. W. S. McClanahan's *Community Property Law in the United States* (Rochester, 1982) compared the early growth of the Hispanic matrimonial property law in Texas, California, and Louisiana. A work that deftly blended both discussion of the antecedents of Texas community property doctrine and the history of early settlement is Joseph McKnight and William Reppy, Jr., *Texas Matrimonial Property Law* (Charlottesville, 1983). Two other useful books are William Q. Defuniak and Michael J. Vaughn, *Principles of Community Property*, 2d ed. (Tucson, 1971), and Harriet Spiller Daggett, *Legal Essays on Family Law* (Baton Rouge, 1935).

Several works have examined the extent to which the community property system constituted a conservative power of family organization within traditional Hispanic society. For a discerning study of traditional culture undergirding the Hispanic matrimonial property regime, see Ann M. Pescatello, *Power and Pawn: The Female in Iberian Societies and Culture* (Westport, 1976). A more recent survey of the ideological structure of the legal system prevalent in the Spanish borderlands on the eve of the Anglo-American invasion can be found in Charles R. Cutter, *The Legal Culture of Northern New Spain, 1700–1810* (Albuquerque, 1995). In his article "Community Property—A Critique of Its Regulation of Intra-Family Relations," *Washington Law Review* 11 (1936), Richard R. B. Powell described how the Hispanic prohibition of absolute divorce for postmarital causes imbued the matrimonial property system with a decidedly patriarchal cast. George McKay's *A Commentary on the Law of Community Property* (Denver, 1910) and *A Treatise on the Law of Community Property*, 2d ed. (Indianapolis, 1925) also characterized the community property system as essentially conservative, while comparing and contrasting the Texas law with the Hispanic regimes that developed in nineteenth-century California, New Mexico, Idaho, Louisiana, Washington, Arizona, and Nevada.

A large body of scholarship has explored the development of married women's property rights in Texas. For useful early studies examining the pertinent blending of Hispanic and Anglo-American principles, see W. S. Simkins, "Some Phases of the Law of Community Property in Texas," *Texas Law Review* 3 (1925); John Bell, "Powers of Married Women in Texas Aside from

Statutes," *Texas Law Review* 6 (1927); and Frederick L. Paxson, "The Constitution of Texas, 1845," *Southwestern Historical Quarterly* 18(4)(1915). More extensive early works include Lawrence W. Neff, *The Legal Status of Women in
Texas* (Dallas, 1905), and Fred Walter Householder, "The Sources of the Texas
Law of Married Women" (M.A. thesis, University of Texas, Austin, 1909). For
a discussion of nineteenth-century legislative and constitutional definitions of
women's community property rights, see Frank Bobbitt's "Is There More Than
One Class of Community Property in Texas?" *Texas Law Review* 4 (1926).
Mattie Lloyd Wooten's "The Status of Women in Texas" (Ph.D. diss., University of Texas, Austin, 1941) is notable for being the first study to look at the
law from the perspective of women. Her dissertation dealt with the legal status
of nineteenth-century Texas women using a social context, taking into account
demographics, the family, church life, education, and employment. William O.
Huie described the expanding powers of women to manage community rents
and profits through the nineteenth century and early twentieth century in
"The Texas Constitutional Definition of the Wife's Separate Property," *Texas
Law Review* 35 (1957). For documentation of the debates among constitutional
delegates instituting reforms to the law of married women's property in 1845,
see *Journals of the Convention* (Austin, 1845) and William F. Weeks, comp.,
Debates of the Texas Convention (Houston, 1846).

Studies conducted in the second half of the twentieth century have gauged
the extent to which constitutional and statutory alterations of the Texas matrimonial property regime aided or undercut the autonomy of married women.
After World War II, the feminist movement began to generate more critical
assessments of the married women's property acts implemented in numerous
states beginning in the late 1830s. Kay Ellen Thurman first argued that the
1840 statute adopting the Spanish matrimonial property regime in Texas was
part of this national development. See "The Married Women's Property Acts"
(L.L.M. thesis, University of Wisconsin, Madison, 1966). Several works echo-
ing this view include W. J. Williamson, *Texas Marital Property* (Houston,
1973), and American Association of University Women, *Legal Rights of Texas
Women*, 2d ed. (Houston, 1974). The best-known study in this line of scholarship, however, is Kathleen Elizabeth Lazarou's "Concealed under Petticoats:
Married Women's Property and the Law of Texas, 1840–1913" (Ph.D. diss.,
Rice University, Houston, 1980). Lazarou amplified on Thurman's thesis, con-
cluding that the Texas matrimonial property law, after the 1840 adoption and
subsequent modification of the Spanish system, was virtually indistinguishable
from that which married women's property acts established contemporane-
ously in many other jurisdictions of the United States. While rejecting earlier
interpretations that had characterized the Hispanic regime as distinctly liberal
in contrast to the common law, she concluded that Texas marital property law,

in fact, constituted an early system of public assistance for women and children victimized by squandering and abandoning Anglo-Texan husbands.

A number of scholars have posited the utility of the Hispanic matrimonial law in the wilds of early Texas. Building on Roscoe Pound's frontier thesis of legal development, Michael J. Vaughn's "The Policy of Community Property and Inter-Spousal Transaction," *Baylor Law Review* 19 (1967) argued that the community property system in Texas comported with frontier conditions under which women and men worked cooperatively in dangerous and harsh circumstances. In "Texas Community Property Law—Its Course of Development and Reform," *California Western Law Review* 20 (1986), Joseph McKnight traced the adoption of the Hispanic regime, while tying this step directly to the consensus among early Texas lawmakers that the Spanish matrimonial property law was well suited to frontier conditions and the mutual economic designs and interests of settling spouses. His article "Texas Community Property Law: Conservative Attitudes, Reluctant Change," *Law and Contemporary Problems* 56(2)(1993) reiterated that settlement exigencies encouraged Texas lawmakers to adopt and alter the Hispanic rules in ways that took into account the contributions of pioneer women. In "Remember the Alamo(ny)! The Unique Texas Ban on Permanent Alimony and the Development of Community Property Law," *Law and Contemporary Problems* 56(2)(1993), James W. Paulsen maintained that frontier social disorganization in Texas and coequal ownership of marital property reduced the utility of permanent alimony and obviated the need for it, while also shaping unusual temporary alimony rules.

Legal historians have explored intensively the Hispanic and frontier origins of Texas homestead exemption laws. In a 1978 paper delivered before the Texas State Historical Association, entitled "The Spanish Elements in Modern Texas Law," Joseph McKnight emphasized how Hispanic community property law in early Texas was critical for protecting married couples and families against creditors. In "Protection of the Family Home from Seizure by Creditors: The Sources and Evolution of a Legal Principle," *Southwestern Historical Quarterly* 86(3)(1983), McKnight traced Texas homestead exemption laws to their Spanish origins. He also argued that the exemptions were particularly attractive because they protected early settlers, who were commonly in debt, from the loss of their land and chattels. Gary Carman's "Texas' Homestead Provision: A Unique Financial Constraint," *Essays in Economic and Business History* 10 (1992) similarly concluded that, because early Texas was a haven for debtors, legislators there favored a law protecting the homesteads of settlers from foreclosure.

Studies of divorce law in antebellum Texas are rather scarce. For a synopsis of the judicial development of the statutory cruelty ground from 1851 through the early 1930s, including references to English ecclesiastical court antecedents, see J. E. C., "Divorce—Cruelty as a Ground," *Texas Law Review* 15(3)(1937). Other brief treatments regarding the early elaboration of cruelty doctrine and the late-nineteenth-century tightening of it include J. E. Thompson, "Divorce – Condonation – Effect of a Marital Offense Insufficient for Divorce," *Texas Tech Law Review* 24 (1945–46) and Theodore S. Fair, "Divorce – Acts Sufficient to Constitute Cruel Treatment as Ground for Divorce," *Baylor Law Review* 2(3)(1950). While examining almost exclusively the patriarchal aspects of divorce law in the antebellum South, Jane Turner Censer's "'Smiling through Her Tears': Ante-Bellum Southern Women and Divorce," *American Journal of Legal History* 25 (1981) includes quite useful commentary on the Texas rules. Paulsen's discussion of property division upon divorce in "Remember the Alamo(ny)!" also described the introduction of judicial divorce in Texas, beginning in 1837 with the controversial divorce of Sam Houston.

The scholarship of Joseph McKnight provides the most thorough inquiry into the early Texas law of inheritance. In his articles "Family Law: Husband and Wife," *Southwestern Law Journal* 35 (1981) and "The Spanish Legacy to Texas Law," *American Journal of Legal History* 3 (1959), McKnight examined the enduring effect of Spanish legal principles on probate procedure after independence from Mexico. In "Spanish Law for the Protection of Surviving Spouses in North America," *Anuario de Historia del Derecho Español* (Madrid) 57 (1987), he argued that Anglo-Americans moving into Texas Americanized the law but retained Spanish rules that provided protection of the property of surviving spouses. For a recent essay by McKnight tracing the Spanish influence on the early law of succession and other excellent pieces describing the enduring impact of the Spanish legal system on Texas, see José R. Remacha et al., *The Influence of Spain on the Texas Legal System* (Austin, 1992).

Biographies of Chief Justice John Hemphill reflect the key role he played in shaping the Hispanic matrimonial property regime, married women's property law, homestead exemption rules, divorce doctrine, and succession principles. Most of the early treatments eulogized Hemphill as the founder of the Texas legal system, while emphasizing his blending of the common law and civilian legal precepts and his commitment to protecting the rights of women and children. Notable among these are V. O. King, "A Biographical Sketch of John Hemphill," *Docket* 1 (1896), and James P. Hart, "John Hemphill—Chief Justice of Texas," *Southwestern Law Journal* 3 (1949). For a discussion of Hemphill within a broader treatment of the structure and functions of the high court, see S. A. Philquist, "The Supreme Court of Texas," *Texas Bar Journal* 1 (1938). The only book-length Hemphill biography is Rosalee Morris Curtis's *John Hemphill: First Chief Justice of the State of Texas* (Austin, 1971), which traced his early life and experiences in South Carolina, his involvement in the various Anglo-Texan conflicts with Mexico in the early 1840s, his accomplishments as chief justice, and his staunch proslavery politics.

Nineteenth-century Texas criminal law permitting a man the use of deadly force to ensure exclusive sexual relations with his wife has received intermittent consideration over the years. A description of the judicial affirmation of the rule permitting a Texas man to kill his wife's paramour, through the nineteenth century and early twentieth century, can be found in C. S. Potts, "Is the Husband's Act of Killing Wife Taken in Act of Adultery Justifiable Homicide in Texas?" *Texas Law Review* 2(1)(1923). For an exploration of the internal inconsistencies of the statute and a presentation of the theory that legislators designed it to protect wives, conceptualized as the weaker sex, see George Wilfred Stumberg, "Defense of Person and Property under Texas Criminal Law," *Texas Law Review* 21(1)(1942). In "Justifiable Homicide in Texas," *Southwestern Law Review* 13(2)(1959), William M. Ravkind further explored the highly anomalous aspects of the rule and concluded that it was simply representative of the "code of the old west." In *Honor and Violence in the Old South* (Oxford, 1986), however, Bertram Wyatt-Brown argued that the law provided essentially southern men a means to vindicate their honor in the face of threatening cuckoldry.

LEGAL SOURCE MATERIALS

Most of the legal source materials used in this study are contained in published volumes. For a complete English translation of the fundamental Castilian code relevant to domestic relations, see Samuel Parsons Scott, trans., *Las Siete Partidas* (Chicago, 1931). A translated synopsis of the Hispanic law current through early statehood can be found in Gustavus Schmidt's *The Civil Law of Spain and Mexico* (New Orleans, 1851). Particularly useful for assessing local policy changes in the Mexican period is J. P. Kimball, trans., *Laws and Decrees of the State of Coahuila and Texas, to Which is Added the Constitution of Said State* (Houston, 1839). The collected statutes of the Republic of Texas and State of Texas, as well as numerous translations of colonization laws, decrees, and the pertinent laws of New Spain and Mexico, can be found in H. P. N. Gammel, *The Laws of Texas, 1822–1897*, 10 vols. (Austin, 1898), and Williamson S. Oldham and George W. White, *A Digest of General Statutes and Laws of the State of Texas* (Austin, 1854). Oliver Cromwell Hartley's *A Digest of the Laws of Texas* (Philadelphia, 1850) compiled the civil and criminal statutes enacted during the national and early antebellum statehood periods. *The Penal Code of the State of Texas* (Galveston, 1857), the first criminal code the state adopted, contains provisions reformulating prior statutes and common law rules that Texas courts had relied upon since 1836. All of the decisions of the Texas Supreme Court are contained in the *Texas Reports*, vols. 1–26 (1846–61). A good synopsis of the opinions of the high court, through to at least 1860, is contained in William G. Myer, *A Digest of the Texas Reports*, 2 vols. (St. Louis, 1881). For a useful annotated compilation of important judicial rulings in Texas and related ones in other jurisdictions, see George W. Paschal, *A Digest of Decisions: Comprising Decisions of the Supreme Courts of Texas and the United States upon Texas Law, of Force and Repealed, with References to all the Civil, Spanish, and Common Law Decisions and Authorities Cited by the Judges*, 2 vols. (Washington, D.C., 1872–74).

The Texas Supreme Court frequently referred to a number of Anglo-American legal treatises in fashioning its early decisions concerning the family, sex, and childbearing. Although not determinative of its rulings or policy choices, these works often provided useful doctrine. William Blackstone's *Commentaries on the Laws of England*, 4 vols. (London, 1765–69) was an occasional source at least through the antebellum period. Conservative in orientation, it emphasized the merger of a woman's legal identity with that of her husband, the strong natural rights of fathers, the lack of rights for bastard children, and marriage as a civil contract rather than as a sacrament. Tapping Reeve's *Law of Baron and Femme* (New York, 1816) was the first volume on marital relations written in the United States, a work that conceptualized law as policy-making and attempted to Americanize the common law of marriage and the family to bring it in line with republican ideals. James Kent's *Commentaries on American Law*, 4 vols. (New York, 1826–30), a high-water mark in nineteenth-century treatise-writing, sought to establish a uniform postrevolutionary law among the states. Building on many ideas set forth initially in *Baron and Femme*, Kent placed a premium on the republican liberty to contract the marital relation, while reinforcing an egalitarianism within families that included rights for all members. Joel Prentiss Bishop's *Commentaries on the Law of Marriage and Divorce* (Boston, 1852) was the first major synthesis of domestic relations law after Reeve's treatise. Although designed to indicate the strides that common lawyers had made in devising a distinct republican notion of family governance, Bishop wrote his commentaries amid rising alarm in the United States about social disorganization. Both his 1852 treatise and his *Commentaries on the Law of Marriage and Divorce*, 2d ed. (Boston, 1856) thus reflected a renewed judicial commitment to regulating marriage and divorce. As an early innovator of the "classical," or formalistic, nineteenth-century law of domestic relations, Bishop characterized the law as a scientific body of rules, harmonious, self-contained, autonomous, and free of class and other biases. For evidentiary precepts upon which the Texas Supreme Court relied in many of its decisions concerning divorce and family matters, see Simon Greenleaf's

A Treatise on the Law of Evidence, 6th ed., 2 vols. (Boston, 1852). All of the above-referenced treatises contain innumerable citations to important appellate decisions in various jurisdictions of the United States, many of which the Texas Supreme Court adopted or rejected, either wholly or in part.

Through the national and antebellum statehood periods, the Texas Supreme Court routinely adverted to treatises by jurists working outside the postrevolutionary United States legal tradition. Particularly regarding common law marriage and rules about adultery, the high court often relied on Patrick Fraser's *A Treatise on the Law of Scotland as Applicable to the Personal and Domestic Relations*, 2 vols. (Edinburgh, 1846). The court frequently looked to Leonard Shelford's *Practical Treatise on the Law of Marriage and Divorce* (London, 1841), a comprehensive work on the British law pertinent to matrimonial relations and separations from bed and board. When dealing with Hispanic matrimonial property principles and related rules regarding the rights and obligations of women during colonial times, the Texas Supreme Court regularly consulted Joaquín Escriche's *Diccionario Razonado de Legislación y Jurisprudencia* (Madrid, 1851).

A number of postbellum treatises provide useful synopses of the law relevant to the decisions of the antebellum Texas Supreme Court. Through the 1870s and 1880s, Joel Bishop continued to produce books that refined his early discussions of domestic relations law from the American Revolution through the antebellum period. Most useful in this regard are his *Commentaries on the Law of Marriage and Divorce*, 6th ed., 2 vols. (Boston, 1881) and *New Commentaries on Marriage, Divorce, and Separation*, 2 vols. (Chicago, 1891). For discussions of the law regarding the statutory crimes of bigamy and "living in adultery," see Bishop's *Commentaries on the Law of Statutory Crimes* (1873). For a brief sketch of the history of Spanish law and rules regarding heirship and wills, see Joaquín Escriche, *Elements of the Spanish Law*, trans. Bethel Coopwood, 3d ed. (Austin, 1886).

Quite useful in this study were a number of twentieth-century legal treatises and reference books. Ocie Speer's *A Treatise on the Law of Married Women in Texas* (New York, 1901) was the first comprehensive description of the nineteenth-century Texas law relevant to women and the family. This book described the variance of the Hispanic regime from that of the common law, focusing particularly on the rules of marriage and divorce and those touching on homestead rights and the administration of estates. Speer's *A Treatise on the Law of Marital Rights in Texas* (New York, 1916) recapitulated the first work and analyzed numerous cases and statutes that had significantly changed the law since the publication of the initial version. Both treatises were clearly the product of a jurist interested in producing a standardization in the law suitable to a more modern society and professional bench and bar. To the extent that

Speer's volumes echoed the formalism of Bishop, they cloaked the sources of change in the early law. Regardless, both works contain valuable case citations, statutory references, and commentary. Jack W. Ledbetter's *Texas Family Law* (Austin, 1968) constitutes a black letter survey of the state's domestic relations law, including summaries of many of the important decisions of the Texas Supreme Court dating back to the 1840s. A useful encyclopedia for tracing early statutory and judicial developments in the law relevant to the family and the intimate relations of women and men is *Texas Jurisprudence,* 3d ed., 77 vols. (San Francisco, 1979), which includes law journal and treatise references.

Index

abandonment: of Indian wives and Anglo-Indian children by Anglo-Texan men, 28–29; post-independence law on, relevant to deserted Indian wives and Anglo-Indian children, 29–32; of Anglo-Texan wives, 87–88; Anglo-Texan female adultery and remarriage following, 92; of Anglo-Texan husbands, 95; and Mexican law on adultery, 135; attitude of Anglo-Texan husbands toward, 136; as ground for divorce after independence, 137–138; and post-independence divorce rules on male adultery, 144–148, 151; and divorce cruelty doctrine on Anglo-Texan men cohabiting with slave women, 151; and post-independence criminal penalty for living in adultery, 151

adultery: of Native American women, 26–27; conditions encouraging Anglo-Texan men to engage in, 82–92; and Anglo-Texan male gender role, 84–87, 90; and entrepreneurship of Anglo-Texan women, 88–89; of Anglo-Texan men with slave women, 89; policy of Anglo-Texan lawmakers toward, 89; of Anglo-Texan women, 89–92, 95–97; and Mexican religious policy, 93–94; and institutional disarray, 95; and post-independence Protestant church formation, 95; Anglo-Texan tolerance of, 96–99; of Anglo-Texan women and slave men, 96; as post-

independence ground for absolute divorce of wife, 120; Mexican divorce rules on, 135; and post-independence dual divorce standard, 144–145; and post-independence divorce cruelty doctrine on cohabitation of married men with slave women, 145–148, 151; and divorce law sanctioning chastisement of woman for, 148–149; and rule of justifiable homicide, 148, 152–153; defenses to divorce suit for, 149, 155–156; and evidentiary rules in divorce litigation shielding women guilty of, 149–150, 153–154; and post-independence policy on family stabilization, 150–157; relative leniency of post-independence criminal law on, 150–151; policy on delimiting sexual prerogatives of married women and men, 157–158; and Anglo-Texan policy on women and men of different races, 159–160

African Texans: colonial immigration of, 54; Anglo-Texan attitudes toward marriage with, 55; and black-white unions in Mexican Texas, 57–59; increased importation of after Anglo-Texan independence, 58; residential patterns of, 59; families of undermined by Anglo-Texan male sexual exploitation and relevant law, 60; and post-independence law of slavery, 60, 64–65; and female slave concubinage, 61–63; and interaction with

CPSIA information can be obtained at www.ICGtesting.com
Printed in the USA
245363LV00002B/6/P